Reporting Elections

Contemporary Political Communication

Geoffrey Craig, *Performing Politics*

Stephen Cushion & Richard Thomas, *Reporting Elections*

Robert M. Entman, *Scandal and Silence*

Max McCombs, R. Lance Holbert, Spiro Kiousis & Wayne Wanta, *The News and Public Opinion*

Craig Allen Smith, *Presidential Campaign Communication* (2nd edition)

James Stanyer, *Intimate Politics*

Katrin Voltmer, *The Media in Transitional Democracies*

Reporting Elections

Rethinking the Logic of Campaign Coverage

STEPHEN CUSHION
& RICHARD THOMAS

polity

First published in 2018 by Polity Press

Polity Press
65 Bridge Street
Cambridge CB2 1UR, UK

Polity Press
101 Station Landing
Suite 300
Medford, MA 02155, USA

ISBN-13: 978-1-5095-1750-3
ISBN-13: 978-1-5095-1751-0 (pb)

A catalogue record for this book is available from the British Library.

Typeset in 11 on 13 pt Monotype Bembo by Servis Filmsetting Ltd, Stockport, Cheshire
Printed and bound in the UK by CPI Group (UK) Ltd, Croydon

The publisher has used its best endeavours to ensure that the URLs for external websites referred to in this book are correct and active at the time of going to press. However, the publisher has no responsibility for the websites and can make no guarantee that a site will remain live or that the content is or will remain appropriate.

Every effort has been made to trace all copyright holders, but if any have been inadvertently overlooked the publisher will be pleased to include any necessary credits in any subsequent reprint or edition.

For further information on Polity, visit our website: politybooks.com

Contents

Tables and Figure

Tables

Figure

Introduction: Studying Elections

Why study media coverage of elections?

Election campaigns play a fundamental role in democratic systems.
They represent, after all, a time when political parties showcase
their vision for the future and citizens consider, if at all, how best
to cast their votes. Since the news media act as the primary source
of election information for most people during a campaign, they
play a crucial role in communicating news to voters. But what kind
of logic do the news media follow when reporting election campaigns? How well do they inform citizens about their democratic
choices? The aim of this book is to answer these (and many more)
questions by comprehensively examining how election campaigns
are reported. In doing so, we reflect on the value of election
reporting and consider how the logic of campaign coverage can
better serve the democratic needs of citizens.

While scholars have increased their interest in how the news
media report election campaigns over recent years (Strömbäck
and Kaid 2008), many book-length studies deal with *national*
issues and concerns (see, for example, Young 2011 or Oates 2008)

rather than considering broader international trends and patterns.
Moreover, most studies focus exclusively on 'first-order' elections, such as presidential or general elections, which are viewed
as more important to voters than 'second-order' elections, such as
European Union (EU), state or more localised contests (Reif and
Schmitt 1980). The aim of this book is to assess election reporting
in both first- *and* second-order elections. We do so by developing an evidence-based understanding of the media logic shaping
election reporting and consider the democratic value of campaign
coverage.

By 'media logic' we refer to the kind of organising principles
behind the editorial selection and communication of news about
election campaigns (Altheide 2016). In political communication
studies, media logic is widely understood as reflecting 'the institutional, technological, and sociological characteristics of the news
media, including their format characteristics, production and dis-
semination routines, norms and needs' (Strömbäck 2011: 373).
It is the rules shaping election reporting that we aim to uncover.
In understanding the influences behind the day-to-day reporting
of election campaigns, many layers need to be stripped away and
interpreted (Semetko et al.. 1991: 178–9). But the lead protagonists
in agenda-setting, above all, tend to be political parties, journalists
and voters (McCombs 2014; Strömbäck and Esser 2014). While
there is clearly an *interdependence* between these actors, there is
an *independence* from one another as different interests and needs
shape the agenda-setting process during an election campaign
(McCombs 2014; Semetko et al. 1991). We need, in other words,
to consider the main agenda-setting factors that influence coverage
during campaigns.

Writing about US media in the 1960s, Katz was one of the first
scholars to question how election campaigns were reported. He
cast considerable doubt on their democratic value and suggested
that the coverage served primarily a political rather than a public
logic. In his words, 'one is led to the conclusion that election
campaigns are better designed to serve the political parties, particularly the dominant ones, than to serve society or the voter' (Katz
1971: 314). Two decades later, Semetko and her colleagues pub-

lished a pioneering book-length study about US and UK election reporting and identified a strong media logic shaping campaign coverage. They observed that US journalists, in particular, exercised considerable 'discretionary powers' over the agenda-setting process (Semetko et al. 1991: 4). Nonetheless, their comparative focus led them to conclude that 'the formation of the campaign agenda is a complex process that varies from one culture and one election to another' (ibid.: 179). In the 2000s, Strömbäck and Kaid's edited collection of nationally themed chapters was another major contribution to understanding media coverage of elections. Overall, they argued that media logic had become a pervasive force in many advanced democracies during election times. In their words, 'almost all the countries discussed in this volume have developed media coverage systems where "horserace" coverage is prominent or even dominant' (Strömbäck and Kaid 2008: 425). A more process-driven agenda in campaign coverage is consistent with broader debates about the increasing power of the media to influence political coverage. The concept of mediatisation, in this context, has been widely used to interpret media influence in different facets of society, such as religion, marketing, fashion and, most relevant to this book, politics. Put simply, *the mediatisation of politics refers to how the media have increasingly set the political news agenda over recent years and influenced the behaviour of politicians* (Strömbäck and Esser 2014).

This book will develop a comprehensive evidence-based assessment about the dominant logic shaping election campaign coverage almost two decades into the new millennium. From news about policy issues to the process of politics – including the rise of horserace reporting – we aim not only to establish empirically *how* elections are reported but to consider *how the logic behind campaign coverage can be rethought*. In doing so, we examine the evidence about how people engage with and interpret both coverage of issues and horserace news. Historically, however, the most researched aspect of election coverage is assessing how fair and balanced news media are during a campaign (D'Alessio 2012). We examine how the media agenda is policed during campaigns, considering the regulatory environment in which journalists operate between countries and different media systems, and how concepts such as objectivity and impartiality are understood and operationalised. While scholars have highlighted the partisan tendencies of particular media – whether US cable news channels or UK tabloid newspapers – we also consider their intermedia agenda-setting role. To explore the logic of campaign coverage in greater detail, we focus on election reporting in the UK and the US more closely, engaging with debates about remaining impartial, objective and balanced in a post-truth political environment. In particular, we consider Donald Trump's electoral strategy during the 2016 presidential election and how the news media reported the campaign. By way of conclusion, we bring together the salient findings of the book to interpret how well the media inform and engage the electorate during an election campaign. Overall, we ask:

> *How are different types of electoral contests reported? What is the main logic shaping news agendas during election campaigns?*

> *How well do the media serve citizens during an election campaign? How can the logic of campaign coverage be rethought to better inform and engage voters?*

Before examining how election campaigns are reported, we begin by providing some context to how most people access political information. We explore the information environments of different countries and the wider political and cultural contexts in which journalism operates, and we consider the role this plays in how different types of election campaigns are routinely reported.

Electoral integrity, political information environments and different types of campaign

Since a key normative goal of the news media is to enhance informed citizenship (Blumler and Cushion 2014; Christians et al. 2009), an election campaign is one of the most important points in time to supply voters with information about the policies of competing parties and to engage them in the process of politics. It is, after all, fundamental to democratic theory that citizens understand politics and public affairs before casting their vote. As the introduction to a UNESCO handbook about election reporting put it:

> For an election to go well, it must be free and fair. There must be free speech so all citizens and all political candidates can speak without fear. The media must be free to tell everyone what was said without pressure to twist the truth. That is the job of professional journalists – to fully inform citizens of the issues and their choices so they can decide for themselves for whom to vote. (Ross 2004: 1)

Of course, the normative aims of journalism do not always match the reality of election reporting in different countries or between competing media systems. By media systems, we mean different types of media that operate around the world. These are not always easy to distinguish or classify between nations, but generally they refer to whether media is funded by commercial means or by the state via general taxation or a licence fee. State media, such as Russia Today, are distinctive from public service broadcasters, such as the BBC, because the latter aims to be editorially independent from the government of the day. At the same time, some commercial media may have public service responsibilities in their licence agreements, reflecting a hybrid public–commercial media system (see Cushion 2012a). When making sense of election reporting throughout the book, our analysis explores the comparative differences between media systems.

Over recent years, scholars have increasingly sought to compare the information environments of different countries to help make sense of people's understanding of politics and public affairs. While demographic factors such as age and education play a role in how people understand politics and engage with election campaigns, individual-level effects have their limits. Greater emphasis, instead, has been placed on the media to which people are increasingly exposed, but this information supply of political news can vary considerably between nations. This point was comprehensively made in the study by Esser et al. (2012a), which examined television schedules in thirteen European countries over a thirty-year period (1977–2007). Taken together, their findings show that the opportunity for viewers to learn about politics was greater in countries where public service media was stronger. This was because such countries tended to schedule more informative formats of news, from news in briefs and newscasts to interview or discussion-type programming, than their commercial counterparts. While the quality of news provision could not be evaluated, Esser et al.'s study highlighted the comparative volume of political information between countries with different media systems.

A smaller-scale schedule analysis study of the US, the UK and Norway similarly found that the largely market-driven media system in the US supplied less political information for viewers than the UK's mix of public and commercial broadcasters and Norway's more public service regulated television channels (Aalberg et al. 2010). In making sense of the differences, the study pointed towards the political culture of each country and the role it played in safeguarding the media environment from commercial forces or lighter regulation. So, for example, while Norway and UK broadcasters follow strict rules about scheduling newscasts in prime time, the US regulation of television news is far more 'light touch'. Consequently, the US has both less news programming and fewer options for viewers to choose from than many European broadcasters because the three most popular networks – ABC, CBS and NBC – schedule their main evening newscast (6.30 pm) at the same time.

Viewed in this context, it is important to understand the political systems in different countries and the influence they might play in shaping the media landscape and the regulation of news reporting during an election campaign. As Norris's (2014) electoral integrity project demonstrated, the conduct and standards of election campaigns differ markedly between countries. Her wide-ranging study drew on over 2,000 experts examining 180 election campaigns in 139 countries, evaluating issues such as voter registration, campaign finances and the performance of media. Norris's study revealed that the Scandinavian countries – Denmark, Finland, Norway and Sweden – provided the fairest election coverage according to the project's measures. Some of the most impoverished developing countries, such as Ethiopia, Equatorial Guinea, Burundi, Djibouti and Syria, where state interference and corruption is rife, ranked lowest.

But perhaps most striking in the global survey were the positions of the US and the UK, since both countries champion the virtues of their democratic systems. While the UK was ranked bottom within Europe, the electoral conduct of the US was considered the worst in the Western world. Moreover, both countries were ranked below nations not necessarily viewed as historically upholding democratic standards, such as Argentina and Rwanda. Norris's (2014) study showed it should not be assumed that the integrity of elections is higher in the developed world. While the role of media was part of the electoral integrity project's global survey, the measures to evaluate performance were relatively broad. The aim of this book is to paint a finer picture of standards in election reporting. In doing so, we examine the weight of evidence about election campaign coverage and consider how well the media engage voters in the political process and inform them about their democratic choices. Of course, making judgements about news standards or quality journalism is not empirically straightforward. There are competing ways in which people interpret the normative value of news and assess the democratic health of political information environments (Cushion 2012a). While we explain how we evaluate election coverage in each chapter, broadly speaking we agree with van Aelst et al. (2017: 8) that 'media coverage should help people to make informed choices and hold politicians accountable, in essence providing people with the information they need to be free and self-governing.' The next chapter develops more fully a framework for analysing the value of election news and how competing logics of campaign coverage will be interpreted.

However, as already pointed out, in making sense of election reporting, most studies tend to focus on what political scientists call 'first-order' elections, such as presidential or general election campaigns (Reif and Schmitt 1980). 'Second-order' elections, such as the EU, state or local electoral campaigns, by contrast, are seen as less important by voters. While much research focuses on the reporting of first-order elections, they may be different in volume and character compared to second-order elections. Indeed, according to Reif and Schmitt, second-order election campaigns have distinctive characteristics. So, for example, while the European Union parliamentary elections are, in theory, about EU policy-related matters, the campaigns may be national in focus and informed by domestic issues, such as voting against the government of the day. This is also because turnout is far lower in second-order elections compared to first-order contests, which often means smaller parties are electorally successful.

Nevertheless, since second-order campaigns tend to be low-key affairs, with 'less being at stake' (Reif and Schmitt 1980: 9–10) than in first-order campaigns, how far they are reported by different types of media systems – particularly by more market-driven outlets – has not been subject to a great deal of empirical attention. There have, for instance, been several cross-national comparative studies examining how different European media report the EU parliamentary elections, considering both the quantity and the quality of coverage from a range of perspectives (de Vreese 2003; de Vreese et al. 2006). But how far more localised electoral contests differ between countries and competing media systems is less clear. In chapters 2 and 3 we explore how far the order-type of elections influences both the amount and nature of campaign coverage. We also consider the national context of different electoral contests in order to understand better why elections are reported differently.

Overall, then, in making sense of election reporting around the world, it is important to acknowledge the integrity of a country's political system and the information environment as well as the type of electoral contest under analysis. Over recent years, scholars have also placed greater emphasis on analysing election news *in more empirical detail*. As the next section now explores, studies have increasingly sought to isolate the influence of different sources of news and consider the effect on people's political knowledge and understanding of politics.

Mobilisation or malaise? Towards a more content-focused understanding of election coverage

The role played by news media during election campaigns has been the subject of fierce debate among political communication scholars over several decades. At its broadest, one branch of scholarship argues that news media mobilise citizens and encourage them to participate in the electoral process. Another puts forward a media malign effect, which discourages voter engagement and promotes cynicism in the political process (Newton 1999). Norris's (2000) proposition that the media create a 'virtuous circle' was a particularly significant intervention at the turn of the century. In a study of twenty-nine countries, Norris found people regularly exposed to news media were more likely to participate in politics, know more about public affairs and invest greater trust in the political process than those who did not have such contact. Put more simply, regularly being exposed to political news had a mobilising effect on citizens in advanced democracies.

But debates about media effects – particularly during election campaigns – often focus more specifically on *how* the media frame politics, such as reporting game- or strategy-type coverage over issues of policy. According to Aalberg et al. (2012: 163): 'the framing of politics as a strategic game is characterized by a focus on questions related to who is winning and losing, the performances of politicians and parties, and on campaign strategies and tactics. This framing is often contrasted with a focus on political substance and issues.' In the US there has been a long-standing complaint that the news media have increasingly reported politics as a strategic game. More than two decades ago, Cappella and Jamieson (1997) put forward a media malaise theory that news reporting may be fuelling a 'spiral of cynicism'. Drawing on field experiments with members of the public, they found that citizens were less cynical when news coverage was about political *issues* rather than the process of politics. Since then, this theory has been both contested and reinforced in various ways. On the one hand, factors such as political interest and knowledge have been used as explanatory factors that lead to cynicism about politicians and parties (de Vreese 2005; Valentino et al. 2001). On the other hand, portraying politics as a strategic game has been found to reduce interest in political affairs (Shehata 2014) and trust in news media (Hopmann et al. 2015). Other variables, including age and levels of education, have also been used by scholars to support or challenge theories about media mobilisation or malaise. Holt et al. (2013), for instance, established that the use among young people of social media during the 2010 Swedish elections enhanced their interest and participation in politics.

Although many scholars continue to interpret media effects by a mobilisation or malaise framework, when forming conclusions about the impact of political reporting this binary distinction often tars all news media with the same brush. As Curran et al. (2014: 828–9) have observed:

> researchers are typically encouraged to choose between 'media malaise' and 'virtuous circle' interpretations; that is, to side either with the view that the media radiate democratic influence in a nimbus of virtue or the opposing view that the media turn people off politics by distorting its true nature. In essence, we are asked to choose between perceiving the media as being an exclusively positive or negative force.

The authors advocated a new approach that understands more flexibly the effects of political news and argued that the news media can both discourage people from politics and empower citizens in the public sphere. As comparative communication studies has grown and become more sophisticated in recent years (Esser and Hanitzsch 2012), the differences between media systems across different countries and the specific content of news produced have become more central to understanding effects. So, for example, Schuck et al. (2016), in their comparative study of twenty-one countries during the 2009 EU parliamentary elections, discovered that conflict news-framing mobilised people to vote. However, their combined content analysis and two-wave panel survey identified that mobilisation was stronger in countries with proportional political systems, in information environments where people are more exposed to public service broadcasting and broadsheets, and where the EU was more positively reported. In other words, understanding the political culture and media system shaping coverage, *as well as* the specific tone of EU reporting, was crucial to interpreting the degree to which conflict-framing had a mobilising effect.

This point was well made in the study by de Vreese and Boomgaarden (2006) of the ways in which European integration was portrayed in Dutch media. Their study examined the topics and institutional sources of stories across television and radio, along with whether an item featured political conflict. Consuming a high volume of news that included coverage of conflict, they suggested, enhanced people's knowledge and likelihood to vote. In reaching this conclusion, they emphasised 'the importance of taking content into account when investigating the relationship between media and political knowledge and engagement' (de Vreese and Boomgaarden 2006: 333). Further still, they argued that 'it is not sufficient to rely on exposure measures and to merely speculate about media content' (ibid.).

In more recent years, interpreting the comparative differences in news *content* between competing media systems has taken greater prominence in exploring the possible influence of political reporting during election campaigns. Hansen and Pederson's study during the 2011 Danish parliamentary elections, for example, discovered the type of newspapers consumed over the campaign was significant in a number of ways. In their words: 'Broadsheet readers experienced a significant increase in both knowledge and internal efficacy. In contrast, tabloid readers became significantly less externally efficacious, suggesting that the tabloids may be partially to blame for cynicism and mistrust among the electorate. In other words, voters tend to be affected by what they are exposed to; you become what you read' (2014: 319). Similarly, Strömbäck's four-wave survey considered knowledge effects during both the Swedish 2014 general election and the EU parliamentary election and during a non-election period in the same year. It found conclusively that public service media – in all three contexts – enhanced people's understanding of issues. Moreover, particular public service programmes had a stronger effect, further reinforcing the importance of investigating *specific news content* rather than just media ownership. Conversely, commercial television was identified as having a negative impact on people's knowledge about the election. But Strömbäck's findings went further. He concluded that 'knowledge effects are stronger for one public service TV news show than for the other. This indicates that it is not ownership per se that is decisive. The format and *the content also matter*' (Strömbäck 2016: 13; emphasis added).

Of course, both these studies were based in Scandinavian countries, which – as already acknowledged – have a comparatively high degree of conduct and standards policing the integrity of elections, including in the provision of news media (Norris 2014). Both Denmark and Sweden have well-funded and widely watched public service broadcasters and a broader journalism culture committed to fair and impartial election reporting. The information environments in other parts of the world are not as reliant on public service broadcasting, with election reporting being shaped more by market-driven or state-controlled media. As a consequence, regular exposure to news media in other countries *might not necessarily* enhance people's knowledge about election issues.

As this section has explored, over recent years, debates about media effects have increasingly stressed the significance of understanding the comparative differences in *news content*, moving beyond broader claims about whether the media *generally* mobilise or malign voters. This is the central aim of the book – to examine, in detail, how similar or distinctive election reporting is between nations, different media systems and types of election campaigns. In doing so, we develop an evidence-based understanding of the logic shaping election reporting and consider its democratic value.

The scope of the book: reporting (and researching) elections

Although the 'new' online and social media platforms often dominate debates during election time (particularly as political parties

Table 1.0 Sources of information about the 2016 presidential election campaign

	Percentage of news audiences
Television	78
Local TV news	57
Cable TV news	54
National nightly network TV news	49
Late-night comedy shows	25
Digital	65
New websites or apps	48
Social networking sites	44
Issue-based group websites, apps or emails	23
Candidate or campaign group websites, apps or emails	20
Radio	44
Print newspaper	36
Local daily newspapers	29
National newspapers	23

Source: Adapted from Gottfried et al. 2016.

increasingly rely on them for campaigning purposes), in most advanced Western democracies 'old' media continue to act as the primary source of information. As table 1.0 shows, a representative survey of 3,760 US adults conducted by the Pew Research Center in March 2016 found that television was more regularly used as a source of learning about the election than digital media, radio or newspapers (Gottfried et al. 2016).

Likewise, in the UK, a representative poll found that 62 per cent of people considered television to be the most influential source of election news (Bold 2015). This was almost six times more than the 11 per cent who indicated social media. Above all, the televised leaders' debates were viewed as the most influential programme on television during the election campaign, but second best were national newscasts. Even's (2015) summary of voters' main information sources during the 2015 UK general election campaign is worth quoting at length:

TV news still remained the way most voters experienced the general election and for many this was further underlined by another recent trend. For the 90% or so of non-marginal constituencies, there were no posters, billboards, hoardings, leaflets, canvassers, election meetings, walkabouts, photo-ops or politicians. If you were not living in a marginal seat, election activity might as well not exist unless it were on TV. These really were the forgotten voters. And this was even truer for parts of the electorate who were not frequent users of Facebook or Twitter. Or whose broadband still wasn't up to scratch. Apart from local radio and newspapers, TV – especially TV news – would shape the campaign for them. For parties, even though there had been an increasing movement to the internet, television and news bulletins were still the primary battleground of the so-called air campaign and still (just about) the most important means of communicating with voters. These things were true of every campaign since the 1960s. They were still by and large true of 2015.

During the 2017 UK election campaign, a survey showed more people thought TV influenced their voting intention than sites such as Facebook, but the difference was just 1 per cent (Weber Shandwick 2017). Since 2016, the annual study of audiences published by Reuters has found that news consumption online is marginally greater than that on television, especially for younger age groups (Newman et al. 2017).

Indeed, television news viewing has fallen over the past few decades in most Western democracies (Nielsen and Sambrook 2016), with more people – notably in lower age groups – relying on online media and social media platforms (Newman et al. 2016). But, while it remains unclear how future generations will consume news, especially about politics, at present the evidence shows that television remains a dominant source of information about election campaigns (Bold 2015; Even 2015; Gottfried 2016; Weber Shandwick 2017). This is especially the case for older people, who, studies have repeatedly shown, are the age group most likely to vote. Put simply, *television is the medium of news that informs most voters about election campaigns and, despite the many transformative developments in the age of online and social media consumption, should remain*

*a critical site of inquiry for understanding how well informed and engaged
citizens are in a democracy.*

Given its continued centrality to most people's information
diet, television news reporting of election campaigns is the main
focus of this book. The scope of our study, however, was designed
to be wide-ranging, engaging with a number of timely debates in
political communication and journalism studies but through the
lens of election campaigns. We explore issues relevant to understanding media systems and information environments, media
ownership and regulation, political news and horserace journalism,
objectivity and impartiality, agenda-setting and intermedia agenda-
setting, and the relationship between media and democracy more
generally. However, the overarching focus is on debates about the
mediatisation of politics (Strömbäck 2008; Strömbäck and Esser
2014). The concept of mediatisation has rightly been criticised for
its narrow application, such as assessing the influence of media in
cross-sectional data or within a national context (Cushion 2015;
Deacon and Stanyer 2014). But we consider the mediatisation
of politics to be a valuable *comparative concept to apply when empirically assessing coverage longitudinally, cross-nationally or between media
systems.* As we explain, the book draws on a comprehensive range
of news studies: each chapter engages with different debates but
concludes with an assessment about the prevailing logic shaping
campaign coverage. Exploring different aspects of coverage, we ask
which logic best explains how election campaigns are reported.

Different chapters are informed by our extensive experience
of conducting research into the reporting of elections over the
past decade (Cushion 2017a, 2017b, 2017c, 2017d; Cushion and
Thomas 2016; Cushion et al. 2006, 2009, 2015a, 2015b, 2016a,
2016b). We draw on several of our own large-scale content analyses of some of the most high-profile election campaigns, including
the 2015 and 2017 UK general elections and the European Union
and/or local elections in 2009, 2013 and 2014. This analysis is
supported by a series of interviews that we have conducted with
the heads and/or senior editors at the BBC, ITV, Sky News,
Channel 4 and Channel 5, as well as media regulators and senior
party officials, including spin-doctors, to consider the logic shaping

campaign coverage and reflect on the wider challenges facing journalists when reporting at election time.

Our interviews allowed us to move beyond analysing just media content and dig deeper into the decision-making process behind campaign coverage. As Semetko et al.'s landmark study about US and UK elections acknowledged more than two decades ago, there is 'a tendency [in political communication scholarship] to focus on agenda-setting as a matter of selection and prioritization of news items, while ignoring the role of the media in framing election stories and thus defining and constructing their meaning' (1991: 180). This should not mean, of course, uncritically accepting the views and opinions of practitioners working in the field of political communications. We agree with Semetko et al. that 'only content analysis can show whether such orientations and aspirations have real consequences for what actually gets into the news' (1991: 183). By combining content analysis with our interviews, we gain many important insights throughout the book about the logic driving campaign coverage. Some of these, we argue, challenge conventional academic wisdom about the causes and consequences of mediatisation in political reporting.

In order to produce a thorough international assessment of election reporting, overall we drew on a wide range of empirical studies examining campaign coverage in specific countries or cross-nationally. Many of these studies were located within different disciplines, ranging from journalism studies and political communication to media studies and political science, along with other industry-related sources. Our review of relevant literature was extensive and time-consuming but was made easier by the rise of open-access publishing and globalised research networks. It was also helped by improvements in academic literature search engines, such as Google Scholar and Metalib. However, election data was not always easy to find, and we are grateful to many people for sharing their research studies and, at times, for sending their raw data sets so we could interrogate them more closely.

While our review of empirical news studies was exhaustive, we would not claim it delivers a complete picture of television news coverage of election campaigns in most Western democracies.

To ensure that we had the space not just to unpack findings but to explain the context in which news was produced, our primary focus was on election studies in the UK and the US. This was also because we had to rely on English-language material. Nonetheless, we do explore campaign coverage beyond our Anglo-American focus, particularly in several Scandinavian countries. These countries have a vibrant research culture in journalism studies and political communication, with many reports being published in English. Although we concentrate mostly on television news, at times we present more general findings about media coverage because data was not always disaggregated by medium and there were no alternative studies about the topic. Indeed, some content-based studies have been excluded because data was too difficult to reproduce accurately (in graphs or charts) or to explain adequately the context in which findings were generated and analysed (in more statistically orientated studies, for example).

Our aim was to explore the most recent election campaigns, but this was partly informed by the availability of data. At times we explored coverage longitudinally, making it necessary to revisit findings that were several decades old. But this was not straightforward. As van Aelst et al. (2017: 20) have pointed out, 'in the international communication literature it is often hard to find descriptive data of developments over time. Most journals give premium to methodologically and theoretically sophisticated articles, and when space is scarce, many scholars do not include the descriptive data that their analyses are based on.' We searched extensively for relevant data but, needless to say, could not examine every aspect of campaign coverage. As we explain, each chapter has a specific focus that allows us to explore election reporting in comparative detail. Many of the studies on which we draw were based on the most popular forms of news programming, such as newscasts, which are relatively easy to analyse in quantitative content analysis studies. This meant important forms of television news – TV debates, one-on-one interviews, documentaries, and more besides – were not part of our analysis. There remain other forms of news during election campaigns that go beyond the scope of our study (see Ekström and Patrona 2011, for example).

Nevertheless, drawing on our own studies of the most recent UK elections, as well as extensively researching the most up-to-date industry reports and academic literature, *the book was informed overall by a comprehensive range of well over a hundred empirical news studies related to election campaign coverage.*

Chapter 1 begins by explaining the conceptual framework of the book. We consider the main actors – the media, political parties and the public – involved in the agenda-setting process during election campaigns. While there is a clear interdependence between them, we suggest there is a degree of independence from each other as they compete to set the news agenda. Drawing on the mediatisation of politics framework, we introduce how media, political and public logics have been theorised and consider their relevance to interpreting election reporting. Above all, the aim of this chapter is to unpack the main editorial influences behind campaign coverage, which explains how the book will analyse and assess the quality of election reporting.

Chapter 2 develops a big picture analysis of election reporting by comprehensively reviewing studies that have investigated how campaigns are generally framed in news coverage. We examine the degree to which election news agendas focus on policy issues compared to campaign-process stories. After all, learning about competing policy positions above the game frame is more likely to help voters make an informed judgement about which party best represents their interests. According to conventional mediatisation of politics theory, the balance of process above policy coverage also reveals how far a media or political logic might shape campaign coverage (Strömbäck and Esser 2014). Our review explores first-order elections, principally American presidential and UK general elections over recent decades, campaign coverage between media systems and political cultures, and the reporting of second-order elections. It is a data-heavy chapter, but the aim is to build a macro-picture about how elections are predominantly framed across different countries, media systems and electoral contests.

Chapter 3 digs deeper into one of the previous chapter's key findings – the rise of process-driven news in campaign cover-age. We explore the historical development of horserace reporting and consider its value in campaign coverage. Horserace news, of course, is nothing new or particularly novel in election reporting, but, since it has become more dominant in election news, this chapter aims to consider how it shapes campaign coverage. We look at why horserace news thrives in broadcast news and consider its value in engaging and informing people ahead of election day. In doing so, we examine the extent to which opinion polls are reported in election campaigns and, drawing on a case study of coverage of the 2015 UK general election, investigate how far a media logic was responsible for the editorial selection of horserace news. Overall, the chapter asks: *Whose agenda is best served by horserace journalism during an election campaign?*

Chapter 4 considers how fair and balanced reporting is during election campaigns. Bias, of course, is not always easy to detect and evidence. But we begin by examining studies that have measured forms of bias, such as tonal or agenda balance, focusing on US news media. Unlike most other Western countries, the US does not have any formal regulations ensuring the objectivity, impartiality or balance of election coverage. In this chapter, we show how these terms represent different philosophical aims and are applied (and understood) according to different national media systems and political cultures. To explore how impartiality is interpreted in more detail, we draw on a case study of the 2015 UK general election, supported by interviews with regulators, editors, politicians and spin-doctors and a large content analysis of television news. We ask how impartiality was interpreted by practitioners during the campaign and consider the intermedia agenda-setting influence of newspapers.

Chapter 5 focuses largely on coverage of the 2016 US presidential race and the media logic of election news. As we explain, Donald Trump was not a typical presidential candidate and, in a number of ways, redefined campaign logic by his use of social media and his ability to command media attention. We characterise this as a Trumpification of election reporting, with campaign coverage having been influenced by the rise of partisan media, post-truth politics and the increasing commercialisation of news values. We explore the limited range of studies (at the time of writing) that examine the nature of coverage during both the primary campaigns and the general election. Drawing parallels with how Trump and Clinton were reported, we examine EU referendum coverage and enter into debates about false balance and impartial journalism. Finally, we ask whether the Trumpification of election reporting is likely to spread around the world.

The final chapter reflects on the overall findings of the book to develop an evidence-based assessment about the value of campaign coverage. We consider how well the news media enhance people's engagement with and understanding of politics ahead of election day. In understanding the logic behind campaign coverage, we question how the mediatisation of politics has been theorised and interpret new logics that shape how elections are reported. Since political parties have become increasingly sophisticated in how they campaign during an election, we argue that journalists need to find new ways of holding power to account. In doing so, we consider how the logic of campaign coverage can be rethought in ways that better serve the democratic needs of citizens. This, above all, is the central focus of the book – *to understand comprehensively the logic of campaign coverage and to rethink how election reporting could strengthen democracy.*

1

Setting the Campaign Agenda

Campaign agenda-setters: towards an understanding of media, political and public logics

An electoral contest is fought principally *between* political parties competing for power. They do so by campaigning in 'air' and 'ground' warfare, drawing on increasingly sophisticated communication strategies and practices to appeal to voters. While the ground war broadly represents direct ways of party campaigning, such as meeting voters face to face or targeting them digitally, the air war primarily involves parties influencing mass-media content on television or in newspapers or online or social media platforms. A voluminous literature about how each type of campaign warfare is planned and executed has steadily grown, with painstaking research and first-hand accounts of how elections are won or lost on the 'ground' or in the 'air' (see, for example, Kreiss 2012, 2016; Nielsen 2012; Vaccari 2008; West 2014).

The focus in this chapter – and, indeed, the book in general – is on the *air war* during a campaign and, more specifically, making sense of the influences behind the editorial selection of election reporting in television news. After all, while the race for power is between political parties during an election, the air war is fought by *a far wider range of actors* that, in different ways, contribute to the formation of media agendas (McCombs 2004; Semetko et al. 1991). McCombs's metaphorical onion provides a vivid illustration of the many layers of influence shaping news agendas. In peeling back the onion to its core, McCombs (2014: 111) argues that the metaphor 'illustrates the sequential nature of this process in which the influence of an outer layer is, in turn, affected by layers more proximate to the core of the onion.' The outer core is represented by sources of news, such as leaders of political parties, particularly the president or prime minister, or other external influences, for example lobbyists, think tanks, academics and voters. Deep inside the onion lie the professional norms and values of news outlets, which operate according to their own regulatory framework and editorial goals. News media can also feed off each other, known as intermedia agenda-setting.

Our emphasis in this chapter is not just on the agenda-setting power of the media but on the role played by political actors and voters in shaping election coverage. Although there is a clear *inter-dependence* between these three primary actors, each has a degree of independence from the others, as competing interests and needs shape the agenda-setting process during an election campaign (McCombs 2014; Semetko et al. 1991). We consider, in particular, the intense power struggle between media and political actors and unpack a wide range of empirical news studies that have explored the battle to control the agenda during election campaigns. While external actors such as lobbyists or special interest groups also play an agenda-setting role, they all influence the actions and behaviour of media, political parties and voters in different but overlapping ways. So, for example, business lobbies may influence the content of election coverage, the manifestos of parties or people's voting attitudes based on their assessment of the state of the economy. Different stakeholders, in other words, play an important, if not always visible, role in the formation of agenda-setting during an election campaign and beyond.

Extending the metaphorical onion of news selection, previous election news research – as the introductory chapter argued – has focused too heavily on the layers of influence shaping campaign reporting *generally*, most prominently in the US or in first-order elections. As a result, our understanding of news agendas in different types of electoral contests, across media systems and between political cultures or levels of voter engagement, is limited. We need to develop a more comparative and empirically richer mode of inquiry in political communication research and bring to light the range of factors that shape news agendas internationally and between different types of elections. We consider the agenda-setting influences of election reporting by drawing on the mediatisation of politics framework, introduced in the opening chapter. Our focus is not only the editorial influences shaping media and political logics during an election campaign – which dominate debates about the mediatisation of politics (Esser and Strömbäck 2014) – but how, and in what ways, a public logic informs the agenda-setting process. Since a key aim of the book is to explore how well the media inform citizens about an electoral contest, the final part of the chapter considers how a public agenda – or logic – can be evaluated when interpreting campaign coverage.

Overall, the aim of this chapter is to consider the editorial influences behind election reporting, beginning first with how scholars have explored the role of the media in setting the election agenda, then moving on to the role played by political actors and the general public. In doing so, we develop a framework that explains how subsequent chapters will analyse and assess the quality of campaign coverage.

Agenda-setting power in a fragmented environment: interpreting media vs. political logic

At the core of the metaphorical onion, the media have a central role in election agenda-setting. While politicians can canvass voters face to face or communicate with them directly on social media or in large rallies, established news outlets, such as the BBC, CNN or

ABC, remain the most influential platforms for informing people about politics. Why else, for example, was the US president – Donald Trump – so incensed by negative post-2016 election coverage when he has nearly 50 million followers on Twitter, Facebook and Instagram? Since most democracies allow the media to have the editorial freedom to decide on what to report – or exclude – it would appear journalists and editors, above all, have the decisive agenda-setting power when reporting elections. However, the theory and practice of agenda-setting is far from that straightforward, with editorial decision-making influenced indirectly by political forces, as well as by wider economic and cultural factors that shape the production of news (McCombs 2014).

In recent years it has been claimed that media agenda-setting power has been diminishing, since people can access a greater range of news outlets (Johnson 2014). So, for example, where once the three US television networks ABC, CBS and NBC were unquestionably key sources of news that reached tens of millions of Americans, the emergence of dedicated cable news channels, online news and, more recently, social media platforms has meant that their ability to influence people has gradually waned (Mitchell and Holcomb 2016). Between them, they still attract audiences of approximately 25 million – far more than cable or online platforms reach. But their *degree* of agenda-setting influence is waning in a more fragmented media environment.

In isolating *particular* news outlets, however, we risk overlooking the *collective* and *systemic* process of media agenda-setting power. McCombs (1997) has labelled this the consensus-building role of the media, which sets a framework of issues that inform public debate and people's priorities. As research in political communication and journalism studies has long revealed, a broadly shared agenda is driven by economic, social and ideological factors that police the boundaries of news across different media systems and political cultures (Herman and Chomsky 1988; Philo 1990). The editorial selection of political news, for example, is not left to the discretion of individual journalists but broadly navigated by a set of news values that help constitute 'what's news'. Harcup and O'Neill's (2001, 2016) systematic analysis of news values over time has shown, on the one hand, that the selection of news is fluid and informed by many factors, such as the resources at the outlet's disposal, the time sensitivity of a story, the type of media and who owns it, and internal organisational pressures, along with other less tangible influences. On the other hand, their evidence shows that, for the most part journalists share a taxonomy of stories that signal greater newsworthiness than others. Put more simply, despite the growth of news media outlets over recent years, the power of agenda-setting has not necessarily diminished or led to a more diverse agenda of news reporting. There remains a conformity of reporting which, as Harcup and O'Neill's (2016) latest study points out, bursts the bubble of many new media enthusiasts who had predicted that the media environment would become radically fragmented. However, there are signs that the gatekeeping power of established media is being challenged. During the 2017 UK election campaign, for example, some of the most shared online stories came from alt-left sites, such as *The Canary*, *Evolve Politics* and *Another Angry Voice* (Waterson and Phillips 2017). Nevertheless, the evidence generally shows the most widely shared news on platforms such as Twitter or Facebook, for instance, tend to be established mainstream media brands, such as Fox, the BBC, CNN, *The Mail* and *The Guardian* (Newman et al. 2016). In other words, while the consumption of news may have changed in the age of social media and smartphones, it has not been radically transformed, since many people in today's online world continue to rely on the same offline sources.

In considering the editorial power of media in election coverage or political reporting more generally, scholars have increasingly turned to the concept of mediatisation. Broadly put, the mediatisation of politics asks whether political coverage has increasingly succumbed to a media logic, promoting its own set of news values to make the editorial decisions as to what should – and should not – be reported. Within this framework, media logic is defined in opposition to a political logic, both of which – it is argued – can be empirically measured according to a set of criteria. As Strömbäck and Esser put it:

The media can be *more* or *less* important as a source of information, and *more* or *less* independent from political institutions, and media content as well as political institutions and actors can be *more* or *less* guided by media logic as opposed to political logic. There might also be variations across different media and, not least importantly, different political actors, organizations and institutions, both within and across countries. The degree of mediatization along different dimensions is ultimately an empirical question and most often contextual. (2014: 7; original emphasis)

By following this framework, our aim is to answer this empirical question by drawing on a comprehensive range of studies that have examined media coverage of elections across different media systems, political cultures and advanced Western democracies. In doing so, we can draw evidence-based conclusions about the editorial power of the media during different election campaigns, asking if a media logic supersedes a political logic or whether the media agenda is influenced to a greater degree by political parties.

Comparing how media and political actors influence an election campaign is not a straightforward empirical task. As we argue throughout the book, while we can examine macro-ways of broadly understanding whether more of a media or political logic was pursued over an election campaign, it remains important to consider the micro-factors that influenced the editorial selection of coverage (Semetko et al. 1991). This requires more background and contextual analysis of specific election campaigns, which we provide in different chapters by developing relevant UK and US case studies. Comparative analysis is easier in a macro-approach, such as examining the quantitative supply of news in campaign reporting or the types of sources used to inform election coverage. So, for example, if a news item was principally about the process of politics, such as reporting the razzmatazz behind a campaign event, the personality of a candidate or the horserace contest between political parties, it could be seen as symptomatic of a media logic (Takens et al. 2013). Broadly speaking, these types of stories are viewed as reflecting the strategic game frame, which is seen to inject excitement and drama into routine political reporting (Aalberg et al. 2012). By contrast, if an election item is primarily about a policy issue, such as the economy, public health, crime or international affairs, within the mediatisation framework it is generally viewed as representing a political logic (Strömbäck and Esser 2014). At various points throughout the book we question this premise, in particular when understanding the 2015 UK general election and the 2016 US presidential campaign (see chapters 2, 4 and 5). Overall, according to the mediatisation of politics framework, reporting *policy issues* rather than campaign process represents evidence of party political influence during an election campaign.

The influence of political actors informing media agendas during an election campaign is more empirically visible by assessing how far they actually *appear* in coverage, rather than when journalists speak for them. After all, when political actors have the opportunity to speak in person, they can exercise at least *some* control over how they are represented. This is most commonly measured by the length of soundbites – the period of time that politicians speak uninterrupted on-screen. But, generally speaking, research has shown political actors have been granted less time to appear in television news. This was established by Hallin's (1992) longitudinal study of presidential election reporting in US network news, which revealed that the average length of political soundbites was reduced from 43 seconds in 1968 to just 9 seconds in 1988. Of course, this period witnessed a major transformation in communication technology, allowing broadcasters to edit raw footage more easily.

But technology alone cannot explain how far politicians were allowed to appear on television news, since comparative studies have revealed the political and journalistic culture of different countries can influence editorial decisions (de Vreese et al. 2017; Semetko et al. 1991). As far back as the 1980s, for example, the study of election reporting by Semetko and her colleagues discovered that US network television news gave far less space and time for political parties to articulate their messages than UK broadcasters. In their view, US media exercised greater 'discretionary power' over political coverage, with journalists interpreting rather than simply conveying the views and behaviour of political actors (Semetko et al. 1991: 4). Put more simply, the US media set the election campaign agenda to a greater degree than their counterparts in the UK.

Semetko et al. (1991) outlined a number of macro- and microfactors that accounted for the differences between nations in editorial power, but chief among them was the role played by public service broadcasting in the UK. Whereas the loosely regulated system of network television in the US was driven largely by commercial decisions, UK broadcasters operated within a public service framework, with stricter editorial guidelines about balance and impartiality. UK broadcasters thus considered it editorially appropriate to grant political parties greater airtime to articulate their messages. However, according to Blumler and Coleman (2010), subsequent decades witnessed an erosion of public service values in the UK and a shift towards a more American style of interpretive journalism. In doing so, journalists appear to have greater autonomy and control in setting the election campaign. The chapters that follow both examine whether UK coverage remains distinctive from that of the US and explore wider shifts in journalism that might influence who sets the campaign agenda.

Within the mediatisation framework, greater journalistic interventionism represents a victory of media over political logic. This has been measured not only by the relative length of political soundbites but by the role played by journalists according to certain criteria. So, for example, enhanced interventionism – or discretionary power – has been interpreted as journalists becoming more visible in coverage, reporting in live two-ways, wrapping up news packages, talking over political speeches or providing more commentary than description (Cushion 2015; Esser 2008; Strömbäck and Dimitrova 2011; Semetko et al. 1991). All of this, it is argued, grants journalists greater editorial agency in setting the election agenda (Strömbäck and Kaid 2008). How far this agency is exercised is partly a consequence of journalistic culture and how adversarial or deferential reporters are when they report on the behaviour and actions of political actors. Within this culture, a 'pack journalism' can often exist where mainstream reporters work, travel and socialise together, meaning they often share similar expectations and perspectives about how they should cover the same events or issues. It is what Barbie Zelizer (1993) calls 'interpretive communities', with journalists policing the boundaries of what and how they decide to report.

However, despite holding a powerful gatekeeping role in the editorial selection and exclusion of news reporting, there remain long-standing conventions that limit how far the media rather than political parties and politicians shape election agendas. With the exception of partisan outlets such as MSNBC or Fox News in the US, most broadcasters around the world strive to report politics impartially, attempting to balance party perspectives and to interpret events and issues objectively (Cushion 2012b). As chapter 4 explores, impartiality, balance and objectivity represent different philosophical goals, and how they are applied editorially can have important consequences for election reporting. So, for example, during the EU referendum, UK television newscasts – which follow 'due impartiality' guidelines – largely balanced competing perspectives from the Leave and Remain camps with limited journalistic arbitration or expert verification (Cushion and Lewis 2017). As we argue in chapter 5, a more objective approach would have been to draw on a wider range of sources – think tanks, say, or economists and academics – to counter the sometimes dubious claims of campaigners. In doing so, the agenda-setting power of political elites might have been lightened and more fact-based reporting might have informed campaign coverage.

The impartiality framework, in this context, aims to ensure particular political parties are given due weight during an election campaign. After all, the role of the media is often viewed as *reflecting* rather than *constructing* the democratic will of the people. Thus, the extent to which political parties are reported in coverage is generally guided by their current opinion poll ratings or their past performance in electoral contests (Hopmann et al. 2012). In the 2017 UK general election, for example, the Conservatives and Labour together received over 80 per cent of the vote. This may justify broadcasters' decision to give less airtime to smaller parties such as the Liberal Democrats than in the 2015 election campaign

(Cushion 2017a). But that overlooks the power broadcasters have, not just in reflecting but in constructing public opinion. Of course, not all media systems are shaped by rules about balance and impartiality. As chapter 5 reveals, Donald Trump's populist brand of politics attracted a considerable amount of airtime during the run-up to the 2016 presidential election campaign even before he was nominated as the Republican candidate. After that point, coverage focused almost exclusively on Trump versus his Democratic opponent Hillary Clinton, leaving little airtime for any third or fourth challenger, such as Gary Johnson or Jill Stein, representing Libertarian and Green Party perspectives.

Far from the media setting the terms of the election agenda, this suggests that political actors from mainstream parties exercise a considerable degree of influence on the *range* of issues and policies that shape campaigns. Put simply, they help set the ideological parameters of election reporting. We thus need to understand the power of politicians and political parties during electoral contests more closely and consider the various ways parties have professionalised their campaigning to help set the media agenda.

The professionalisation of political campaigning: interpreting party political logic

Over recent decades, scholars have increasingly explored how political parties have become ever more professionalised in election campaigning. Professionalisation, of course, is a broad process and, in political communication studies, has become a catch-all term to describe changes that are difficult to pin down empirically (Lilleker and Negrine 2002). Nevertheless, broadly speaking, it is often used in political communication scholarship to represent how, since the Second World War, political parties have been 'transformed by the gradual evolution of the permanent campaign in which the techniques of spin-doctors, opinion polls, and professional media management are increasingly applied to routine everyday politics' (Norris 2000: 173). As a result, the range of personnel involved in election campaigning has grown in terms of size and specialism. As Strömbäck (2009a: 95) put it, 'If the campaign warriors of yesterday were activists and volunteers, today they are . . . professional political persuaders and consultants for hire.'

The professionalisation of election campaigning was brought into sharper focus after the release of the 1993 documentary *The War Room*, which followed James Carville and George Stephanopoulos, two Democrat spin-doctors, during the 1992 US election campaign. It revealed the extraordinary time and resources behind Bill Clinton's presidential communication strategy, from handling the aggressive pack of journalists, rebutting fierce attacks from opponents and carefully crafting soundbites. The rebranding of the New Democrats in the US foreshadowed the transformation of New Labour in the UK, symbolised by the appointment of the spin-doctor Alistair Campbell, a Carville-esque figure who sought aggressively to control the media agenda and to keep his party relentlessly 'on message' (Norris 2000). Into the new millennium, 'spin' became a term of abuse in British politics, with the Labour Party in particular associated with a cynical misuse of information and presentation for political gain. Immediately after the terrorist attacks on 11 September 2001, for example, a Labour spin-doctor suggested in a leaked email that today would be 'a very good day to get out anything we want to bury'. The extent of New Labour's enhanced focus on communication was revealed when a report showed that, while in 1997 the government had employed 300 press officers, by 2006 this number had risen more than tenfold, to 3,200, including 77 politically appointed special advisers (Hencke 2006).

At the same time, the beginning of the twenty-first century witnessed a huge expansion in the media, with the arrival of multi-channel television and rolling online coverage. The government, viewed in this light, was thus understandably responding to this changing culture of information and communication. As a government spokesperson said in 2006, 'The world of communications has changed dramatically over the last decade. The phenomenon of the web, explosion in 24/7 multi-channel media and investment in staff and stakeholder communications make comparisons with 1997 largely meaningless' (Hencke 2006). A decade on and the infra-structure of communication has been further enhanced, with more digital tools and social media platforms opening up new ways of micro-managing electoral campaigning and influencing the media agenda. Kreiss's (2014) study of the use of Twitter during the 2012 presidential election, for example, found that the Democrats' better resourced and more autonomous staff of digital campaign-ers was able to influence how journalists interpreted fast-moving events and issues. In 2016, Donald Trump's campaign used social media to bypass the mainstream media, allowing him to com-municate directly with voters. But it also helped exercise greater control over Trump's campaign messages, as his tweets were often reported in full. Ahead of the 2016 presidential election, according to Enli (2017), Trump's use of Twitter ran counter to conventional and professionalised ways of campaigning – as Clinton's did – but this amateurism and lack of professionalism were highly effective. As chapter 5 further explores, Trump's campaign self-consciously sought to side-step conventional interaction with journalists, lim-iting questioning at press conferences and even attacking some reporters. Since the mainstream media are increasingly mistrusted by Americans, particularly by registered Republicans, social media proved an effective means of communicating with voters and exer-cising greater control over the campaign.

However, the transformation of political communication over recent decades cannot be explained by technology such as Twitter or Facebook alone. As Negrine (2008) has argued, the profes-sionalisation of politics is the product of a multiplicity of forces that change the culture of communication, including technology, but also the result of wider political, economic and social charac-teristics, such as mistrust towards mainstream media, that may be unique to a particular country. Indeed, the US's political system is often regarded as hyper-professionalised, since electioneering is fuelled by billions of dollars that fund specialist practitioners to campaign and influence the agendas of the world's largest media market-place (Nichols and McChesney 2013). By contrast, many European countries, including the UK, impose strict limits on how much political parties are allowed to spend on campaigning during the election period. But it is not just a question of campaign resources that differentiates professionalisation from the kind of campaigning that Trump displayed in 2016. There are also more subtle differences in style and character between nations. American political campaigning is often singled out for its more negative approach, notably in (largely unregulated) television advertising, where candidates spend a huge amount of money (although Trump spent comparatively little on adverts in 2016 compared to previous candidates). Hence, beyond the US, when interpreting any changes to specific countries, scholars sometimes refer to an 'Americanisation of' campaigning or political reporting (Blumler and Gurevitch 2001). In other words, the *degree* of professionalisation in campaigning needs to be understood comparatively according to wider macro-influences, such as different media and political systems, as well as micro-influences between parties (Strömbäck and van Aelst 2013).

Gibson and Römmele (2009), for example, developed a thirty-point index to show how professionalised campaigning was in a German federal election. They sought to measure and compare the depth of parties' campaign infrastructure according to variables such as telemarketing, direct mail, an intranet system, an email network, a headquarters, the use of PR and opinion poll experts. This party-centred focus on election campaigning has also been applied in different national contexts in first-order elections (cf. Strömbäck 2009a). However, perhaps more revealing are cross-national studies that compare the level of professionalisation not only between parties and countries but also in different types of electoral contests, such as second-order elections. Tenscher and his colleagues, for instance, examined twenty-eight parties in four nations – Austria, Finland, Germany and Sweden – and identified striking differences in the level of campaign professionalisation during the 2009 EU elections. Their study concluded that 'the differences in professional campaigning between countries are smaller than the differences between political parties within one and the same country' (Tenscher et al. 2012: 159). They further argued that smaller parties adopted distinctive ways of appealing to a media logic than did bigger parties, using their more limited resources to find ways of attracting attention, and thus voters, more widely. While, overall, they found a Western style of political campaigning, they also suggested there could be 'two levels of professionalization: an upper level with higher degrees of professional communicative activities at national first-order elections and a lower level at European and second-order elections'. De Vreese's analysis of electioneering in eight EU countries during the 2004 EU elections found candidates' campaigning could be considered second rate. He concluded that 'campaigning in second-order types of elections, such as the European Parliament elections, is less extensive than in first-order elections' (de Vreese 2009: 15).

For the purposes of this book, understanding the *extent* of political campaigning across different types of election and between countries clearly has implications for the degree of power – or logic – parties can exert in setting the media agenda. After all, the level of professionalisation (however that is measured) could enhance a party's ability to influence editorial decisions during an election campaign. As Strömbäck and van Aelst have explored, political parties have increasingly adapted their own political logic to appeal to the dominant norms and values of the media environment. In their view, this represents the fourth and final phase of the mediatisation of politics, where political parties modify their behaviour and actions as a consequence of a media logic. As they put it, 'More than ever, political actors try to anticipate how media will react to their words or deeds and incorporate this reaction in their decision-making' (Strömbäck and van Aelst 2013: 354). Figenschou and Thorbjørnsrud's analysis of how the Norwegian government communicated its policy about immigration, for example, revealed how its messaging was consciously designed according to a human interest narrative that reflected atypical immigrants who threatened ordinary people's lives. In their words, the study showed how 'media work in government is adjusted to the dominant news logic, based on sophisticated public relations and media competency and resources, but also constrained by central civil service norms and rules' (Figenschou and Thorbjørnsrud 2015: 1959).

There is arguably a greater urgency and sensitivity to a media logic among political actors during an election campaign, since they are desperate to promote their messages to an electorate about to cast their vote. Indeed, in the age of online and social media communication, political actors have become adept at appealing to competing media logics across multiple platforms. So, for example, a day before the second US presidential election in October 2016, a recording of Donald Trump making lewd remarks about women dominated campaign coverage. Although he apologised later that night, an hour before the Sunday night debate Trump organised a press conference with women who had previously accused Bill Clinton (the husband of his Democratic opponent) of inappropriate sexual behaviour more than two decades previously. With the three women invited guests of Trump at the evening broadcast, it was, in short, an attempt to overshadow the live television contest and the debates between candidates. According to Poniewozik (2016), a *New York Times* journalist, Trump 'gave the women front-row seats at the debate – with Mr Clinton in the crowd – counterprogramming his unscripted video scandal by staging a daytime talk-show drama.' Viewed in this context, the reality TV star turned presidential candidate was appealing to a media logic that might turn the campaign spotlight onto Clinton's past. As Poniewozik further observed, 'what happens in the 90 minutes of a modern debate matters less than the conversation before and after. It's less about sustaining an argument than creating moments – generating news clips and viral memes, setting up your opponent to misstep . . . trying to drive the narrative.'

When Richard Nixon and John F. Kennedy participated in the first ever televised presidential debate in 1960, it was during a time when Marshall McLuhan (1964) argued that the medium was the dominant force behind the shaping of a message. But today politicians are savvy enough to communicate beyond one platform. After all, the hybrid nature of contemporary media means that a speech or TV debate will rarely be watched – or judged – in its entirety but, rather, cut up into tiny newsworthy pieces and endlessly replayed and shared online or social media (Chadwick 2013). The heightened awareness of how politicians appear in the news was well illustrated in a 2011 interview with Ed Miliband, the then UK Labour leader, about public sector strikes. Much to the annoyance of the journalist, Miliband repeated the same responses over and over again, despite being asked different questions about the issue. The next day the journalist opined in a 1,200-word blog that, 'If news reporters and cameras are only there to be used by politicians as recording devices for their scripted soundbites, at best that is a professional discourtesy. At worst, if we are not allowed to explore and examine a politician's views, then politicians cease to be accountable in the most obvious way' (cited in Sweney 2011).

In the age of shrinking soundbites, however, carefully scripted responses from politicians are perhaps an understandable reaction to the limited power they have in controlling the message. After all, if their perspective is limited to little more than ten seconds on the evening news, speaking in repetitive soundbites grants them greater agency in how that clip is edited. Although there is a clear battle to control the agenda between political and media actors, the relationship has been described as not only adversarial but deeply intimate or even collusive. Both actors want to exert their political or media independence from each other, but there remains an *interdependence*. As discussed earlier in the chapter, since most broadcasters are impartial, they attempt to balance the perspectives of competing political parties, allowing them a platform to communicate their campaign messages. In representative democracies, the media view their role as legitimising the terms of the debate. Indeed, during elections or beyond, political elites have long been viewed as a routine and credible institutional source in news coverage. The parameters of their views help police the boundaries of what is – and is not – considered rational territory to debate issues in politics and public affairs (Bennett 1990). But, in relying so heavily on politicians, journalists build close relationships with them which, at times, have to be carefully negotiated, since coverage can be advantageous but also critical. Moreover, most journalists have editorial guidelines or, at least, a wider professional ideology that promotes independence from politics and champions holding power to account. There remains, in this sense, an uneasy but necessary tension between journalists and politicians, with both sides mutually benefiting from their relationship.

Against this backdrop, subsequent chapters examine the evidence about the power dynamic between journalists and politicians during an election campaign, asking which actors typically lead the election agenda across different countries, media systems and electoral contests. But, before we begin reviewing the evidence, the role played by citizens must be explored in the agenda-setting process. Citizens, above all, have the power to vote politicians in and out of office. But how do they shape a public logic in campaign coverage?

How do citizens make – or shape – election news agendas? Towards a public logic in campaign coverage

According to Gamson (2001: 56), 'in a democracy, public discourse can and should empower citizens, give them voice and agency, build community, and help citizens to act on behalf of their interests and values.' Viewed in this light, the media play an essential role for citizens, not only in informing them about the burning issues of the day but in representing their concerns and encouraging engagement. Since elections represent a decisive moment in any democracy, understanding how far citizens help set the campaign agenda clearly matters. Interpreting the public agenda, in this context, is not incompatible with exploring a media or political agenda. It is more an attempt to isolate, where possible, how far coverage is driven from the bottom up (by citizens) rather than top down (by media and political elites). This, of course, lies at the heart of agenda-setting theory, which seeks to establish how – and why – people acquire knowledge and understanding of politics and public affairs by watching, listening to or reading media (McCombs 2004).

However, since the turn of the century, there has been widespread debate about a so-called democratic crisis in Western countries, with generally declining levels of voting and enhanced cynicism towards party politics (Franklin 2004). As our introductory chapter explained, the media have been caught up in debates about discouraging political engagement, with broadcasters often singled out for promoting a style and approach to reporting that turns viewers off (Lloyd 2004). And yet the media, in particular public service broadcasters, are acutely aware of their democratic significance during an election campaign. Regulatory guidance is often enhanced during official campaigns, with specialist programming and television debates scheduled to inform and foster democratic engagement.

A sense of journalistic responsibility – even civic duty – was revealed at the beginning of the new millennium in the UK, when the proportion of people voting in the 2001 general election – 59 per cent – reached its lowest level for over eighty years. Far from blaming party politicians or citizens, the BBC – the UK's main public service broadcaster – launched an internal review of its programming to find ways of promoting political engagement (Kevill 2002). At the subsequent election in 2005, broadcasters attempted more generally to explore voters' attitudes and opinions towards the campaign, as a then Sky News presenter, Julie Etchingham, conceded: 'Everybody was aware that the 2001 coverage had bored people, so I was interested to see how each broadcaster had scratched their heads.' At the time, ITV editor-in-chief David Mannion argued that their programming tried to 'get out there, presenting from the doorsteps of floating voters (Ballot Box Jury)', while Nick Pollard, then head of Sky News, revealed that their channel had made a concerted effort to speak to 'ordinary people'. According to Chris Shaw, then senior programme controller of Channel 5, 'the idea of getting closer to the real people got out of hand' during the election campaign (all quotes taken from Cushion et al. 2006). In other words, the *public agenda* was pushed too far up the election agenda.

During the 2010 UK general election campaign, one citizen – Gillian Duffy – played a significant role. A long-standing Labour councillor, she was asked to talk to Gordon Brown, the then Labour prime minster, during what has become common practice in recent UK election campaigning – a seemingly casual but highly stage-managed walkabout. In the full glare of the media, they had a long discussion covering topics such as the number of Eastern European immigrants arriving in her Rochdale constituency.

While returning to his car, and unaware that his microphone was still on, the prime minster called Mrs Duffy a 'bigoted woman'. This moment dominated media coverage that day and was widely replayed over the course of the campaign. Moreover, coverage of immigration as a policy issue subsequently rose (Deacon and Wring 2011), with Gillian Duffy's views used by the media – particularly by right-wing newspapers – to reflect public disquiet with increasing numbers of immigrants. Not only that, as chapter 3 explores further, Gillian Duffy's intervention arguably shaped the logic of party political campaigning during the 2015 general election. To avoid any 'Duffy moments', political parties exercised a greater degree of control over events such as walkabouts, limiting how far 'ordinary' members of the public could interact with senior politicians in front of the cameras (Cushion et al. 2016b).

But beyond moments when a citizen grabbed the headlines or when journalists voiced their impressions about how involved voters were in campaign coverage, how can we assess how far the public shape media agendas? Lewis, Inthorn and Wahl-Jorgensen (2005) carried out a systematic analysis of public opinion in US and UK television news and press coverage over four months *outside* of an election campaign. Examining 4,398 references to public opinion in 2,720 news items, they found that, while citizens were often visible in coverage, they were represented in quite passive ways. So, for example, between 52 and 58 per cent of references to public opinion in the US and UK items were conjectures, where journalists *infer* what citizens think about an issue or event without supporting evidence. Between 39 and 41 per cent of references, meanwhile, were vox pops – where citizens were granted the opportunity to voice their opinion within a news item. But although vox pops act as a conduit for public opinion, Lewis and his colleagues argued that broadcasters largely featured citizens responding to political parties rather than reflecting their own policy preferences. This was, they argued, primarily because broadcasters were attempting to be impartial, constructing public opinion according to the positions of political parties rather than the views of citizens. Public demonstrations and forms of protest, by contrast, represented a tiny fraction of references to public opinion – 1.5 to 2.8 per cent – despite many occurring over their period of analysis. The authors also identified that opinion polls – arguably the most systematic way of interpreting public opinion – made up between 1.8 and 3.6 per cent of references to the public. Overall, they found that, 'while news *is* replete with references to public opinion . . ., they remain remorselessly apolitical and passive' (Lewis et al. 2005: 50; original emphasis).

During election campaigns, however, the public become more of a focal point in coverage, with polls and vox pops more regularly used to navigate people's voting intentions and attitudes towards competing parties (Brookes et al. 2004; Cushion 2017b). As we explore in several chapters, this is widely known as horserace reporting, since opinion polls are endlessly pored over to forecast which party is currently 'winning' or 'losing' the electoral battle. Chapter 3 takes a closer look at the relative merits of horserace reporting, considering how it might, on the one hand, engage audiences in the electoral contest but, on the other, distract voters from being exposed to more serious policy issues.

Of course, polls tell us much more than simply people's voting intentions and can reveal the issues most affecting their lives or their policy positions (Lewis 2001). But during election campaigns public opinion has to compete with the agendas of the media and political parties, which, for the reasons discussed throughout this chapter, means entering into an editorial struggle about which voices prevail. However, the public can be elusive and difficult to represent, since citizens have competing and often contradictory perspectives. To paraphrase Raymond Williams, there is no such thing as the masses, just ways of seeing people as masses. Broadcasters, in this sense, will claim that reflecting audience interests is central to their journalism, while political parties will argue that their policies represent people's everyday anxieties and concerns and are pitched at improving voters' lives. But turning to audience ratings or counting the number of votes cast for a party does not necessarily reflect a public logic. After all, pursuing a populist brand of politics or approach to reporting does not always serve the public's interest.

Beyond journalists referencing public opinion, either explicitly or implicitly (Lewis et al. 2005), how can we interpret a public logic in election reporting? Recent debates about the mediatisation of politics have pointed out that audiences have been marginalised by scholars, since the dominant framework centres on the competing logics driving media and political agenda-setting. According to Witschge (2014: 345), 'the focus is on the autonomy of media institutions and lack thereof by political institutions. But in this discussion the missing component is the audience. Do they have any agency in the constellation? Are they silent accomplices or unaware casualties?' Further still, Witschge argues that 'Media logic as understood in mediatization theory remains a matter that is between political actors and media actors' (ibid.: 346). Likewise, Brants and van Praag (2015: 403) have argued that many studies about the mediatisation of politics largely ignore or fail to appreciate 'the place and importance of considerable parts of the public as a potentially empowered, active and participating force'. They suggested that the 'powers of the public . . . are implicit – but, with that, not less powerful. It is relative, indirect power in that media and politicians anticipate what they assume to be the public's wishes, wants, irritations and angers – assumptions that can be wide of the mark' (ibid.: 404). Overall, they concluded that it is difficult if not impossible to interpret a public logic in political reporting, since there is 'an often unpredictable interaction between public, media and politics' (ibid.: 405).

Landerer (2013) developed an alternative mediatisation framework to the dominant model (Strömbäck 2008), which more explicitly included the role of the public. Both political and media logics were interpreted according to whether a commercially oriented audience logic or a more normatively informed public logic was followed. The former is guided by market considerations, such as a media logic of profit and ratings or an electoral logic of winning elections, whereas the latter is driven by the normative aim of advancing a public interest agenda. Although there is an attempt here to theorise a public logic when interpreting the mediatisation of politics, the difference between a normative and a market approach is empirically difficult to pin down. As Downey and Neyazi (2014) have pointed out, a normative logic in journalism might be radically different, from remaining impartial and balanced to advocating a cause and championing an issue. What is in the public interest, in other words, could be achieved according to competing ways of communicating politics.

More broadly, interpreting what is meant by 'the public interest' in election reporting might also prove challenging because its precise meaning has long been contested within both journalism and the wider legal profession. A normative logic, according to Landerer (2013: 248), enables 'democratic society to take informed decisions'. But this is distinctive from 'the market-oriented primacy of newsworthiness according to which certain issues are selected, organized, and presented, using particular formats.' While this might appear a clear enough theoretical distinction, distinguishing between a *normative* and a *newsworthy* editorial decision about election coverage is not empirically straightforward. After all, a sexual exposé of a senior politician clearly meets the market's demand for salacious news, but it might also perform an important democratic function, exposing an elected representative for misusing his power and authority in office. Put simply, what *interests* the public might also *serve* the public's agenda.

In order to examine how far a public agenda – or logic – informs campaign coverage, the chapters that follow go beyond isolated election stories. We avoid legalistic discussions about what is – and is not – in the public interest. Instead we draw a comprehensive picture about the logic shaping campaign coverage in different countries, media systems and electoral contests. In doing so, we can then consider *how far a media, political or public agenda can be detected.* Of course, these agendas are not mutually exclusive and may involve the logics of all three actors shaping campaign coverage. Our approach, in this sense, is consistent with Downey and Neyazi's analysis of mediatised politics in an Indian context. They argued that future studies should:

> investigate three groups of actors – mediatized publics, media actors, and political actors and see three logics at play simultaneously – a political logic (driven by the goal of electoral success), a commercial logic (driven by the goal of profit maximization), and a professional logic

(driven by the goal of serving the public interest). These logics interact in a complex fashion; at times they are complementary, at other times they are competitive. (Downey and Neyazi 2014: 492)

While they referred to 'mediatized publics', they interpreted a public agenda according to whether a professional logic acted in the 'public interest'. In other words, when comparing the nature of coverage between competing media throughout this book, we *make judgements about how well it informs voters' democratic decision-making.*

Interpreting editorial decision-making: towards an understanding of who sets the agenda

This chapter considered the main actors involved in setting the media agenda over the course of an election campaign. We introduced McCombs's (2014) metaphorical onion to explore the many layers of influence shaping news agendas. While many actors are involved in the agenda-setting process, we identified three – the media, political parties and the public – that can be described as the lead protagonists during an election campaign. Each, of course, has independent interests, but – we argued – there is a clear interdependence between them, and there is a particularly intense power struggle between political parties and the media in the battle to control the agenda.

On the face of it, the media might appear to be the most powerful agenda-setter. It is the media, after all, which have the final editorial say about whether one election story is selected over another. Moreover, they can frame coverage in certain ways, such as focusing on the process of politics to a greater extent than policy issues. Or they can control how much time a candidate has to articulate their perspective, epitomised by the widely used term 'soundbite'. By either framing politics as a game or strategy – for instance, in horserace reporting – or limiting the length of a politician's soundbite according to the mediatisation of politics framework, this represents that a media rather than political logic is being pursued. The agenda, in this context, appears to be set by the editorial interests of news media rather than by political elites.

However, as we further explored, the theory and practice of agenda-setting is far from straightforward, with many different factors shaping the editorial content of political news. Following news values, of course, means editorial discretion is exercised about story selection, but there are long-standing practices, norms and routines that also shape media agendas. With the exception of the US, most advanced democracies have relatively strict impartiality guidelines in broadcast news, and particularly so during election campaigns. This ensures a level of fair and balanced coverage between the main political parties, while also recognising that the media attempt to reflect rather than construct the democratic choices people face when voting. How far that balance is achieved, of course, remains open to debate, and future chapters will carefully consider the evidence across different countries and electoral contests. The broader point is that media agendas are not entirely at the mercy of editorial discretion but follow a set of news values and journalistic practices that give political parties a platform to put forward their positions.

Indeed, this chapter explored how political parties have become increasingly professionalised in setting the media agenda and controlling their messages. However, the level of professionalisation, according to how this concept is measured, can vary between countries and different types of election, with fewer resources invested in second-order campaigning. Moreover, tracing the impact of party political logic in agenda-setting can be difficult in media coverage, since the close, if often combative, relationship between journalists and politicians is often conducted behind closed doors. It is empirically difficult, in other words, to know whether and to what degree editorial decisions about the reporting of elections are influenced by a political or a media logic. To explore how far political parties set the media agenda during an election, debates about the mediatisation of politics often focus on how far political actors or policy issues appear in coverage. Future chapters will consider how useful this framework is in establishing the power dynamics between media and political logics, particularly as parties become increasingly sophisticated in their understanding of news values and journalistic practices. Many party political practitioners are now hired from the media world so that their experience and expertise can be drawn on to influence editorial decision-making.

Finally, the chapter examined the role the public play in setting media agendas during an election campaign. Citizens, after all, have the power to elect and eject governments. But with fewer people voting at the beginning of the twenty-first century, and increasing levels of public scepticism towards the political class, many broadcasters have attempted both to inform and to engage voters during a campaign. Several studies have suggested citizens are represented in largely passive ways in routine political reporting (Cushion et al. 2006; Lewis et al. 2005), which can be exacerbated during election campaigns when their voice is most visible in opinion polls (covered in chapter 3). As later chapters explore, while this helps fuel horserace-type reporting, it is debatable how useful or informative they are in coverage of election campaigns.

But while the use of polls is an explicit instance of the public informing coverage, citizens can shape media agendas more indirectly. Broadcasters would argue their agendas *routinely* reflect the public's interest. As with political parties influencing editorial decisions, however, it can be difficult to isolate how and in what way citizens influence day-to-day agendas. This perhaps explains why – scholars have argued – citizens have been largely excluded from debates about the mediatisation of politics (Witschge 2014). A public logic has been theorised within mediatisation debates, but, since 'the public' can be elusive and contradictory, there are limited ways of measuring their involvement in setting the agenda. We concluded by drawing on Downey and Neyazi's (2014: 492) mediatisation of politics framework, which involved a professional logic that is 'driven by the goal of serving the public interest'. In other words, in order to assess whether citizens make and shape election agendas, we need to interpret how far a public interest agenda is pursued over the course of a campaign.

Needless to say, what is interesting to the public may be different from what is in the public interest. But in the chapters that follow that will be our central focus – *to develop an evidence-based understanding of election reporting and to rethink how the logic of campaign coverage could strengthen democracy.*

The next chapter begins by exploring the extent to which election coverage is informative. We examine how far the media report the policies of competing political parties during election campaigns or focus, instead, on the game, strategy and wider processes of politics.

2
Reporting Election Campaigns

Policy versus process: which logic prevails in campaign coverage?

In order to understand *how* elections are reported we need to establish *what kind of news agendas* are typically pursued during the campaign. After all, the issues reported ahead of election day help define the character of a campaign and represent most people's main information source just before they cast their vote. To paraphrase McCombs (2004), the media not only create an agenda of issues for people to think about, they often tell people what to think – or how to vote. In this chapter we examine news agendas during election campaigns across a range of countries, media systems and electoral contests by considering how campaign coverage is generally framed by the news media, paying particular attention to the proportion of news about *policy issues* compared to *campaign-process coverage*.

The concept of media 'framing' is widely used in political communication and journalism studies to understand how one perspective is privileged over another (Entman 1993). We can interpret election news, in this sense, by exploring the 'emphasis, exclusion and elaboration' (Tankard 2001: 100) of issues reported during an election campaign. Of course, campaigns come in all shapes and sizes, making it hard to compare and contrast not just between countries but between types of electoral contests. Friedman (2016), for example, observed that the American presidential election process was so long that, between the time Ted Cruz announced he was running as a Republican candidate and his eventual withdrawal and endorsement of Donald Trump, France could have repeated its own campaign cycle forty-one times.

While there are many possible ways of understanding how an election campaign is reported, the 'issue versus non-issue' binary has become a dominant way of categorising political reporting in academic research (Aalberg et al. 2012). This, broadly speaking, means interpreting the prevailing logic of campaign coverage in two ways. On the one hand, election reporting is viewed as supplying information about particular issues, such as the positions of party policies or topics such as the economy or healthcare. On the other hand, coverage is viewed in terms of the process of politics, such as reporting campaign rallies or tactics, TV debates, coalition deals, polling data or, more generally, the horserace between parties. In more recent years, this last category has been further nuanced to differentiate the 'game' type aspects from the 'strategy' of political parties (ibid.).

In order to compare and contrast political news cross-nationally, international scholarly networks have sought to standardise how particular concepts are operationalised. As Esser et al. (2012b: 140) have pointed out, 'while there are many different scholars in different countries doing research on the extent to which news journalism frames politics as a strategic game . . . and they largely share the same terminology, there is no agreement on how this framing of politics should be conceptualized and measured.' If resources allowed, this chapter would draw on a large-scale content analysis of standardised variables that could be tested in the most recent election campaigns across many Western countries (see, for example, de Vreese et al. 2017). Our aim instead is to explore comprehensively the latest empirical research examining election coverage between countries, media systems and electoral contests. We acknowledge that there will be some variations in the sampling and interpretation of variables (Esser et al. 2012b), but *our focus is on comparing the weight of evidence about how the media frame election news according to whether coverage is primarily about campaign process or about the policies of competing parties and candidates.* We largely rely on quantitative content analyses of single and cross-national studies, extrapolating data that can convey whether campaign coverage was characterised by policy issues or process-driven news. We begin by exploring first-order elections, looking principally at how American presidential and UK general elections have been reported over recent decades. We then focus on comparing coverage between media systems, asking whether the evidence supports the proposition – as the introduction to the book suggested – that public service media report election news differently from more market-driven outlets. Finally, we turn to how second-order elections are reported, drawing primarily on our own studies to establish whether this type of electoral contest influences the way campaigns are framed.

In order to help understand and explain the editorial judgements behind media agendas, subsequent chapters will explore the micro-contexts of particular electoral campaigns in more detail. This chapter, by contrast, is unapologetically data-heavy, with the aim of building a macro-picture about how election reporting is generally framed across many countries, media systems and electoral contests.

First-order elections: a longitudinal picture of campaign reporting

Farnsworth and Lichter (2011a) have examined television news coverage of US presidential elections extensively over recent decades. Focusing on ABC, CBS and NBC – the three major television networks – they identified some clear and significant longitudinal trends in presidential reporting between

Table 2.0 Amount of network television news coverage of presidential primary campaigns between 1998 and 2008

	Number of stories	Minutes per day	Total time in minutes
1988	597	13.3	1,126
1992	370	10.7	738
1996	699	16.9	1,202
2000	550	13.4	882
2004	356	11.2	684
2008	932	17.6	1,710

Source: Adapted from Farnsworth and Lichter 2011a.

1988 and 2008. Their analysis is based on 3,504 news reports, during six presidential election campaigns, lasting 6,342 minutes.

Table 2.0 shows the quantity of US network coverage during the most competitive part of past presidential races – the period in the election cycle between December and March known as the primaries, when the Republicans and Democrats select their candidate. Overall, it reveals how the coverage differs between presidential campaigns, with 2008 the most newsworthy primary contest. However – as Farnsworth and Lichter (2011a) pointed out – this was partly explained by the longer nomination period in 2008. Nevertheless, the longitudinal analysis shows the race to be president of the US consistently attracts a significant proportion of time on network news television during the campaign.

Indeed, 'race' is the operative term in US election reporting. As another study by Farnsworth and Lichter (2014) revealed, coverage of policy issues has been superseded by horserace reporting during the last six presidential campaigns – with the exception of 1992 (see table 2.1). Into the twenty-first century, the horserace angle was enhanced during primary contests, with between 71 and 78 per cent of coverage in 2004 and 2008 focusing on which candidate was winning or losing. Issues, by contrast, made up less than 18 per cent of election stories in the same period.

However, the study discovered that, once the primaries were over and the presidential race had begun, issues typically appeared in approximately 40 per cent of election stories, with less emphasis

Table 2.1 TV news coverage of the US presidential primary campaigns, 1988–2012 (percentages)

	1988	1992	1996	2000	2004	2008	2012
Horserace	49	55	56	78	77	71	61
Policy issues	16	72	44	22	18	14	22

Source: Adapted from Farnsworth and Lichter 2014.

Table 2.2 TV news coverage of the US presidential elections, 1988–2008 (percentages)

	1988	1992	1996	2000	2004	2008
Horserace	58	58	48	71	48	41
Issue coverage	39	32	37	40	49	35

Source: Adapted from Farnsworth and Lichter 2011b.

on the horserace in 2004 and 2008 (see table 2.2). The slight drop in horserace coverage during the 2008 campaign might suggest a shift in policy focus compared to other campaigns. However, Farnsworth and Lichter (2011b: 361) pointed out that, in 2008, 'Little more than one third of the news stories contained significant discussion of policy issues or other substantive matters, far below the 49% level of 4 years earlier.'

A study by the Pew Research Center (2012) helps to shed further light on the level of policy compared to process coverage, since it looked at the 2008 and 2012 election campaigns across a range of media – newspapers, online news, network TV, cable TV and radio. In the run-up to the 2012 election, the study showed 'policy debates accounted for 22% of the overall coverage; in 2008 that figure was 20%. This year [2012], the candidates' personal stories and public records accounted for 10% of the coverage; in 2008 that number was 11%.'

However, in the 2016 presidential election – examined more closely in chapter 5 – several studies established that the level of policy information was remarkably low. Thomas Patterson of the Shorenstein Center examined CBS, Fox, the *Los Angeles Times*, NBC, the *New York Times*, *USA Today*, the *Wall Street Journal* and the *Washington Post* between January and June 2016 and discovered

Table 2.3 News topics in the US presidential election coverage, 2016 (percentages)

	Opening contests	Super Tuesday	Middle stage	Final month
Competitive game	65	71	57	40
Substantive content	6	5	12	16

Source: Adapted from Patterson 2016a.

that, at four points during the primary contests, substantive content of the issues accounted for – as table 2.3 indicates – between 5 and 16 per cent of all election news items (Patterson 2016a). By contrast, items including a competitive game angle made up 40 and 71 per cent. As Patterson put it, curtly, primary coverage of candidates was 'long on the horse race and short on substance'.

The decline in the level of attention paid to policy issues was further uncovered by Tyndall's[*] analysis of network television news coverage during the 2016 US presidential election. As table 2.4 reveals, in 2012, 114 minutes were dedicated to issues, compared with 220 and 203 in 2008 and 2004 respectively. With just two weeks before election day, the 2016 study found just 32 minutes had been dedicated to issues over the campaign period. Tyndall's (2016b) conclusions about the 2016 presidential election warrant quoting in full:

> This year's absence of issues is an accurate portrayal of the turf on which the election is being played out. It has turned into a referendum on the candidates' fitness for office, hinging on attributes such as honesty, trustworthiness, judgment, temperament, stamina, good health, comportment and boorishness. If the candidates are not talking about the issues, the news media would be misrepresenting the contest to do so. With just two weeks to go, issues coverage this year has been virtually non-existent. Of the 32 minutes total, terrorism (17 mins) and foreign policy (7 mins) towards the Middle East (Israel–ISIS–

---

[*] We are grateful to Andrew Tyndall for providing us with his raw data about network coverage of the 2016 US presidential campaign.

Table 2.4 Coverage of issues in US presidential elections, 1988–2016 (in minutes)

	ABC	CBS	NBC	Total
1988	36	40	42	118
1992	112	38	60	210
1996	29	53	17	99
2000	45	39	46	130
2004	40	119	44	203
2008	41	119	66	226
2012	13	70	32	115
2016 (up until approx. two weeks before election day)	8	16	8	32

Syria–Iraq) have attracted some attention. Gay rights, immigration and policing have been mentioned in passing. No trade, no healthcare, no climate change, no drugs, no poverty, no guns, no infrastructure, no deficits. To the extent that these issues have been mentioned, it has been on the candidates' terms, not on the networks' initiative.

Overall, longitudinal studies of US presidential election coverage suggest that, while the campaign continues to be a highly newsworthy story into the twenty-first century, the focus has increasingly turned from the policy agendas of competing parties to the competition between the two candidates, their characters and strategies. In a 1991 book, *The Formation of Campaign Agendas*, Semetko and her colleagues carried out a comparative study of US and UK election coverage during the 1980s. The study was wide-ranging, but the authors' conclusion about the differences between election coverage in the US and the UK was emphatic:

Our study of the nature of campaign news coverage in the two countries shows that British election coverage on television is almost *comprehensively* different from campaign news on U.S. television . . . It is more ample, more varied, more substantive, more party oriented, less free with unidirectional comment, and more respectful. By contrast, American election television is more terse, concentrated, horse-racist, guided by conventional news values, ready to pass judgment, and ready to be occasionally disrespectful in passing such judgment. (Semetko et al. 1991: 142; original emphasis)

We explore the comparative degree of journalistic interpretation and reliance on news values in later chapters, but Semetko et al.'s conclusion that UK election reporting places far greater emphasis on substantive policy reporting than on horserace coverage was striking. However, more than two decades on, does this observation stand up to empirical scrutiny?

Academics at Loughborough University – led by David Deacon – have carried out systematic reviews of news coverage over recent UK general election campaigns (Deacon et al. 2001, 2005; Deacon and Wring 2005; Loughborough University 2015). Between 1992 and 2005, they observed a steady if not necessarily uniform decline in the amount of election coverage on the UK's major evening newscasts. As far back as the 2001 election campaign, they suggested that the agenda had become more trivialised. As they put it, 'The evidence presented here speaks of a politics reduced to a few elemental issues, focussed on a very limited range of key dominant personalities, and mediated as performance rather than policy' (Deacon et al. 2001: 677). According to their systematic analysis of television news coverage in subsequent campaigns in 2005, 2010, 2015 and 2017 (see table 2.5), with the exception of 2017, the proportion of coverage focused on campaign process has remained broadly the same. The 2017 campaign, of course, was a snap election. The decision behind it, according to the prime minister, was to strengthen the government's Brexit negotiations (although these were actually weakened because the outcome was a hung parliament). Nevertheless, the agenda may have been more policy driven because the UK voted to exit the EU – and Brexit

Table 2.5 TV news coverage of the 2001, 2005, 2010, 2015 and 2017 UK general elections (percentages)

	2001	2005	2010	2015	2017
Campaign-process news	45.0	44.0	43.0	45.9	32.9

Source: Adapted from Deacon and Wring 2005, 2011; Loughborough University 2015, 2017.

Table 2.6 The percentage of time spent reporting election, policy and campaign-process items in UK newscasts during the 2015 and 2017 UK general elections

	2015	*2017*
Proportion of all news about election	47.1	45.7
Policy issues	37.6	53.3
Campaign process	62.4	46.7
Totals	100.0	100.0

Source: Adapted from Cushion et al. 2016b.

was a dominant issue reported by the media during the campaign (Loughborough University 2017).

In our study of the 2015 general election (focusing on a different sample of television news to the Loughborough University election team), we found an even greater emphasis on campaign-related news. As table 2.6 shows, while campaign coverage accounted for nearly half of all news coverage – 47.1 per cent – close to two-thirds of items were about campaign process rather than policy issues. The proportion of coverage about the 2017 election was roughly the same as in the 2015 campaign, but with a greater emphasis on policy stories. Nevertheless, overall the evidence suggests that UK coverage of elections is no longer as 'substantive' or 'policy oriented' as Semetko et al. (1991:142) observed more than two decades ago.

Beyond the US and the UK, how far do other Western countries focus on the policy differences between parties rather than on campaign process? Strömbäck and Dimitrova (2011) compared television news coverage of the 2008 US and 2006 Swedish election campaigns. As table 2.7 shows, they found that Swedish coverage paid more attention to issues during the campaign than that in the US – 41.7 per cent of the agenda compared to 18.5 per cent – with less emphasis on the strategic game frame.

Shehata (2014) examined Swedish election coverage in three news programmes during the 2010 election and identified a similar degree of game (between 46 and 59 per cent) versus issue coverage (between 40 and 52 per cent). In a study of Danish and German elections between 1990 and 2010, Zeh and Hopmann (2013) also

Table 2.7 The framing of politics in Swedish and US TV news (percentages)

	Sweden	US*
The issue frame is dominant	41.7	18.5
The framing is balanced	10.4	14.9
The strategic game frame is dominant	47.9	66.7

Note: *Due to rounding up or down, columns in this and subsequent tables may not add up to exactly 100 per cent.

Source: Adapted from Strömbäck and Dimitrova 2011.

discovered a high degree of horserace and campaign reporting in television news stories about the candidates. In Germany, the proportion of campaign-process stories was just under 10 per cent in 1990 and slightly above 40 per cent in 1994. While by 1998 this had risen to almost 80 per cent of stories, in 2002 it dropped to just below 60 per cent, and it remained at this level up until 2010. By contrast, in Denmark, approximately 50 and 70 per cent of candidate stories between 1994 and 2007 involved horserace- or campaign-related issues. Overall, Zeh and Hopmann concluded by observing: 'our data indicate a substantial increase in the proportional attention to horse-race and hoopla stories. However, these changes occurred in Germany, and not in Denmark, where there always has been a fairly high proportion of horse-race and hoopla stories with regard to the incumbent and opponent' (2013: 232).

Meanwhile, Takens et al. (2013) examined television and press coverage of elections in the Netherlands between 1998 and 2010. They discovered that reporting had not become more horserace driven into the twenty-first century, but, in the authors' words, 'The attention for contest news is high, ranging from 54.4% in 2006 to 66.4% in 2002 . . . media pay more attention to the electoral contest than to the political issues at stake' (ibid.: 287). In their study of the 2014 New Zealand general election, Boyd and Bahador (2015) broke down newspaper and television coverage over five weeks ahead of election day. As table 2.8 outlines, policy issues were consistently superseded by campaign-process stories, which amounted to almost two-thirds of the overall agenda.

So far we have focused mostly on how television coverage gen-

Table 2.8 Mixed TV and newspaper coverage of the 2014
New Zealand general election (percentages)

	Week 1	Week 2	Week 3	Week 4	Week 5	Total
Non-issue coverage	61.7	75.5	57.9	66.8	61.9	65.1
Issue coverage	38.3	24.5	42.1	33.2	38.1	34.9

Source: Adapted from Boyd and Bahador 2015: 156.

erally reports first-order elections. We now explore studies that *compare* coverage between public service broadcasters and more market-driven news media.

Media systems matter: comparing public and market-driven media

Previous research has identified that public service broadcasters supply a more distinctive agenda than commercial media in political reporting and public-affairs news more generally (Cushion 2012a; Strömbäck 2016). But how far does this stand up to empirical scrutiny during election campaigns cross-nationally?

In the UK, studies have shown that the degree of public service obligations shaping a newscast can influence the level of policy information supplied during an election campaign. Table 2.9 reveals how the broadcaster with the most public service broadcast

Table 2.9 The level of policy information during the 2010 UK election campaign in television news (percentages)

	BBC1 10 pm	ITV 10.30 pm	Channel 4 7 pm	Channel 5 7 pm	Sky News 9 pm
Entirely about policy issues	20.4	7.4	17.2	7.4	14.9
Significantly about policy issues	20.4	17.5	12.9	11.1	13.4
Limited references to policy issues	28.1	38.1	34.4	30.9	19.4
No reference to policy issues	31.1	37.0	35.4	50.6	52.2

Source: We are grateful to David Deacon at Loughborough University for supplying us with this data.

Table 2.10 Election news coverage of the 2015 and 2017 UK general elections (percentages)

	2015					2017				
	BBC	*ITV*	*Ch 4*	*Ch 5*	*Sky*	*BBC*	*ITV*	*Ch 4*	*Ch 5*	*Sky*
Non-issue	56.8	65.6	60.7	63.9	68.6	46.5	47.5	44.3	50.0	48.5
Issue (policy)	43.2	34.4	39.3	36.1	31.4	53.5	52.5	55.7	50.0	51.5

Source: Adapted from Cushion et al. 2016b.

responsibilities – the BBC – reported the most substantive news about policy matters during the 2010 general election.* Conversely, Sky News and Channel 5, broadcasters with either no or limited public service obligations, supplied the least amount of news about policy issues.

Our study of the 2015 UK general election campaign also identified a more distinctive policy agenda on more public service television newscasts. As table 2.10 demonstrates, over the campaign in the 2015 election, the BBC reported the most issue-based news – 43.2 per cent. Sky News's agenda, by contrast, was made up by less than a third of campaign-process stories – 31.4 per cent. In the 2017 election campaign, Sky News and Channel 5 spent the least proportion of time focused on policy issues.

In a study of television and radio coverage of the 2011 election campaign in Ireland, Rafter et al. (2014) compared their findings of public and private media with those from four other European countries (see table 2.11). With the exception of Poland, all four public service media outlets supplied a greater proportion of policy issues than did private broadcasters.

Strömbäck and Dimitrova's (2011) comparative study of Swedish and US elections (unpacked, in part, earlier in the chapter) showed a clearer distinction between campaign coverage on public service broadcast and commercial television news. As table 2.12 indicates, almost half of coverage on public service media in Sweden was issue based – 47.3 per cent – compared to just over a quarter – 27.4

---

* We are grateful to David Deacon for providing us with his raw data about television news coverage of the 2010 UK general election campaign.

Table 2.11 International variance of issue and non-issue coverage, 2003–2011 (percentages)

		Issue percentage minus non-issue percentage
Public media	Belgium	40
	Sweden	21 (average)
	Poland	−22
	Ireland	12
	Netherlands	−9
Private media	Belgium	−3
	Sweden	−26
	Poland	32
	Ireland	−6
	Netherlands	−46

Source: Adapted from Rafter et al. 2014.

Table 2.12 TV news coverage of the 2008 US presidential election and 2006 Swedish parliamentary election (percentages)

	Sweden		US
	Public service news	*Commercial news*	*Commercial news*
Non-issue coverage	43.0	60.3	66.7
Issue (policy) coverage	47.3	27.4	18.5
Balanced coverage	9.7	12.3	14.9

Source: Adapted from Strömbäck and Dimitrova 2011.

per cent – on commercial media. By contrast, a fifth of market-driven US coverage – 18.5 per cent – was about issues. There was, however, a slightly higher proportion of balanced coverage in US media – 14.9 per cent – than in Swedish public and commercial reporting (9.7 and 12.3 per cent, respectively).

Strömbäck and Dimitrova (2011: 42) pointed out that, 'if we exclude public service news, there are no longer any significant differences across countries. This suggests that media commercialism is one of the main factors explaining the degree to which TV news frames politics as a strategic game.' At the same time, they concluded that, because there was a higher degree of issue-driven news reporting on commercial television news in Sweden than the US, 'the effects of media commercialism may be moderated by

national journalism cultures and national political news or political communication cultures' (ibid.: 44). The presence of a strong
public service media system, in other words, encouraged a higher
issue-based agenda *within* a particular country. Since American
public media is limited in both resources and audience size, it
follows that it cannot exercise the same influence on the culture of
election journalism.

Strömbäck and van Aelst's (2010) comparative study of the 2006
Swedish and 2008 Belgian general elections reinforces this perspective. As table 2.13 shows, public service broadcasters all have
a far higher degree of policy-related coverage than do commercial
broadcasters (between 55 and 70 per cent of the agenda over the
campaign). However, in the case of Het Nieuws, a commercial
programme in Belgium, the emphasis on campaign process over
policy was not as apparent (51 vs. 49 per cent) as it was in the US,
where a more commercially dominant media system operates. The
Swedish commercial programme, by contrast, reported a far lower
proportion of issues – 37 per cent – but this was still only approximately 20 to 30 per cent behind the amount of policy news covered
by their public service media counterparts. As Strömbäck and van
Aelst concluded, the relative degree of difference between public
and market-driven media systems was related not just to the type
of media but also to the political culture of a particular country. In
their words, 'Media type . . . appears to trump media channel as
an antecedent of the media's framing of politics.' However, 'there
were also differences across countries, suggesting the conditionality

Table 2.13 Television news coverage of the 2006 and 2008 Swedish
and Belgian elections in public service and commercial broadcasters
(percentages)

	Public service broadcasters			*Commercial broadcasters*	
	BEL Het Journaal	*SWE Rapport*	*SWE Aktuellt*	*BEL Het Nieuws*	*SWE TV4 Nyheterna*
Non-issue coverage	30	34	45	51	63
Issue coverage	70	66	55	49	37

Source: Adapted from Strömbäck and van Aelst 2010.

of the impact of media types: regardless of country, commercial as well as public service news . . . operate in a context that is largely nation specific' (ibid.: 56).

The evidence of a national shift among public service programming towards more process-orientated coverage was identified in Nord and Strömbäck's (2014) analysis of Swedish election campaigns. In a comparative study of public and market-driven media, Nyheterna, a commercial programme, featured the most process-related coverage – between 55 and 64 per cent in the 2008, 2002, 2006 and 2010 election campaigns (table 2.14). But the public service programmes (Aktuellt and Rapport) increased their emphasis on non-policy issues in the two most recent campaigns. Viewed in this context, while public service programming in Sweden remained distinctively issue-based during election campaigns, they also increasingly resembled the character of commercial news reporting. As this section showed more generally, there is not necessarily a uniform shift among public service broadcasters towards more campaign-process coverage. Several studies suggested trends can be unidirectional, a consequence of micro-factors that shape news agendas *within* a particular nation. To conclude the chapter, we also need to consider whether the type of electoral contest influences the kind of news agenda pursued over an election campaign. We need, in other words, to move beyond presidential or general elections to examine second-order elections.

Table 2.14 Longitudinal split between private and public broadcasters in Sweden (percentages)

	1998			2002			2006			2010		
	A	*R*	*N*	*A*	*R*	*N*	*A*	*R*	*N*	*A*	*R*	*N*
Non-issue coverage	40	46	64	32	30	55	45	33	62	47	52	60

Note: A = Aktuellt (public broadcaster); R = Rapport (public broadcaster); N = Nyheterna (commercial broadcaster).
Source: Adapted from Nord and Strömbäck 2014.

Electoral contests also matter:
reporting second-order elections

So far the focus of this chapter has been on first-order elections, which are viewed as being more electorally significant than second-order contests such as localised campaigns or the EU elections. But, as political scientists have long recognised, second-order elections exhibit a set of characteristics (Reif and Schmitt 1980) that are distinct from first-order contests. This may result in journalists following a different type of logic in campaign coverage.

However, there is a limited supply of national or cross-national studies that compare media coverage of first- and second-order elections. The EU elections have attracted more interest than local contests, but much of the literature focuses on the quantity rather than the quality of news. The study by Schuck and his colleagues (2011) of the 2009 EU elections discovered that the visibility of coverage differed markedly between countries. As table 2.15 shows, while television news in Belgium, the Czech Republic, Luxembourg and France dedicated 10 per cent or less to the 2009 campaign, Slovenia, Poland, Malta and Greece reported between three and five times more coverage as a proportion of all television news.

Clearly, the significance of EU elections can vary considerably between European nations. In Malta and Greece, for instance, the amount of second-order coverage appears roughly the same as the attention paid to first-order elections (cf. Cushion et al. 2016b). Strömbäck et al. (2013) also examined campaign coverage in a range of countries during the 2009 elections and found an alarming disparity (see table 2.16). Comparing the number of items over the campaign, they revealed that, while television news in Portugal and Spain reported 299 and 162 items respectively, Germany featured 23 and the UK just 17 items.

The evidence suggests that *the type of media system* plays a more important role in reporting second-order elections than in first-order elections. A comprehensive study of television news during the 2009 EU election campaigns also discovered that the visibility of coverage was far greater on public than on more market-driven

Table 2.15 Visibility of EU news in television newscasts during the 2009 European parliamentary elections (by percentage time of all news)

	Percentage of all news
Belgium	8.5
Czech Republic	9.8
Luxembourg	10.4
France	10.5
Lithuania	11.1
Italy	11.2
Estonia	12.5
Romania	12.7
Belgium	13.1
Germany	13.3
Hungary	14.0
Spain	16.2
UK	16.3
Netherlands	16.9
Denmark	17.3
Slovakia	18.4
Bulgaria	18.9
Latvia	19.1
Finland	19.6
Portugal	23.3
Ireland	23.4
Cyprus	23.9
Sweden	27.1
Austria	27.6
Slovenia	30.4
Poland	33.4
Malta	48.7
Greece	57.1

Source: Adapted from Schuck et al. 2011.

channels. In twenty-one out of the twenty-six EU countries examined, public service television newscasts reported a greater level of news about the election than more commercial outlets. In Finland, the same level of coverage was found on both media systems. But, as table 2.17 further reveals, in Slovenia, Poland, Bulgaria and Malta – where private broadcasters had more coverage than public service newscasts – the differences between them (apart from in

Table 2.16 Number of television items reporting the 2009 EU elections

	Television news
Portugal	299
Spain	162
Austria	91
Sweden	95
Romania	133
Czech Republic	53
Poland	79
Finland	49
Italy	78
Denmark	49
Germany	23
UK	17
N	1128

Source: Adapted from Strömbäck et al. 2013.

Malta) were marginal. It is important, however, to compare the level of coverage between broadcasters within a nation rather than cross-nationally. Different formats and programming limit how far comparisons can be meaningfully compared between nations. This notwithstanding, table 2.17 shows public service broadcasters were responsible for a large majority of coverage about EU elections during the 2009 elections.

However, as previously acknowledged, beyond the quantity of news it is difficult to establish the *comparative nature of coverage*. The relative degree of coverage about policy or campaign-process reporting, for example, is not available between EU countries. But research has established that conflict and strategy framing of EU elections tends to be greater than an emphasis on horserace coverage (Schuck et al. 2013). However, the framing of EU elections was different cross-nationally. Political systems with proportional representation, for example, were less likely to report horserace coverage because, as the authors put it, 'in other systems the question of who is in the lead and will ultimately win the election becomes more important' (ibid.: 20). This again demonstrates how *the culture of journalism* helps shape the agenda of election reporting. At the same time, the relative degree of horserace coverage in second-order campaigns appears less common than in first-order electoral contests. This is perhaps because, as Schuck et al. (ibid.: 21–2) concluded, the 'absence of a clear formation of a government after such elections . . . is likely to have depressed the use of the horse-race frame and the focus on who is leading in the polls.' The electoral system, in other words, can shape the propensity to report a horserace perspective during an election campaign. Nevertheless, once again the evidence shows public service broadcasters report policy to a greater extent than do commercial broadcasters. Hanretty and Banducci (2016) consistently found that, between 1999 and 2009, public service broadcasters in the original EU member states had fewer horserace stories in coverage of the EU elections than commercial news outlets.

Our analysis of the 2009 and 2014 EU elections in the UK and the local election in 2013 sheds further light on the degree to which second-order contests are reported across media systems. We begin with an analysis of the 2009 and 2013 EU and local elections, which allowed us to explore any differences in the extent and nature of news reporting about different second-order elections on UK evening television newscasts. While many second-order election studies compare their findings with those concerning first-order contests, our aim was to explore whether citizens' attitudes towards both affected coverage. After all, local elections have been viewed as being more significant to voters than EU elections. Indeed, an Electoral Commission (2004: 24) study comparing both type of elections found that, because voting in the EU elections is so low, 'one might almost describe European Parliament elections as "third order".' A representative opinion poll from 2009 reinforced this perspective, since it found 'European elections are viewed as somewhat secondary in comparison with the locals', with one in ten revealing that, had both elections been on the same day, they would not have voted in the EU election (Electoral Commission 2009: 3). So how did the perceived relevance of both elections influence how television newscasts reported the campaigns?

Table 2.18 shows that, across the board, election coverage of

Table 2.17 Number of 2009 EU election campaign news items across European countries on public and commercial television nightly newscasts★

Country	Public/state	No.	Commercial	No.	Public	No.		No.
Austria	ZiB (ORF1)	45	Aktuell 19.20 (ATV)	12				
Belgium	Het Journaal (VRT)	21	VTM-Nieuws (VTM)	13	JT Meteo (La Une)	32	Le Journal (RTL–TV)	7
Bulgaria	BNT (Kanal 1)	33	bTV (bTV)	40				
Cyprus	RIK1	83	Ant1 (Antenna)	61				
Czech Republic	Udalosti (Ceska televise)	23	Televizni noviny (TV Nova)	4				
Denmark	TV-avisen (DR1)	26	Nyhederne (TV2)	12				
Estonia	Aktuaalne Kaamera (ETV)	21	Reporter (Kanal2)	8				
Finland	TV-uutiset ja sää (YLE TV1)	20	Kymmenen (MTV3)	20				
France	Le Journal (F2)	37	Le Journal (TF1)	29				
Germany	Tagesschau (ARD)	10	Aktuell (RTL)	8	Heute (ZDF)	14	SAT1	4
Greece	Net (bulletin at 21.00)	148	Kentriko deltio (Mega)	134				
Hungary	Hirado (M2)	41	Esti Hirado (RTL-Klub)	16				
Ireland	Nine News (RTEI)	20	TV3 News (TV3)	10				
Italy	TG1 (RaiUno)	18	TG5 (Canale5)	16				
Latvia	Panorãmas (LTV)	19	T Ziņas (LNT)	11				
Lithuania	Panorama (LTV)	15	TV3 žinios (TV3)	8				
Malta	L-Ahbarijet TVM (TVM)	56	One News (One TV)	150				
Netherlands	NOS Journaal	23	RTL Nieuws (RTL)	10				
Poland	Wiadomósci (TVP1)	30	FAKTY (TVN)	35				
Portugal	Telejornal (RTP1)	87	Jornal Nacional (TVI)	57				

Romania	Telejurnal (TVR1)	21	Stirile (Pro TV)	4		
Slovakia	Spravy (STV1)	37	Televizne Noviny (TV Markiza)	21		
Slovenia	Dnevnik (TVS1)	32	24UR (POP TV)	47		
Spain	Telediario-2 (TVE1)	74	Telecinco (Tele5)	35	Noticias 2 (Antena 3)	51
Sweden	Rapport (TV2)	19	Nyheterna (TV4)	17		
UK	News at Ten (BBC)	14	News at 10 (ITV)	6		

★ This data was generated by using SPPS files available at the PIREDEU data centre (www.piredeu.eu). We are grateful to Ingo Linsenmann for her guidance on downloading the relevant data sets.

Table 2.18 The percentage of time spent on the most reported categories of news during the 2009 EU and local elections and the 2013 local elections on UK television newscasts (seconds in parentheses)

	BBC		ITV		Channel 4		Channel 5	
	2009	2013	2009	2013	2009	2013	2009	2013
Election	(1,565) 5.9%	(1,262) 4.6%	(1,397) 5.2%	(292) 1.3%	(1,396) 3.0%	(1,784) 3.6%	(243) 1.1%	(213) 1.0%
National politics	(10,621) 40.1%	(5,576) 20.3%	(11,238) 41.5%	(4,570) 20.6%	(15,172) 33%	(11,109) 22.2%	(3,170) 14.5%	(4,164) 20.2%
Crime	(1,828) 6.9%	(5,741) 20.9%	(2,497) 9.2%	(4,874) 22.0%	(4,287) 9.3%	(10,905) 21.9%	(2,434) 11.2%	(5,930) 28.7%
War	(3,240) 12.2%	(2,626) 9.6%	(2,201) 8.1%	(1,578) 7.1%	(6,034) 13.1%	(4,633) 9.3%	(1,538) 7.1%	(1,219) 5.9%
Sport	(918) 3.5%	(1,884) 6.9%	(1,681) 6.2%	(908) 3.4%	(476) 1.0%	(1,850) 3.7%	(1,355) 6.2%	(737) 3.6%
Accidents/disasters	(964) 3.3%	(879) 3.2%	(1,672) 6.2%	(1,774) 8.0%	(1,594) 3.5%	(1,550) 3.1%	(1,194) 5.5%	(1,233) 6.0%
Business	(1,390) 5.3%	(1,434) 5.2%	(771) 2.9%	(1,098) 5.0%	(3,175) 6.9%	(2,689) 5.4%	(668) 3.1%	(935) 4.5%
Foreign affairs	(1,830) 6.9%	(1,624) 5.9%	(1,613) 6.0%	(794) 3.6%	(2,736) 5.9%	(3,495) 7.0%	(233) 1.1%	(463) 2.2%
Entertainment/culture	(706) 2.7%	(861) 3.1%	(792) 2.9%	(124) 0.6%	(2,398) 5.2%	(,2080) 4.2%	(2,502) 11.5%	(760) 3.7%
Health	(449) 1.7%	(1,993) 7.3%	(80) 0.3%	(2,504) 11.3%	(284) 0.1%	(1,645) 3.3%	(1,320) 0.6%	(1,764) 8.5%
Celebrity	(177) 0.1%	(161) 0.1%	(851) 3.2%	(22) 0.1%	(1,089) 2.4%	(431) 0.1%	(2,039) 9.4%	(302) 1.5%
Home affairs	(247) 0.1%	(1,385) 5.0%	(363) 1.3%	(1,387) 6.3%	(760) 1.7%	(2,353) 4.7%	(542) 2.5%	(1599) 7.7%
Human interest	(331) 1.3%	(414) 1.5%	(495) 1.8%	(98) 0.4%	(365) 0.1%	(596) 0.1%	(2,022) 9.3%	(129) 0.1%

Source: Adapted from Cushion and Thomas 2016.

the 2009 EU and 2013 local elections represented a small share – between 1.0 and 5.9 per cent – of the overall news agenda during the respective campaigns. The BBC – the main public service broadcaster – reported the most coverage, while Channel 5 – the newscast with the fewest regulatory obligations – provided the lowest proportion of coverage in both campaigns. Put more broadly, *the more public service responsibilities a broadcaster held, the more likely they were to report news about a second-order election.*

Our study also explored which second-order election – local or EU – was reported more widely across these broadcasters. Some local (primarily English) council elections were also being contested during the 2009 EU campaign. In 2013 it was just local council elections (although a mayoral and by-election occurred in this campaign period too). As table 2.19 shows, as a proportion of all airtime granted to the election campaigns, the BBC reported the most focused coverage of the EU and local elections in 2009 and 2013. The more commercial broadcasters, with the exception of Channel 4, featured news stories that blended together EU and local election issues, focusing mostly on how the campaigns were developing. Contrary to more UK citizens valuing local elections above the EU election (Electoral Commission 2009), it was the latter that received more attention on television news.

Beyond the quantity of second-order coverage during the 2009 and 2013 EU and local elections, we also examined how far news

Table 2.19 Percentage of airtime (as a proportion of all news) reporting different elections in 2009 and 2013 on UK television newscasts where the type of election is specified (seconds in parentheses)

	2009			2013	
	Local	*EU*	*Mixture (EU and local)*	*Local*	*Mixture (local, mayoral and by-election)*
BBC	(196) 0.7%	(1,105) 4.2%	(264) 1.0%	(676) 2.5%	(38) 0.1%
ITV	—	(484) 1.8%	(501) 1.9%	(224) 1.0%	(68) 0.3%
Ch. 4	(265) 0.6%	(647) 1.4%	(315) 0.7%	(514) 1.0%	(398) 0.8%
Ch. 5	—	—	(118) 0.5%	(196) 0.9%	(17) 0.1%

Source: Adapted from Cushion and Thomas 2016.

Table 2.20 The percentage of time spent on different types of election coverage during the 2009 EU and local elections and the 2013 local elections on UK television newscasts (seconds in parentheses)

	2009		2013	
	Policy as % of election coverage	*Non-policy % of election coverage*	*Policy as % of election coverage*	*Non-policy as % of election coverage*
BBC	(837) 53.5%	(728) 46.5%	(649) 51.4%	(613) 48.6%
ITV	(250) 17.9%	(1,147) 82.1%	—	(292) 100%
Ch. 4	(289) 20.7%	(1,107) 79.3%	(895) 50.1%	(889) 49.8%
Ch. 5	—	(243) 100%	—	(213) 100%

Source: Adapted from Cushion and Thomas 2016.

was primarily about policy or campaign process. Table 2.20 indicates that the BBC was more likely to focus on policy, which made up between 53.5 and 51.4 per cent of news during the 2009 and 2013 election campaigns respectively. Indeed, apart from Channel 4 in 2013, the commercial broadcasters reported either a low level of policy coverage or none at all. Channel 5's coverage of second-order elections, for example, was completely devoid of *any news items* where the primary focus was on policy issues.

We can develop this focus on second-order elections further by examining how the 2014 EU election campaign was reported by UK television newscasts. Our study, once again, examined all the major evening newscasts to compare how much coverage was dedicated to the campaign and the kind of issues that were discussed. We found that, proportionally speaking, the BBC spent more airtime covering the campaign than commercial broadcasters. But perhaps more striking was how much more policy driven the UK's main public service broadcaster was compared to its commercial counterparts (see table 2.21).

The BBC spent 78.3 per cent of its campaign coverage reporting policy issues – far more (as we explore below) than it did during the general election (Cushion et al. 2016b). By contrast, Channel 5's policy agenda made up 44.9 per cent of airtime, Channel 4's made up 30.0 per cent and ITV's just 7.6 per cent. As table 2.22 shows, this meant that, for the commercial broadcasters, far more time – particularly on ITV – was spent reporting the

Table 2.21 The framing of the 2014 EU election news in UK
television news

	Strategic game frame	*Policy frame*
BBC	11 mins 35 secs	41 mins 43 secs
	21.7% of election coverage	78.3% of election coverage
ITV	31 mins 22 secs	2 mins 34 secs
	92.4% of election coverage	7.6% of election coverage
Ch. 4	90 mins 7 secs	38 mins 33 secs
	70.0% of election coverage	30.0% of election coverage
Ch. 5	10 mins 2 secs	8 mins 12 secs
	55.1% of election coverage	44.9% of election coverage
Total	143 mins 6 secs	91 mins 0 secs
	61.1% of election coverage	38.9% of election coverage

Source: Adapted from Cushion et al. 2015b.

horserace aspects of coverage, the tensions between and within
political parties, their strategies or candidates, and more generalised
stories about the campaigns.

Based on our analysis of how television news reported different first- and second-order elections, table 2.23 shows the amount
of time spent on campaign process compared to policy issues. It
reveals that, with the exception of the 2014 EU election, policy
matters were reported to a far greater extent in first-order campaigns than in second-order elections.

However, our analysis also revealed the distinctive nature of
the UK's main public service broadcaster – the BBC – compared
to other commercial channels in first-order elections, most strikingly in second-order contests. As table 2.24 shows, the BBC had
a far greater focus on policy issues in the local and EU elections,
whereas commercial television overwhelmingly led with news
about the horserace, game or strategies behind the campaigns. *If not
for the BBC*, in other words, *second-order election reporting would have
been largely about the parties' campaigns rather than their policy agendas.*

Table 2.22 The focus of game-frame items in 2014 election coverage on UK television news

Focus of game reporting	BBC	ITV	Ch. 4	Ch. 5	All
Campaigning strategies	38 s 5.5%	—	7 m 59 s 8.9%	2 m 56 s 29.2%	11 m 33 s 8.1%
References to chosen daily topics determined by broadcaster	1 m 42 s 14.7%	2 m 0 s 6.4%	19 m 39 s 21.8%	21 s 3.5%	23 m 42 s 16.6%
Party spin/PR/news management	21 s 3.0%		28 s 0.5%	—	49 s 0.6%
Horserace/opinion polls	2 m 6 s 18.1%	16 m 43 s 53.3%	14 m 21 s 15.9%	5 m 14 s 52.2%	38 m 24 s 26.8%
Political tensions/infighting	—	2 m 25 s 7.7%	13 m 34 s 15.1%	51 s 8.5%	16 m 50 s 11.8%
Campaign launch	3 m 8 s 27.1%	3 m 7 s 9.9%	8 m 28 s 9.4%	15 s 2.5%	14 m 58 s 10.5%
Candidate values/integrity	3 m 40 s 31.6%	7 m 7 s 22.7%	25 m 38 s 28.4%	25 s 4.1%	36 m 50 s 25.6%
Totals	11 m 35 s 100%	31 m 22 s 100%	90 m 7 s 100%	10 m 2 s 100%	143 m 6 s 100%

Note: s = seconds, m = minutes; percentages refer to all game-frame time on each channel.
Source: Adapted from Cushion et al. 2015b.

Table 2.23 The amount of policy- and process-driven news in television news coverage of second-order elections (percentages)

	2009 local and EU	2013 local	2014 EU	2015 general
Non-issue coverage	77.0	74.6	61.1	62.4
Issue coverage	23.0	25.4	38.9	37.6

Source: Cushion et al. 2015b, 2016b; Cushion and Thomas 2016.

Table 2.24 The amount of policy- and process-driven news in television news coverage of second-order elections on public and commercial broadcasters (percentages)

	2009 local and EU elections		2013 local elections		2014 EU elections		2015 general election	
	Policy	Game/ strategy	Policy	Game/ strategy	Policy	Game/ strategy	Policy	Game/ strategy
BBC	53.5	46.5	51.4	48.6	78.3	21.7	43.2	56.8
Other commercial	12.9	87.1	16.7	83.3	27.5	72.5	35.3	64.7

Source: Cushion et al. 2015b, 2016b; Cushion and Thomas 2016.

What issues are addressed in election campaigns? Towards a more process-driven news agenda

Our review of studies examining television news coverage of election campaigns revealed some clear and, at times, striking conclusions. Taken together, the evidence showed that most Western countries have a relatively high degree of campaign-process coverage (above 40 per cent share of all election news). While not every country has experienced a uniform increase in campaign-process reporting, broadly speaking, many recent studies have observed that policy matters have gradually been relegated in favour of stories focused on the horserace between candidates and parties. Because of the different methodological approaches between studies and the various ways of categorising election stories, it is hard to compare directly the proportion of issue-based news as opposed to process coverage. Nevertheless, overall the empirical evidence suggests that coverage of the US presidential election is the most policy-lite in the Western world. This was apparent during the 2016 campaign, where, according to several studies, very few stories contained substantive policy content (the consequences of which are explored in chapter 5).

This chapter also established that *media systems matter* in election reporting. When national and cross-national studies have compared the nature of election coverage, the weight of evidence clearly shows that public service broadcasters reported a greater level of policy than campaign-process news. Indeed, our studies of UK election campaigns identified that the more public service obligations a broadcaster holds, the more policy-orientated their news agendas will be. Comparative analysis also revealed that, when a popular public service broadcaster operates within a national media system, it appears to moderate how far commercial television reports campaign process. This was apparent in several European countries, whereas in the US – which has a market-dominated system and a weak public service broadcasting sector – network television coverage was, relatively speaking, policy-lite. At the same time, longitudinal studies have shown that, into the twenty-first century, public service broadcasters have gradually taken on the character of commercial television, with a greater emphasis on horserace coverage, party strategy and candidate-centred stories. As our next chapter explores further, this suggests that the micro-context of national journalism cultures and political systems plays a decisive role in shaping campaign coverage.

Finally, we considered whether second-order elections were reported differently to first-order elections. While we had a limited supply of studies on which to draw, generally speaking we found that localised electoral contests or EU elections did not receive the same level of attention as presidential or general elections. This was most striking in EU election coverage, with some countries widely reporting the campaign whereas in others, notably the UK, it barely registered on the news agenda. Once again, however, we found that media systems played a crucial role in how much a second-order election was reported. Cross-national studies not only showed that most European public service broadcasters reported the EU elections to a far greater extent than their commercial counterparts, but in the original member states they focused less on horserace coverage or soft news issues (Hanretty and Banducci 2016). Our case studies of UK television news coverage in the 2009, 2013 and 2014 EU and local elections confirmed the disparity between the amount of coverage given to second- and first-order elections and the significance of public service broadcasters. The BBC, in most election campaigns, pursued a far more policy-driven news agenda than commercial outlets. This was particularly striking in second-order elections, where the share of policy news was above 50 per cent of the overall agenda (compared to 43 and 53 per cent in the 2015 and 2017 general election), and during the 2014 campaign it was as high as 78 per cent.

Overall, our findings broadly point towards an increasing reliance on process-driven reporting in many Western election campaigns, but to different degrees across competing media systems, electoral contests and journalism cultures. For many scholars, this represents a deterioration of the political public sphere, as citizens are exposed to less policy information about the issues of competing parties and candidates. However, it has also been argued that some aspects of campaign-process reporting, such as horserace coverage, can engage audiences in the campaign and the candidates involved in the electoral contest. The next chapter considers the relative merits of horserace coverage, drawing on relevant academic studies about whether it enhances or discourages voters' understanding of and engagement with election campaigns.

But beyond exploring how beneficial horserace journalism is for voters ahead of election day, we also need to examine *why* campaign coverage has become increasingly process driven over recent decades. According to many mediatisation of politics studies, the growing emphasis on game and strategy reporting during a campaign represents a media logic superseding a political logic (Strömbäck and Esser 2014). Put bluntly, the media favour a less policy-driven and more campaign-focused style of coverage. But should the retreat from policy and the march towards campaign-process coverage over recent decades be understood entirely as a commercial media logic shaping broadcast news? As chapter 1 explored, the editorial decisions behind selecting news stories involve several actors making it empirically difficult to unravel who sets the election news agenda. Indeed, the evidence often used to support this mediatisation of politics thesis is based on large-scale content analysis studies which classify horserace and other types of campaign-process coverage as a clear sign that a media logic is stamping its authority on election journalism. In our view, the contention that poll-driven, campaign-related and policy-lite election news agendas reflect a mediatisation of politics needs to be empirically questioned rather than accepted at face value. Potentially, there are other factors influencing the selection of election news, which may involve, for example, a political or a public logic shaping the agenda-setting process.

The next chapter explores in more micro-detail the editorial decisions behind campaign reporting. It begins by examining the rise of horserace reporting and then draws on a detailed case study about the logic shaping campaign coverage of the 2015 UK general election.

3

Making Sense of Horserace Reporting

Understanding the logic and value of process-driven news

Since the previous chapter established that election reporting has become increasingly process driven, the nature and impact of this type of campaign coverage needs to be considered more closely. Horserace coverage was identified as one of the most widely reported campaign-process stories, with who's up or down in the polls a dominant media narrative. This is not a new or sudden development. Several decades ago Patterson (1993) warned of a 'quiet revolution' in US political reporting, with issues having been demoted, or even replaced by news about party strategy, the candidates, campaigning or the latest polling data.

As we showed in the previous chapter, more than two decades into the new millennium it would be hard to argue that the revolution is as quiet as it once was. As Jackson (2014: 159) pointed out, the 'proposition that the news media increasingly report about the "process" of politics over the "issues" has gathered general acceptance among the political class and academic observers.' Non-issue political coverage that focuses on 'who is ahead, who is behind, who is gaining, who is losing, what campaign strategy is being followed, and what the impact of campaign activities is on the candidate's chances of winning' is now widely called 'horserace coverage' (Joslyn 1984: 133). During election campaigns, horserace coverage is broadly viewed as representing a greater emphasis on process rather than policy issues. In *Keywords in News and Journalism Studies*, Zelizer and Allan (2010) define it as 'using opinion poll data, details about campaign strategy and gossip about political personalities [that seek] to give the race a defined shape – an organising narrative – that generates excitement'. Further still, they pointed out that 'Its proponents defend it on the grounds that it increases voter interest in politics, putting a human face on policy abstractions' (ibid.: 55).

In this chapter we explore the characteristics of horserace journalism and consider the proposition that it may enhance people's interest in and engagement with the election campaign. In recent years, scholars have paid closer attention to interpreting the nature of political-process news, since reporting is not just about the horserace or strategy but increasingly about meta-campaign issues, such as how politicians deal with journalists and how the media respond to spin tactics employed by various parties (Esser and D'Angelo 2003; Jackson 2012). As the introduction to this book explained, the concept of framing politics as a strategic game frame has gained greater currency (Lawrence 2000). Above all, it encapsulates how reporters treat campaigning as a game between candidates seeking to win election (Patterson 1993). To bring greater conceptual clarity to debates, Aalberg et al. (2012) have argued that game and strategy aspects of political coverage should be examined separately, since they represent distinctive journalistic characteristics and may cause different effects. More recently, a small but growing body of literature has sought to examine the role and effects of the strategic game frame in depth and micro-detail (Aalberg et al. 2012; de Vreese et al. 2017; Dimitrova and Kostadinova 2013; Shehata 2014; Schuck et al. 2016).

The aim of this chapter is not to enter into these specific debates about political coverage but to paint a broader picture about how far *horserace reporting generally shapes election campaign agendas in television news*. In doing so, we examine the conditions in which horserace news thrives in contemporary journalism and consider the evidence about the extent to which it helps people engage with and understand election campaigns. We look closely at studies exploring how opinion polls are reported in political coverage and consider their value in election campaigns. Drawing on a case study examining the reporting of the 2015 UK general election campaign, we conclude this chapter by exploring how far a media logic drives the editorial selection of horserace news.

While the focus on who's up or down in the polls is conventionally viewed as symptomatic of a commercialised media system (Strömbäck 2008), we ask whether horserace reporting might also reflect a political or a public logic. So, for example, political parties may prefer to avoid debating issues in media coverage, while reporting polls could help communicate the public's agenda. Overall, we ask: Whose agenda is best served by horserace journalism and reporting polls during an election campaign?

Does horserace reporting engage audiences?

Horserace reporting may be on the rise in many countries, but its metaphorical use in political coverage dates back centuries. According to Broh (1980), the *Boston Journal* declared that a 'dark horse' was not likely to appear during the 1888 election campaign, while Sigelman and Bullock's longitudinal analysis of US electoral contests from 1888 to 1988 revealed that horserace reporting existed well before the age of television news. They observed that: 'Newspaper straw polls can be traced all the way back to the 1820s ... election projections of one sort or another were fairly widespread long before the major polling breakthrough of 1936, when Gallup, Roper, and Crossley all correctly forecast Roosevelt's landslide victory' (1991: 22). Nonetheless, they later acknowledged that 'Horse race coverage has surged dramatically during the latter stage of the television era' (ibid.: 23).

Why, then, has horserace reporting played such an enduring and, in more recent decades, enhanced role in election campaigns? There is, needless to say, no single overriding factor that explains why a focus on the electoral race between parties or candidates plays an increasingly prominent part of campaign news. As Iyengar, Norpoth and Hahn have argued, it could simply be that horserace reporting is viewed by journalists as appealing to audiences. Their widely cited experimental audience study of 187 people in the US found that most individuals, when given access to a variety of sources, choose to watch news about the horserace rather than turn to issue-based coverage. In short, they argued that horserace sells, even if – as we explore further below – it may leave 'voters unsold on the campaign and the electoral process' (Iyengar et al. 2004: 174). A horserace angle, from this perspective, is viewed as exciting for many journalists and editors because it generally involves news values such as conflict, human interest and timeliness. As the media environment has become more commercialised in recent decades, the growing presence of horserace news could reflect a greater reliance on news values, which appeal to audiences and help shape election coverage.

But this macro-explanation skates over important structural changes in political journalism. Horserace reporting, after all, meets many of the editorial demands of today's 24/7 culture of dramatic and instant news. It promotes a conflictual frame that can regularly feed the news cycle throughout the campaign, setting up the competition between political elites in the race for power. This has been enhanced by the abundance of opinion polls, at both national and state level, that provide journalists with an immediate sense of who is winning or losing during the campaign. The next section takes a closer look at the extent to which opinion polls feature in election reporting and considers how their use shapes the narrative of campaign coverage. But, above all, the reliance on polls feeds the game aspect to political reporting. As has long been observed, election reporting is often compared to sporting contests, with political journalism akin to 'real life' horserace commentary. This is partly explained by the close connection between sports and political reporters in the 1940s and 1950s, when, incidentally, scientific public opinion polls became more widely available. There has remained an intrinsic link between the culture of politics and sports journalism, as Banville (2016: 285) has recently explained:

> To grow up as a professional sports reporter is to grow up with a love for the strategy and the game itself. For those reporters who move into political reporting, the connections between sport and politics are obvious. The sources are the same – a coach versus a campaign manager – the questions of strategy and the opponent abound . . . group reporting on the horserace will hold a predisposition for the contest of politics.

In most US colleges today, sports culture is closely connected to campus life. Since most journalists have received some form of higher education before becoming a professional reporter (Cushion 2012b), this perhaps helps explain why the form and style of election news has continued to resemble horserace reporting.

As previous chapters have suggested, although concerns have been raised about the greater focus on campaign process over policy reporting, many journalists view horserace reporting as a way of engaging audiences in politics. So, for example, in response to a question about day-to-day life as a lobby journalist, Isabel Oakeshott, a regular commentator on programmes such as the BBC's *Sunday Politics*, revealed that she enjoyed:

> being literally in the corridors of power, having a ringside seat on these huge decisions that affect everybody's lives . . . I love getting to know MPs and special advisors, and enjoy the whole ins and outs of it, the skulduggery, the plotting, the who's up, who's down. I sometimes try to explain the job to people who don't really feel enthused by politics as rather like being a sports reporter, only there are a few more women involved on the teams – but not that many, perhaps not enough – in that you're reporting on who's up, who's down, who's on the benches, who's in trouble for a foul, and in that way it's incredibly entertaining, but it's also intellectually challenging. (Media Focus 2016)

Routinely explaining the polices of competing parties might appear dull and, for many journalists, to be 'old' news. Many reporters may, after all, have been following candidates' positions for several years, whereas opinion polls offer 'new' and exciting narratives about the campaign. Indeed, even in parliamentary systems there has been a greater emphasis in political coverage concerning the leaders of political parties, including understanding their characters and personalities (Blumler and Coleman 2010). Thus, polls exploring the approval ratings of a candidate, how far they are trusted, or whether the public would like to go for a beer with them or not (which, incidentally, is one of the best ways of predicting an election winner in the US) are all viewed as legitimate polling questions in today's media culture.

The journalistic thirst for horserace reporting has been further enhanced by the greater emphasis placed on producing instant news and comment online, on social media platforms or 24-hour television news channels (Cushion and Sambrook 2016). In this continuous news culture, where the new or novel takes precedence over the old or familiar, coverage of the horserace can deliver new twists and turns to campaign coverage. In an increasingly time pressured environment, where journalists are required to file copy around the clock, process news can also be far easier to churn out than policy issues, which often require greater context and background research. By contrast, most horserace news, such as covering the latest polls about which party is ahead or speculating about possible post-election coalition deals, is relatively straightforward to report.

However, it does not necessarily follow that the relative ease and convenience of horserace reporting is left to low-quality news suppliers. In a study of how the 2009 EU elections were reported in 160 broadcast and newspaper outlets in twenty-seven countries, Banducci and Hanretty (2014) found horserace coverage was more likely to be included in broadsheet newspapers than in commercial television news or the tabloid press. They also revealed that horserace coverage was more likely in more professionalised political cultures and more polarised electoral systems, where the electoral outcome is less clear-cut. This demonstrates how both political systems and journalism cultures play an important role in the selection of election news. Indeed, as we discovered in the previous chapter, the amount of campaign-process coverage can differ markedly between countries, particularly in respect of second-order elections. This makes it difficult to draw wider conclusions about Banducci and Hanretty's study, because the significance of the EU (according to citizens) varies across Europe. So, for example, in the UK, the 2014 EU campaign made up a tiny proportion of television news coverage, with the horserace angle focused on the implications of a future first-order contest – the 2015 general election – such as whether the then UKIP leader, Nigel Farage, would stand for a seat at Westminster (Cushion et al. 2015a).

But Banducci and Hanretty's (2014) conclusions about horserace reporting being driven by professional journalists does reinforce the view that reporters often cover the process of politics because it is easier for them to remain objective or impartial. After all, survey 'data' can often appear factual and, most of the time, is produced independently by polling organisations. While later in the chapter we question this perceived neutrality, it is perhaps understandable why journalists feel horserace news is less politically sensitive than issue-based coverage. As the American press critic Jay Rosen (2010) has put it, 'journalists fall into horse-race coverage, where they ask: Who's going to win? What's the strategy? Is it working? Focusing on those things helps advertise the political innocence of the press because "who's winning?" is not an ideological question. By repeatedly asking it journalists underline that theirs is not an ideological profession.' In the UK, where broadcasters have to remain impartial, McNair (2000: 74–5; original emphasis) has similarly observed that 'The constraints imposed by the requirement of impartiality' are 'one of the main sets of factors leading to the broadcasters' emphasis on *process* rather than policy. Where the interpretation of policy leaves broadcasters vulnerable to accusations of journalistic bias, judgements on the process of political competition – the horse race – take place at a distance from policy *per se*, and thus more easily avoid charges.'

From this perspective, horserace journalism appears ideologically harmless because it eschews party politics and 'objectively' presents the latest data. However, there is evidence to suggest that the emphasis on process over policy can have both a direct and an indirect influence on people's understanding and engagement with politics. It can also have a wider impact on the strategies of political parties during a campaign. While later in the chapter we explore more specifically how opinion polls can (mis)inform the campaign agenda, studies spanning decades have suggested that process reporting can be detrimental to public knowledge, while horserace news can adversely affect the public's relationship with politics. So, for example, in a representative survey of US voters in the 1992 election, Lewis and Morgan (1992) found a lack of public knowledge about the policy agendas of the main political parties. One finding was particularly striking:

> When asked facts about the candidates' policies and backgrounds, the only questions that a majority knew the answer to were 'Which candidate's family has a dog called Millie?' and 'Do you recall which TV character Dan Quayle criticized for setting a poor example of family values?' Eighty-six percent knew that Millie belonged to the Bush family, and 89 percent correctly identified Murphy Brown.

Perhaps counter-intuitively, the authors also found that heavy television viewers – television being the overwhelmingly dominant source of information at this time – knew less about each party's policy positions than light viewers. This lack of knowledge, it was argued, could be explained by the limited access most people had to news about *issues*, since network coverage focused on the candidates rather than their policies. Fast-forward twenty years and five presidential elections, when the range of news media has grown expansively, and the evidence suggests that access to information has not dramatically raised people's knowledge of American politics. So, for example, a survey carried out by the Annenberg Public Policy Center (2016) just a few months before the 2016 election found that 87 and 84 per cent, respectively, could name the Democratic and Republican presidential candidates Hillary Clinton and Donald Trump. However, just 37 per cent could name Mike Pence as the Republican candidate for vice-president, while less than a quarter – 22 per cent – could name his Democratic counterpart, Tim Kaine. On matters related to the constitution, close to one in four (39 per cent) thought the president had the power to declare war, with just over half (54 per cent) aware that Congress grants this power. Overall, the poll suggested most people were aware of the dominant personalities involved in the campaign – Trump vs. Clinton – but were less knowledgeable about basic civics underpinning the election. As mentioned in the previous chapter, this is perhaps not that surprising given the paucity of issue-based reporting during election campaigns.

Beyond public knowledge, several studies have shown horserace journalism promotes greater cynicism about election campaigns, since audiences become more exposed to the self-interested strategies of parties rather than how their policies might enhance the public good. As the introduction to the book briefly examined, this was most compellingly proposed in Cappella and Jamieson's (1997: 238) research into the spiral of cynicism. Their study suggested that, because politicians and journalists endlessly obsess about the process of politics, much of the public tune out and turn off from the issues. Over twenty years later, several studies have reinforced this perspective beyond the US, finding an empirical relationship between exposure to game-frame news and enhanced cynicism (de Vreese 2005; de Vreese and Elenbaas 2008; Shehata 2014). Indeed, Shehata's large-scale survey of Swedish audiences not only discovered that watching game-type news increased cynicism but also revealed that it reduced public trust and interest in politics. However, as already explored, scholars have suggested that game frame news can interest people in politics (Iyengar et al. 2004; Norris 2000), with opinion polls, in particular, viewed as generating excitement and human interest about the horserace. But whether or not one accepts that horserace reporting is more beneficial than detrimental to the democratic health of politics, it is important not to generalise its impact cross-nationally. As Banducci and Hanretty's (2014: 637) comprehensive study of twenty-seven European nations established, 'exposure to opinion polls is not distributed uniformly across countries, or across individuals. Consequently, any literature that attempts to identify the effects of exposure to opinion polls . . . will need to take account of these differences in exposure.'

The next section goes some way towards addressing this issue by examining the way opinion polls are reported during election campaigns. We assess how far they inform news coverage of election campaigns and the type of agenda they promote, and we consider their wider impact on people's knowledge and understanding of politics.

Reporting polls: how do they inform the campaign?

The polling industry rapidly expanded in the latter half of the twentieth century, and in many countries it has become intrinsically connected to politics, particularly during election campaigns. American politics has long embraced the use of surveys during elections, with campaign fundraising significantly influenced by the performance of candidates' relative poll ratings in the primaries. As Traugott (2005) has pointed out, it is difficult to trace precisely how many polls are issued in the US ahead of election day, since many are published at local, state and nationwide levels. But his analysis of polls between the 1972 and 2004 elections identified a substantial increase in one of the longest-standing questions being asked: 'If the election were held today, who would you vote for?'. According to Traugott (2005: 644), 'The explosion of polls started in the 1980s, and the shift from 1984 (27 questions retrieved) to 2000 (245 questions retrieved) is about 900 percent. Most of this was due to the increase in daily tracking polls, as in the 2000 campaign three firms (Gallup, Voter.com and Zogby) each released results from more than 35 tracking polls.' One estimate of the number of horserace polls in the run-up to the presidential election was that well over a 1,000 had been carried out (FiveThirtyEight 2016). In the UK, polling has also steadily increased, albeit not to the same degree or intensity as in the US. According to Cowley and Kavanagh (2016), the 2015 UK general election was the most polled election in British political history, with ninety-two having been published during the six-week campaign. As we examine further below, these also influenced the parties' tactics and campaign coverage.

But beyond the steady growth in the use of polling during election campaigns, what role can and do polls play in shaping the logic of political coverage? George Gallup pioneered opinion polling in the US and, in his appropriately titled book published in 1940, famously argued that it had the potential to take the 'Pulse of Democracy'. Of course, public opinion polls have developed more sophisticated modelling and sampling strategies since then, not least in recent years with the reliance on internet polling. They continue to hold, as Gallup observed, long-standing democratic functions that potentially help the media report elections. Above all, they can help represent 'the public' in the most scientifically accurate way possible, rather than vox pops or journalists being relied on to interpret more subjectively 'the mood' of a country or demographic. This allows reporters to use polls to understand the public's reaction to candidates, parties and the issues during an election campaign. Moreover, polls can help journalists orientate their news agenda according to the needs and interests of the public. But while there is much potential for polling in order to better inform journalism – and shape a public logic in election coverage – how have surveys been reported during election campaigns?

Generally speaking, the abundance of data produced by an ever growing polling industry has produced more media coverage of polls (Kohut 2009). This is about not just the availability of polling but also the changing culture of journalism in often under-resourced newsrooms. As Dunaway (2011: 80–1) observed, 'the constant demand for 24-hour news means that whenever possible outlets will take free and available poll results that can be easily crafted into a news story.' However, while this may be the case with cable news and online media, there is little recent empirical research that systematically tracks the volume and nature of poll television coverage in news generally and election reporting specifically. Lewis et al.'s (2005) study of US and UK news reporting, for example, found polls represented a tiny fraction of references to public opinion over a nine-month sample period. Meanwhile,

Table 3.0 Number of polls reported in public and commercial television news during the 1998, 2002 and 2006 Swedish election campaigns

	1998	2002	2006	N
Public service TV	7	6	14	632
Commercial TV	5	6	10	231
Total	12	12	24	863

Source: Adapted from Strömbäck 2009b.

Toff (2015) carried out a longitudinal study of US network coverage of polls between 1991 and 2013 and discovered, over time, that stories involving surveys remained broadly the same. However, during election cycles the reliance on polling grew, particularly on CBS. In Toff's words, 'the CBS time series demonstrates clear spikes in references for most presidential elections (with the exception of the somewhat less competitive re-election campaigns of 1996 and 2012), but also during the contentious primary periods of 2000 and 2008.'

Strömbäck's (2009b) longitudinal analysis of reporting in Swedish elections between 1998 and 2006 found a small but steady increase in opinion polls over time. As table 3.0 shows, on both public and commercial television news the volume of polls reported doubled within eight years, with a greater proportion reported in more market-driven channels. Although television news was not isolated in this part of the study, table 3.1 reveals that, in media coverage generally (including newspapers, TV and online news), the type of poll responses reported were primarily about party preferences – the classic horserace story – in all three election campaigns and, in 1998, perceptions towards particular candidates. Strömbäck also discovered a positive and significant statistical relationship between the inclusion of an opinion poll and horserace-type coverage. However, in 2002 and 2006 the reporting of issues increased, making up in respective campaigns between one in five and one in four of election news items. Despite the greater focus on issues and the overall prominence towards game- and horserace-type coverage, Strömbäck concluded that:

Table 3.1 Type of opinion polls reported in public and commercial television news during the 1998, 2002 and 2006 Swedish election campaigns (percentages)

	1998	2002	2006
N	98	88	117
Party preferences	67.3	60.2	44.4
Candidate perceptions	20.4	15.9	21.4
Issues	7.1	19.3	24.8
Other	5.1	4.5	9.4
Total	100.0	100.0	100.0

Source: Adapted from Strömbäck 2009b.

the media seldom use opinion polls in ways that suggest a genuine interest in the people and their thoughts and opinions . . . the results of this study thus show that if the media indeed use opinion polls to give voice to the people, they fail. As used by the media, opinion polls very seldom serve as *vox populi*. Rather, opinion polls serve as *vox media*. Even if we assume that opinion polls do a good job at measuring public opinion, which often is highly questionable. (2009b: 68)

Kolbeins's study of TV, radio, online and newspaper reporting during Iceland's 2013 parliamentary elections found less than one-third − 29.8 per cent − included a primary focus and only 7.2 per cent a secondary focus involving public opinion polls. She found much of the poll coverage concentrated on horserace news, with experts from political science departments used widely to interpret coverage. Instead, '41.4% (n=170) of election stories that had public opinion surveys as their primary angle didn't talk to or mention a human being while only 7.2% (n=12) of the party platforms' stories did so' (Kolbeins 2016: 140). Once again, the focus on the game aspect of election campaigns overshadowed more issue-based polls based on the public's interest.

In their study of the UK 2001 general election, Brookes and his colleagues identified a similar level of stories − 29 per cent − involving polls during the campaign. Furthermore, they found that 93 per cent of references were made by reporters and 7 per cent by politicians. Once again, there was an overwhelming focus on horserace polls – a total of 86.1 per cent – rather than on policy issues. Overall, the authors concluded that 'the use of polls in the media coverage of elections actually has very little to do with an attempt to understand or represent public opinion. Polls are used – to develop the horse-race analogy – as a kind of "form guide" to structure the narrative of the campaign' (Brookes et al. 2004: 69).

Our analysis of television news coverage of the 2015 UK general election also found that polls informed all the major newscasts during the campaign (Cushion et al. 2016b), with between two to three news items in ten featuring a survey (see table 3.2). However, over two-thirds of election items involving polls were referenced just briefly. This was particularly the case on the BBC, with 93 per cent of such items mentioned in passing. Once again, policy-based polls featured marginally in coverage, with just ten in total across all newscasts and none on the BBC over the six-week campaign. The overwhelming focus of polls was on the horserace, with Labour and the Conservative Party neck and neck, and, to a far lesser extent, on the performance of the leaders. In the 2017 election campaign, polls were reported in 15 per cent of election items – roughly 10 per cent less than in 2015 – with almost all of them about the horserace between the two main parties. As the next section explores, since the opinion polls were so misleading in the 2015 contest, in 2017 broadcasters were reluctant to publish polls or let them inform coverage to the same degree as the previous campaign (Kanter 2017).

Among the few studies that have systematically examined how opinion polls are used in the coverage of election campaigns, the broad consensus shows that they promoted horserace coverage and paid limited attention to policy issues. According to Dunaway (2011: 83), for instance, 'poll-centered coverage is non-substantive, on the rise, and is even crowding out more substantive coverage. Taken together, it seems that the disproportionate emphasis on poll-centered news coverage brought on by the digital age poses problems for the pool of information available to citizens for democratic decision-making.' Indeed, a study by Searles, Ginn and Nickens of all surveys released by polling organisations during the 2008 election campaign suggested not just that the media were

Table 3.2 Percentage of election items featuring a poll and the nature of such polls (N in parentheses)

	BBC	ITV	Ch. 4	Ch. 5	Sky	Total
Election items where poll is featured	20.5	31.1	20.7	22.2	28.1	24.2 (204)★
Of these, percentage mentioned in passing	93.0	55.8	66.7	67.6	59.0	67.6 (138)
Horserace poll	84.1	79.2	81.1	82.3	72.5	79.8 (166)
Leaders' poll	15.0	15.1	10.8	11.8	22.5	15.4 (32)
Policy poll	0.0	5.7	8.1	5.9	5.0	4.8 (10)
Total	100.0 (44)	100.0 (53)	100.0★★ (37)	100.0 (34)	100.0 (40)	100.0 (208)

Notes: ★This value is not identical to the total, since on some occasions more than one poll was referenced.

★★ A small number of items on Channel 4 did not fit into any of these categories and were omitted from this table.

Source: Adapted from Cushion et al. 2016b.

highly selective in which polls they aired; more than a hint of bias in cable news coverage of the campaign was found. The authors concluded emphatically: 'television media present a picture of the presidential race via coverage of public opinion that differs from the results of polls . . . the data demonstrate that gatekeepers' decisions to cover some polls while not covering others appear to have a significant impact on the nature of poll coverage' (Searles et al. 2016: 957–9).

Overall, many studies of election campaigns have concluded that opinion polls tend not be used in news coverage to interrogate the public's views on issues or to understand the kind of agenda they would like pursued. As Brookes et al. (2004: 70) put it, 'television elections are about what politicians talk about rather than what the public want them to talk about.' In their view, this is partly a consequence of how impartiality is interpreted, since journalists can appear objective if they rely on scientific data to report people's preferences for parties rather than issues. The public's views on policy issues, by contrast, are more complicated to represent, with conflicting views and opinions that may not easily fit with how people decide to vote. While issue-based polls may reflect the public's aggregate view about a specific policy, they could also represent a respondent's party political preference. For journalists attempting to remain impartial or objective, this means that shining a light on a poll dealing with policy could be seen as ideologically siding with one party, whereas horserace polls provide a more neutral way of interpreting public opinion.

However, horserace polls should not be seen as ideologically neutral. After all, they typically focus on the race between major parties (the Democrats and Republicans, for example), crowding out alternative left- or right-wing perspectives. Since they contain few references to policy preferences, they also do little to inform citizens about competing parties' and candidates' stances on issues such as healthcare, immigration and education. In this sense, polls do not live up to normative claims – to act, in the words of Gallup, as the democratic pulse of a nation long associated with opinion polling (cf. Lepore 2015). This was even recognised by Gallup in 2015, when the organisation decided to end its horserace polling in the run-up the 2016 US presidential election. According to Frank Newport, Gallup's editor-in-chief, the new aim was to focus on better 'understanding where the public stands on the issues of the day, how they are reacting to the proposals put forth by the candidates, what it is they want the candidates to do, and what messages or images of the candidates are seeping into the public's consciousness can make a more lasting contribution' (cited in Clement and Craighill 2015). He added 'This may not be the focus that gets the most "clicks" or short-term headlines, but is one which hopefully can make a real difference.' Given the relative paucity of policy coverage during the 2016 presidential election (see chapter 2) and the evidence presented in this chapter, Gallup's retreat from asking horserace questions appears not to have dampened media interest in process-driven opinion polling. Now more than ever, the use of polls to fuel horserace news appears a deeply ingrained journalistic convention during election campaigns.

To explore further the extent to which polls (mis)inform coverage of election campaigns, and to consider horserace coverage and its wider ideological impact, we now draw on a case study of our research about television news coverage of the 2015 UK general election (Cushion et al. 2016b). As we shall see, the reliance on polls was not driven entirely by a journalistic thirst for horserace coverage but also by a political logic to draw attention to how close the contest was and the possibility of electing a coalition government.

Interpreting the logic(s) of campaign reporting during the 2015 UK general election

Up until election day in May 2015, Labour and the Conservatives were reported as being neck and neck in the polls. But, after a shock exit poll forecast a Conservative majority, it soon became apparent that the surveys throughout the campaign were out of kilter with the voting public. Following a review of their sampling and methodology, the polling industry concluded that, among other things, they had underrepresented older Conservative voters and overrepresented younger Labour voters. Since polls had both parties tied throughout the campaign, it was widely believed that a coalition would be formed. As we investigate, television news focused primarily on an alliance between Labour and the Scottish National Party (SNP), despite other possible coalition deals.

Our research examined the UK's leading late-evening television newscasts over the six-week campaign, exploring both the volume and the nature of coverage between different broadcasters. We did so in the context of asking how far a media or political logic shaped coverage, concentrating on horserace reporting, which – as this chapter has explained – is also viewed as reflecting the agendas of journalists. To support our analysis, we interviewed the heads of news and/or senior editors from the BBC, ITV, Sky, Channel 4 and Channel 5. This allowed us to compare and contrast the agenda of broadcasters with the editorial decisions behind the selection of election news (Semetko et al. 1991).

As the previous chapter revealed, campaign-process news made up 62.4 per cent of airtime across the five newscasts examined (Cushion et al. 2016b). Of this coverage, 51.8 per cent was about the campaign, such as staged walkabouts or rallies, 30.8 per cent about the horserace, notably speculation about possible coalition deals, and 17.4 per cent about the televised leaders' debates. At face value, then, campaign coverage appeared to be driven by a commercial media logic, with the more market-driven newscasts – ITV, Sky News and Channels 4 and 5 – reporting more process-driven news than the BBC. However, our analysis of the editorial judgements shaping coverage suggested that a political logic was influencing the agenda of election news.

As previously discussed, opinion polls were widely reported during the election campaign, which might – according to conventional academic wisdom – point towards the media being obsessed with the closeness of the electoral race. And yet, as the editors we interviewed explained, the polls had clear political implications behind them, as they showed not just that a coalition was likely, but that Labour and the SNP would be the most likely government alliance. So, for example, Cristina Squires, head of Channel 5 news, explained how they:

were very conscious of the SNP being of enormous importance, not just to voters in Scotland . . . I think it was legitimate. We'd had five years of a coalition government, the pollsters were all telling us . . . that the most likely outcome was going to be a coalition and, therefore, who was going to make up that coalition was really important.

Some editors not only took their cues from pollsters, they alluded to the influence of the Conservative Party's campaign tactics. As its advertising revealed, the Conservative Party wanted to draw attention to the possibility of Labour going into coalition with the SNP. The party sought strategically to stoke up fear among English voters that the SNP could wield considerable influence at Westminster if in a coalition government. This was even praised by the BBC's Westminster editor, Katy Searle, who said:

> let's face it, the Tories were really successful in pushing this, and they knew because they were saying privately to us that it was coming up again and again on our doorstep, which actually I think it proved to be right – although I slightly didn't believe it when they were saying that, but I think it did. So it was very successful.

Our content analysis revealed just how successful the Conservative Party was in setting the television news agenda. We examined every mention of a possible Labour and SNP coalition deal in all process-driven news about the campaign, including both vague and explicit references to an electoral alliance. As table 3.3 shows, almost a third of all items – 31.3 per cent – connected the SNP with Labour, with close to four in ten on Sky News. Almost three-quarters of references to a potential alliance (74.8 per cent) were subtle references to a relationship between Labour and the SNP that did not clearly spell out a coalition government would be formed. So, for example, a Sky News reporter said that 'it's no surprise that the relationship between Labour and the SNP has gone from bad to bitter. But they could still be forced to work together after May' (10 April 2015). The remaining quarter of references – 25.9 per cent – were more explicit, such as an ITV reporter stating that 'David Cameron once again attacked Labour on Scotland,

Table 3.3 Percentage of campaign news items making a connection between a Labour–SNP coalition and the clarity of these references (N in parentheses)

	BBC	ITV	Ch. 4	Ch. 5	Sky	Total
Percentage among election items referring to a Labour–SNP coalition	27.2	38.6	28.8	23.8	39.6	31.3 (162)
Innuendo references to a Labour–SNP coalition	67.7	71.8	83.3	83.3	68.4	74.8 (120)
Explicit references to a Labour–SNP coalition.	32.3	28.2	16.7	16.7	31.6	25.9 (42)
Total	100.0 (31)	100.0 (39)	100.0 (30)	100.0 (24)	100.0 (38)	100.0 (162)

Source: Adapted from Cushion et al. 2016b.

claiming a vote for them could lead to the frightening prospect of a government propped up by the SNP . . . [Labour has] rattled the prime minister enough to issue a warning about the dangers of a Labour government backed by the SNP' (News at Ten, 19 April 2015). The final part of the package pictured a Conservative poster showing Nicola Sturgeon working Ed Miliband like a puppet. A voice-over added: 'But the Conservative posters are getting blunter. As is their message: vote Tory, to stop an alliance that would only favour the Scots.'

Clearly, broadcasters were aware of the Conservative Party's campaign tactics. Our close textual analysis and follow-up interviews with editors revealed broadcasters' emphasis on the polls and future coalition deals could not be explained entirely by a media logic obsessed with reporting a horserace angle. Editorial decision-making was also informed by the Conservative Party's logic. Only by examining *the micro-context of the campaign* could the political logic of election coverage be understood and exposed (Cushion et al. 2016b).

If we consider the reporting of the campaign more generally, according to many of our interviewees the selection of process news was not the result of an attempt to excite viewers or uncover campaign tactics. It was largely because of the limited access granted to political parties and the unwillingness of candidates to answer policy questions put to them. As Cristina Squires, head of Channel 5 News, described:

> I think it's really important to concentrate on the issues . . . but do you know what, that's what the parties were telling us to do. There was a lot of pressure from the parties and the bottom line is . . . they wouldn't answer the questions. We had David Cameron on our programme live. We asked him about four times, 'where was the £12 billion of cuts going to come from?' and he wouldn't answer it.

In previous elections, all the major political parties held daily press conferences, granting journalists the opportunity regularly to question and interrogate their policy proposals during the campaign. However, in recent campaigns parties have controlled their campaign events more tightly (Gaber 2011), with staged walkabouts or rallies, but with restricted access for both journalists and members of the public. As the head of BBC political programming Sue Inglish revealed, 'the parties, virtually all of them, did not hold morning press conferences. So their press operations . . . went out into the country. They were very small controlled groups of people, often party supporters who were in the so-called press conferences.' In this way, she argued, 'you didn't have any real forum in which the parties were quizzed about their manifestos across a range of different policies, and I think the one issue that one would want to look at next time round is how do you force that examination of policy when the parties don't want to talk about it?'

Many of the editors we interviewed observed how political parties were attempting to exert control over their campaign and the media agenda. So, for example, Geoff Hill, editor of ITV News at Ten, said that 'there is a desire to control something they [political parties] can't control, which is the news agenda, and there's so many bizarre strategic decisions made by the political parties and then at the end of the day you get a lot of complaints saying, why didn't you do this, why didn't you do that?' Meanwhile, the then head of politics at Sky News explained how there's lots of very heated exchanges with all the parties about the way the campaign was being driven – actually let's say the two main ones, because the Lib Dems had a much more . . . they wanted you to feel like you could film everything . . . We have a number of run-ins where we say to them we're not part of your broadcast operation.

In other words, a political logic – not an obsessive journalistic logic – was partly responsible for the high process-driven agenda and horserace approach to election reporting. Many editors pointed out they were highly conscious of the increasingly controlling nature of party campaign tactics and attempted to expose them throughout the campaign. This was reflected upon by the editors of both BBC News and Sky News:

We did a piece that went behind the campaign, and a lot of BBC outlets did this piece because, as I'm sure you know, it was being described as the most carefully controlled campaign and all of that. And we did a piece that went behind the campaign and how we couldn't hold microphones and things like that. (Paul Royall, editor of BBC News at Ten)

. . . we did a couple of pieces actually on all the campaigns, showing the fact that this is where we're allowed to stand – there's Cameron, we're not allowed in, we don't get to ask a question, we're on a bus, he's on a plane ahead of us. So, if they were trying to control the situation too much, then yes we would expose that the way we saw it. (Esme Wren, head of politics at Sky News)

The limited access parties granted to journalists and the public was visibly exposed by a Sky News journalist, Niall Ferguson, who tweeted a picture of a Conservative Party rally in Cornwall. It showed how the rally was being held in a giant cowshed, closed off to the public, with party activists tightly circling the prime minister to give the effect of a crowded gathering. The image was widely shared and retweeted, perhaps because it showed a rare glimpse of a political party's carefully choreographed and controlled rally. Nevertheless, since television newscasts did not provide a wide shot of the proceedings, many people would not have been aware of their constructed nature.

Although many editors claimed they regularly highlighted the parties' campaign tactics during the election, our systematic analysis of coverage suggested the contrary. We examined every item when a reporter was on the campaign trail – over 350 in total – to consider whether a reporter exposed a rally or an event. By 'campaign trail', we mean items involving a reporter with a political party, such as: 'the political correspondent Ian Watson is at the Labour rally in Warrington to hear Miliband make an announcement on housing policy. He does his analysis over the cheers of the crowd and with Miliband waving behind him' (BBC News at Ten, 4 April 2015).

As table 3.4 shows, more than seven in ten items – 73.4 per cent – did not draw attention to the stage-managed way a campaign rally was conducted. Needless to say, we would not expect every item to be comprehensively or partially exposed, but across all broadcasters – notably ITV and Channel 5 – the parties' stage management went unchallenged most of the time.

Channel 4 ran several lengthy packages about the parties' campaign tactics, including one where they asked a war photographer to report. In doing so, as the following example illustrates, he revealed just how far parties went to control the campaign agenda:

Table 3.4 Percentage of election items featuring a reporter questioning politicians on the campaign trail and how far stage management of a party rally was exposed (N in parentheses)

	BBC	ITV	Ch. 4	Ch. 5	Sky	Total
'On the campaign trail'	38.1	43.7	42.0	41.8	48.2	42.3 (357)
No exposing of rally	75.0	68.5	68.8	85.9	68.7	73.4
Some exposing of rally	18.7	30.1	19.2	10.9	22.3	20.4
Comprehensive exposing of rally	6.3	1.4	11.0	3.1	9.0	6.2
Total	100.0 (80)	100.0 (73)	100.0 (73)	100.0 (64)	100.0 (67)	100.0 (357)

Source: Adapted from Cushion et al. 2016b.

A seat on the Lib Dem battlebus costs journalists £750 a day. Hmm. Let's see if it's worth the money . . . I've come all this way and it turns out that this blue rope means I can't get close. I'm not in the pool . . . When it comes to the media, the entire event has been carefully managed . . . The atmosphere seems stifling and controlled. You know, you get a sense in your fingertips. I find everything is scripted, there seems to be no room for surprises . . . There's a fear, they don't seem to want to talk to the people direct, y'know, pump flesh and kiss babies and taste pastries. (Channel 4 News, 5 April 2015)

But, overall, our analysis of the six-week campaign showed this level of scrutiny was the exception rather than day-to-day norm. The parties' campaign logic, in other words, was largely successful, with broadcasters most of the time accepting rather than exposing their events and rallies. In the 2017 UK general election, once again parties tightly controlled their campaigns, limiting access to journalists and members of the public (Cushion 2017c). Despite editors suggesting they might more regularly challenge the spin behind the campaigns, fewer items in the run-up to 2017 election exposed the staged-managed nature of the parties' rallies and walkabouts.

Horserace reporting: a media, political or citizen logic?

The chapter began by discussing the rise of horserace reporting and considering the type of election journalism it promoted. Much of the fascination with horserace news, it was suggested, was based on a journalistic belief – supported by some evidence (Iyengar et al. 2004) – that there was a consumer demand for it because audiences found it exciting and engaging during the campaign. The growth of horserace reporting was attributed partly to the pace of contemporary journalism, with the latest update about who's up or down in the campaign well suited to the rhythms and routines of 24-hour news culture. Opinion polls, we further explored, played an integral part in this horserace narrative, and their increasing presence and availability over recent decades has enhanced the focus on game-type news rather than encouraging more issue-based election agendas. For journalists concerned about the impartiality of coverage, reporting polls as opposed to policies can also appear safer ideological territory. After all, most (although by all means not all) polls are produced by independent (and non-partisan) polling organisations, allowing reporters to produce the latest figures without taking political sides.

According to conventional academic wisdom, the rise of horse-race reporting during election campaigns represents an increasingly media-controlled agenda. However, this chapter has suggested that horserace news cannot be explained by a media logic alone. Our case study of the 2015 UK general election examined senior broadcasters' editorial judgements about campaign coverage and discovered how a political logic was a driving force behind less coverage of policy issues. So, for example, whereas journalists in previous elections quizzed politicians about their policy positions in their daily press conferences, political parties no longer held these and instead opted for tightly controlled campaign events. This limited the opportunities for journalists to scrutinise parties' policies. While journalists have often been blamed for obsessing over the horserace, during the 2015 UK general election there was a clear political logic to drawing attention to the closeness of the race. As we explored, it reinforced the Conservatives' campaign agenda in highlighting a possible coalition deal between the SNP and Labour. Soon after the election result it transpired that the polls had been misleading, but the forecasts still shaped the media narrative of the campaign.

So how can we interpret whose agenda – a political, media or public logic – is best served by the increasing emphasis on horser-ace reporting in election campaigns? According to conventional mediatisation of politics theory, a political logic is often viewed as running counter to horserace reporting. But, when political parties and candidates are not willing to open themselves up to policy scrutiny, it could be in their interest to promote a process news agenda and close down debate about election issues. As our UK case study showed, a political logic helped relegate policy news and enhanced the horserace narrative. A media logic, of course, would have been met by emphasising the closeness of the race and speculating about possible coalition deals. But since media logic is also about exerting editorial power and control, a more independently orientated agenda could have more regularly exposed the fabricated nature of campaigns and challenged party political attempts to manipulate the agenda. This is not to suggest that the parties' voices should be marginalised in coverage or that a more media-led agenda should be encouraged. But journalists could start from a more critical position, where parties are asked to respond to (rather than promote their own) policy issues, even if their aim is to avoid explaining them in any detail during the campaign. Since reporting polls predominately fuels news about the horserace, the emphasis on campaign process does little to enhance people's understanding of the parties' competing policy positions.

As we explore in the final chapter, an election news agenda – or logic – driven by issues could also better represent the public's voice and policy preferences during a campaign. Although there is (limited) evidence to suggest that audiences have an appetite for horserace news (Iyengar et al. 2004), it would be hard to argue that this represents the public's interest, since it appears to crowd out coverage of issues and can even misinform voters about who's ahead in the polls. As Iyengar et al. put it themselves, 'polling on the issues allows reporters to file policy-oriented horserace stories . . . painting the candidates' issue agendas in broad, ideological strokes is more likely to attract attention than reporting on specific issues' (2004: 174). In other words, election reporting could be more sensitive to the public's needs, but this does not necessarily mean replacing all process news with dull and worthy policy discussion. It may involve, as we develop further in the final chapter, splicing together issues and horserace reporting in ways that serve a public logic by exciting *and* informing audiences. Indeed, process news more generally can play an important democratic role ahead of an election, such as explaining to people how to vote or exposing the spin behind a campaign event. But, as the evidence in the previous chapter revealed, the emphasis on process news often overshadows coverage of the parties' policy agendas during an election campaign.

The next chapter considers how fair and balanced broadcasters are during an election campaign. We examine the evidence about media bias in campaign coverage and draw on a UK case study to consider the impartiality of television news in the run-up to the 2015 general election.

4

Regulating Balance and Impartiality

Policing the agenda: how fair and balanced is election coverage?

Considering the fairness and balance of news reporting is one of the most studied aspects of political communication (D'Alessio 2012). This line of inquiry can reveal whether the news media favour one party over another, potentially swaying how people vote and influencing election outcomes. This chapter explores the evidence about how fair and balanced broadcasters are during election campaigns, focusing primarily on recent campaigns in the US and the UK. Bias, of course, is not always easy to detect and evidence. While election reporting may be explicitly one-sided – championing one party or demonising another – bias can also be more elusive and difficult to uncover, with subtle verbal or visual communication undermining the character or positions of politicians (Esser 2008; Grabe and Bucy 2009).

In exploring how fair and balanced broadcasters are during election campaigns, it is important to be aware of any cross-national differences in how they are regulated and policed (Hallin and

Mancini 2004). As previous chapters have explained, different countries have unique media systems with different regulatory environments and professional aims when reporting election campaigns. So, for example, American news media are not subject to any regulatory checks and balances during election campaigns, whereas across Europe most broadcasters have to comply with rules about reporting impartially or objectively (Hopmann et al. 2012; Strömbäck and Kaid 2008). Through education, training and newsroom culture, many US journalists subscribe to an objectivity norm (Schudson 2001), but this is not policed by a formal regulatory body.

On account of the breadth and depth of literature about media bias, the opening part of this chapter focuses on *party political balance and tone in election coverage*. We review studies that have explored stopwatch balance, which quantifies the proportionate time and number of appearances granted to parties and politicians during an election campaign. We also examine tonal balance, which considers the nature of coverage, and whether the language and framing of news is supportive or undermining. Needless to say, there are many other ways of detecting bias, but the chapter begins by *empirically establishing whether most broadcasters broadly remain fair and balanced during an election campaign*.

It is also important to be aware of how concepts of balance are understood cross-nationally (Hopmann et al. 2012). Reporting impartially, for instance, is often used to represent competing positions. The aim, above all, is not to take sides on a story with opposing arguments. Objectivity, by contrast, assumes there is a 'truth' to report even if the facts behind a story may be conflicting or contentious. For objectivity, this makes balanced reporting appear unnecessary, whereas, for impartiality, balance is essential so that claims and counter-claims can be represented. In the UK, achieving impartiality has traditionally been the professional aim of broadcast journalists while, in the US, remaining objective is widely viewed as the normative goal (Cushion and Thomas 2017; Sambrook 2012; Schudson 2001). Given this context, it is not easy comparing and contrasting how fair and balanced election news is cross-nationally. Different countries have specific and bespoke *national* rules and professional aims that measure concepts such as objectivity and impartiality (see Hopmann et al. 2012; Strömbäck and Kaid 2008).

The second part of the chapter addresses this by examining how the UK's impartiality rules are interpreted and applied by scholars and practitioners during an election campaign. Although the stopwatch principle of measuring how much airtime reporters supply for particular candidates and parties remains a dominant way of policing balance during an election campaign (Norris et al. 1999), our research suggests that broadcasters no longer subscribe to this logic (Cushion and Thomas 2017). Drawing on interviews with regulators, editors, politicians and spin-doctors after the 2015 UK general election, we conclude that the 'due' before 'impartiality' gives broadcasters considerable flexibility in balancing coverage of parties during a campaign.

Finally, we explore debates about intermedia agenda-setting and the influence rival media can play in shaping coverage during election campaigns. In our view, this represents an important but understudied aspect of media influence. We draw further on our research about the 2015 UK general election to suggest that the impartiality of broadcasters' editorial judgements was compromised when they relied on the news values of partisan newspapers to select election stories (Cushion et al. 2016a).

How fair and balanced is election reporting?

We begin by exploring US election reporting. Compared with their equivalents in most other advanced Western democracies, American broadcasters have no formal regulations about remaining balanced during election campaigns. This makes US political journalism exceptional for a number of reasons. As chapter 5 explores in detail, the American news environment has changed dramatically since the 1980s when the Fairness Doctrine was abolished and broadcasters no longer had to abide by regulatory rules concerning balance (Cushion 2012b). This helps explain why trust in US media has been falling for many decades. According to Gallup (2016b), trust in journalists reached its lowest point in polling history, with just 32 per cent of Americans stating that they believed US media 'report the news fully, accurately and fairly' in 2016, compared with 55 per cent in 1999. This is symptomatic of a wider polarisation of news audiences in recent years, with people increasingly tuning into programmes according to their own ideological preferences (Iyengar and Hahn 2009; Stroud 2011). This is more apparent among registered Republicans than among independent or Democratic voters. But, overall, whereas 46 per cent of people in a 2014 poll believed a liberal bias existed in US news coverage, only 13 per cent thought there was a conservative bias (Mendes 2013).

But is there evidence that confirms a so-called liberal bias in news reporting? Often used to support this contention is research showing that most journalists in the US are more likely to vote for a Democrat candidate or hold left-wing values. This line of argument dates back most prominently to a 1986 book, *The Media Elite: America's New Powerbrokers*, which surveyed the most influential American journalists at different news organisations and discovered most held liberal views and supported Democratic candidates (Lichter et al. 1986). While the findings have been widely challenged, they reflect a branch of academic inquiry which contends that political bias can be established by analysing the ideological credentials of journalists *rather than news coverage*.

However, empirical studies examining election news have found little sustained or consistent research showing a general media bias in US news media towards either pro-conservative or pro-liberal perspectives. D'Alessio's meta-analysis of ninety-nine academic studies examining presidential election reporting between 1948 and 2008 offers perhaps the most evidence-based assessment of whether a media bias exists. Overall, he argued that: 'the data clearly indicates that the media, on the whole, with the exception of specific individual outlets on either side of the ideological spectrum (that have a strong tendency to offset one another) tend to be neither pro-Republican nor pro-Democratic in their coverage of presidential election campaigns. On the whole, the media are smack dab in the middle' (D'Alessio 2012: 102). This conclusion also included studies of television news, such as network coverage of presidential elections, which dates back many decades (see also D'Alessio and Allen 2000). However, coverage on the cable television news channels that arrived in the 1990s and 2000s has become more explicitly partisan. As table 4.0 shows, during the 2012 presidential election campaign, while the right-wing cable channel Fox News was particularly negative towards the Democratic candidate, President Obama – making up 46 per cent of items with tone (excluding mixed tone) – its left-wing counterpart, MSNBC, was more negative – representing 71 per cent of items – towards his Republican opponent, Mitt Romney. Conversely, both were far more positive about their liberal/conservative-favoured presidential candidates (Rosenstiel et al. (2012).

By contrast, both the morning and evening programming of the main networks – ABC, CBS and NBC – was less one-sided in tonal coverage towards candidates during the 2012 presidential race. Comparing cable and network news coverage, the study concluded that the difference 'reveals the degree to which the two cable channels that have built themselves around ideological

Table 4.0 Positive or negative coverage of presidential candidates during the 2012 campaign (percentages)

	Positive for Obama	Negative for Obama	Positive for Romney	Negative for Romney
Fox News	6	46	28	71
MSNBC	39	15	3	12

Source: Adapted from Rosenstiel et al. 2012.

Table 4.1 Positive or negative US network news coverage of presidential candidates during the 2012 campaign (percentages)

	Positive for Obama	Negative for Obama	Positive for Romney	Negative for Romney
ABC	27	20	18	33
CBS	17	28	15	29
NBC	16	29	18	29

Source: Adapted from Pew Research Center 2012.

Table 4.2 Percentage of stories in network television favouring
Democrats or Republicans during presidential campaign coverage

	2000	*2004*	*2008*
Favour Democrats	45	45	36
Favour Republicans	46	44	53
Balanced	9	11	11

Source: Adapted from Diddi et al. 2014.

programming, MSNBC and Fox, stand out from other mainstream media outlets' (Rosenstiel et al. 2012: 4). As table 4.1 indicates, with perhaps the exception of ABC coverage of Romney, there was no clear imbalance towards a liberal or conservative perspective.

This balanced approach to reporting the two major parties on network television news was also evident in the three previous US presidential election campaigns. As table 4.2 indicates, apart from stories in 2008 favouring Republicans by 17 percentage points, there was no *clear* imbalance towards either of the two main parties.

We take a closer look at how balanced and objective television news was during the 2016 US presidential race in the next chapter. But, generally speaking, the evidence suggests that the news media enhanced its negativity of election coverage in 2016, which reflected the aggressive and personalised campaigns waged by both candidates. Nevertheless, Patterson's (2016b) study of the full campaign as covered by ABC, CBS, CNN, Fox, the *Los Angeles Times*, NBC, the *New York Times*, *USA Today*, the *Wall Street Journal*, and the *Washington Post* (January 2015 to November 2016) found Clinton was reported more negatively than positively (62 vs. 38 per cent) in comparison with Donald Trump (56 vs. 44 per cent). Again, there is not a huge disparity in bias between candidates, but, as chapter 5 explores, this masks the partisanship displayed on some cable television news stations.

But arguably the most biased aspect of presidential election coverage was *the overwhelming focus on the two established mainstream parties*, with limited attention being granted to the independent Libertarian candidate, Gary Johnson, or the Greens' Jill Stein. This meant, as noted in chapter 2, that coverage was ideologically confined to the issue agendas of Republicans and Democrats. Moreover, from the primaries onwards, the two leading respective candidates – Clinton and Trump – were by far the most dominant voices within their parties (see chapter 5). Thus the more left-wing brand of politics of the Democrats' Bernie Sanders was marginalised, while more moderate Republican perspectives received far less media attention. Bias, in this sense, is more about what is *excluded than what is included in election coverage.*

In the UK, broadcasters must abide by regulatory guidelines concerning the relative balance political parties should receive during the official part of the campaign. We consider – and critique – these in detail further into the chapter, but, broadly speaking, they refer to rules about 'due impartiality' that ask broadcasters to cover political parties according to a set of criteria – for example, the number of votes they received in the last election and their level of support in the opinion polls. These are designed to ensure that, unlike in the US, coverage is broadly balanced between both the major and the minor parties. As we argue below, these guidelines are not necessarily followed that closely, but, compared to the laissez-faire approach in the US to regulating balance, the aim is to ensure that a proportional range – according to measures of party success – of political voices is heard over an election campaign.

Overall, the evidence suggests that, historically, the UK's main broadcasters have tended to be even-handed in stopwatch balance towards Labour and the Conservatives, with the party in power gaining a slight 'incumbency bonus' in the amount of coverage they receive. As table 4.3 shows, whereas the Conservatives received the most airtime and the largest number of appearances in broadcast media during the 1992 general election campaign – when they were the party in power – Labour was reported to a similar extent during the 2005 election campaign, when it was the sitting party in government. In the 2015 and 2017 general elections, the proportion of Conservative and Labour coverage was, once again, finely balanced, with just a 2.2 per cent difference in the latter campaign (see table 4.4).

The UK national press, by contrast, reported Conservative Party representatives by roughly 10 per cent more than the Labour

Table 4.3 The amount of quotation time and number of appearances on UK broadcast news coverage (percentages)

Quotation time Political party	1992	2001	2005
Conservatives	41.0	43.6	41.3
Labour	36.0	38.3	34.8
Lib Dems	23.0	18.1	23.9
Number of appearances			
Conservatives	33.4	41.3	40.0
Labour	41.0	38.0	33.3
Lib Dems	26.0	20.7	26.7

Source: Adapted from Deacon et al. 2005.

Table 4.4 Share of party political coverage on TV and in the press in the 2015 and 2017 UK general election campaigns (by percentage time)

Political party	2015		2017	
	Broadcast media	Print media	Broadcast media	Print media
Conservatives	27.9	37.5	34.7	46.9
Labour	28.9	31.8	32.5	37.3
Lib Dems	15.1	10.0	11.4	6.9
SNP	11.1	9.0	6.4	2.3
Plaid Cymru	1.6	0.5	2.4	1.0
UKIP	9.7	8.3	6.1	2.9
Greens	1.9	1.3	2.1	0.3
Others	3.8	1.6	4.3	2.3
Total★	100.0	100.0	100.0	100.0

Note: ★Due to rounding up or down to one decimal place, some columns do not add up to exactly 100 per cent.
Source: Adapted from Loughborough University 2015 and 2017.

Party in both elections. Minor parties, such as the Greens, gained a fraction of coverage – 1.3 and 0.3 per cent share overall in 2015 and 2017 election campaigns respectively. We look more carefully at how even-handed coverage was during the 2015 election later in the chapter by considering other measures of balance and focusing on the agenda-setting influence of the UK national press. But in terms of the tonal balance – positive and negative – while past Loughborough University studies (Deacon et al. 2005: 32–3) have identified mixed coverage of parties, there has not been a tendency to target any political party in particular. During the 2015 general election, for example, Loughborough University (2015) concentrated exclusively on tonal balance in press coverage, excluding the results of their analysis of broadcast news (on account of the comparatively lower level of intercoder reliability than in their study of newspapers). As we might expect in a media system with due impartiality guidelines and a professional commitment towards fair and balanced reporting, there was no *explicit* party political bias in broadcast news.

Our analysis of second-order election reporting during the 2009 and 2014 EU and local campaigns found a similar degree of relative balance between the main parties on UK television news (Cushion et al. 2015a). As chapter 2 confirmed, there was limited coverage of both campaigns, but the time allocated to spokespeople from the 'major' parties was broadly even-handed. However, there was an imbalance in coverage during the 2014 election campaign, with UKIP – the most Eurosceptic party – dominating the issue agenda. We quantified the number of times one party dominated a news item – as shown in table 4.5 – and discovered UKIP's issues gained by far the most prominence. We argued that the focus on UKIP did not breach the UK's formal rules on impartiality. But it did reflect a narrow focus on a limited range of issues – with immigration high on the agenda – and on whether the UK should be in or out of the EU (of the four major parties, only UKIP supported leaving at the time). In other words, the issues favoured UKIP's agenda to a greater degree than those of the other major parties.

Several studies of European countries have also identified a media logic influencing election reporting, such as a greater prominence being paid to controversial political leaders or smaller parties that increased their public opinion poll ratings (see Hopmann et al. 2012). Nonetheless, Hopmann, van Aelst and Legnante's review of many European studies examining political balance in the news suggested there was also little evidence of *any sustained explicit bias in broadcast news where one party was favoured over another.* They found mixed results without any clear pattern. However, one consistent finding was the identification of an 'incumbency bonus'

Table 4.5 Number of news items dominated by one party in TV coverage of the 2009 and 2014 EU elections

Party	2009	2014
Labour	7	15
BNP	7	1
Lib Dems	4	12
Conservatives	3	14
Greens	2	6
Other parties in Europe	2	5
UKIP	0	35
Other UK parties	8	2
No party dominated item	26	28

Source: Adapted from Cushion et al. 2015a.

across several national elections, such as those in the Netherlands, Denmark, Austria and Belgium, with the government in power receiving greater media attention than its opponents. In explaining this repeated bias, Hopmann et al. (2012: 245–6) observed that 'These studies argue that this type of bias towards incumbents has nothing to do with partisan preferences but should be seen as the result of "media routines". Even in France, where strict control of electronic broadcasting is in force, a bonus on dominant parties' candidates was found in presidential elections.'

In a longitudinal study of Danish election reporting between 1994 and 2007, for example, Hopmann, de Vreese and Albæk identified clear evidence of an incumbency bonus with the visibility of the party in power. The study found 'change over time within the country [Denmark], further confirming the relationship between political power and the incumbency bonus: Governments with more support (i.e., expected winners of an election) had a larger incumbency bonus than weaker governments' (Hopmann et al. 2011: 277). The authors thus concluded that, 'The more powerful you are, the more attention you receive' (ibid.: 276–7). Likewise, the analysis of television and press coverage of the 2003 Belgian election by van Aelst et al. (2008) concluded that 'the politicians who topped the electoral lists of the larger parties and who were running simultaneously for a seat in the Senate were attributed much more media attention than candidates of smaller parties (or the extreme-right party).' In their view, this challenged the notion that election coverage was dominated by a media logic, since a political logic was evident by an equal balance of the main political parties.

Needless to say, our review of how fair and balanced election reporting is in just a handful of countries cannot possibly account for all national and local electoral contests that may have been unique, with one party receiving greater or more favourable coverage than its rivals. There are, in this sense, exceptions to the norm. But, generally speaking, the evidence from most Western democracies suggests that, with the exception of cable television news channels in the US, most broadcasters *did not explicitly favour one party over another during election campaigns*. Studies showed that both the visibility of the big parties and the tone towards them was relatively even-handed. As discussed in the introduction to this chapter, this reflects the regulatory rules and wider professional commitment towards *reporting the major parties*. This, in turn, polices the boundaries of how impartiality and balance are interpreted by broadcast news editors during an election campaign. Moreover, it is reinforced by the pressure exerted on broadcasters during the campaign by mainstream politicians (a pressure that minor parties cannot exert to the same degree).

However, as already acknowledged, this broad-brush perspective masks more subtle ways in which the impartiality of election news can be compromised. It also overlooks how journalists understand and apply impartiality as distinct from the objectivity norm (Schudson 2001). In the next section, we focus on the UK's impartiality guidelines and consider how they were interpreted during the 2015 general election campaign not just by editors but by regulators, politicians and party political spin-doctors.

Interpreting impartiality: towards a looser regulatory environment?

Although detecting bias in the news is widely researched, few studies have explored how objectivity, impartiality or balance are understood and applied by editors and regulators (with notable exceptions – see Rafter 2015). As the opening part of this chapter explained, these terms can be conceptually difficult to put into practice, but they remain fundamental journalistic aims for many broadcasters, particularly during election campaigns. The BBC's editorial guidelines, for example, boldly state that 'Impartiality lies at the heart of public service and is the core of the BBC's commitment to its audiences . . . We must be inclusive, considering the broad perspective and ensuring the existence of a range of views is appropriately reflected.'* Central to this editorial aim is how 'appropriately' is understood and operationalised by editors. It refers to the 'due' that precedes 'impartiality' in the guidelines that shape UK broadcast news regulation, which provides flexibility for editorial judgements.

All UK broadcasters are regulated by Ofcom. But during the 2015 election campaign – the focus of this section – Ofcom regulated only commercial broadcasters, while the BBC Trust was the corporation's watchdog and helped set the parameters of its output. During the 2015 election campaign, both regulators adopted a broadly similar interpretation of 'due impartiality'. However, Ofcom classified parties by whether they were major or minor (depending on past electoral support, rating in public opinion polls and other measures). This was led by Adam Baxter, an executive in editorial standards at Ofcom, whom we interviewed as part of our study. According to Ofcom's criteria, while Labour, the Conservatives and the Liberal Democrats were viewed as major parties in Great Britain, UKIP was considered 'major' only in England and Wales. The SNP and the Greens, by contrast, were

---

* This quotation is taken from the BBC editorial guidelines; see www.bbc.co.uk/editorialguidelines/guidelines/impartiality.

both considered minor parties in Great Britain. But, understandably, the SNP was considered a major party *in Scotland* as was Plaid Cymru *in Wales*. Because of the different status of parties across the nations, it is not straightforward for network television news editors to apply the rules to their UK national programming (covering, as this does, all four nations). Given their mission to serve UK viewers, it seems reasonable to assume that network newscasts would give due weight to the major parties from Great Britain or England and Wales (since both represent the vast majority of their audiences), rather than in, say, Scotland or Wales. We apply these distinctions in our analysis of how impartial broadcasters were during the 2015 UK general election campaign.

Although the BBC Trust did not formally label parties major or minor, in practice the BBC guidelines are similar to Ofcom's, recommending that the 'relative amount of coverage given to political parties in each electoral area . . . should reflect levels of past and/or current electoral support' (BBC 2014). For further guidance, staff are asked to contact the BBC's advisor, Ric Bailey, whom we also interviewed in our study. During the negotiations for parties to appear in the televised leaders' debate in 2010, the SNP complained that its exclusion was not consistent with the BBC's impartiality guidelines. However, the BBC Trust rejected the SNP's challenge because it was not a UK-wide party and its leader would not become prime minister. Following Ofcom's guidelines and the BBC Trust's previous rulings, it would be reasonable to assume that, at least in BBC UK network programming, the SNP was considered a minor party.

Our interviews with two regulatory professionals were central to our study's approach to interpreting how impartiality is understood and applied. As we will see, the way scholars explain the impartiality guidelines appears contradictory to how regulators police them. So, for example, Semetko (2000: 353) has suggested that, 'To guarantee balance, tradition has it that the coverage of each of the parties in the news is "stop-watched" during the election campaign . . . So, for example, every five minutes devoted to the Conservatives was matched somewhere in the bulletin with five minutes devoted to Labour and four minutes devoted to the

Liberal Democrats.' Likewise, Norris (2009: 333) has stated that 'election news TV and radio broadcasts in Britain display internal diversity, with stop-watch balance regulated and monitored across party coverage.' The review of studies exploring political balance by Hopmann and his colleagues also points out that, 'In the UK, the public service broadcaster, the BBC, is required to balance news coverage of the political parties according to specific shares allocated to the parties' (Hopmann et al. 2012: 244). In other words, the predominant scholarly view is that UK regulators should adopt a quantitative method towards impartiality by balancing the proportion of coverage granted to different political parties. And yet, since the 1992 election, ITN has no longer quantified the allocation of time for each party, while the BBC in the 2001 election campaign also signalled it would no longer use a stopwatch approach to policing impartiality (Harding 2001).

We analysed television news coverage of the 2015 UK general election campaign to assess whether broadcasters adopted a quantitative or a more qualitative approach to balancing party political perspectives (Cushion and Thomas 2017). The results informed our interviews with regulators from both Ofcom and the BBC Trust, as well as fourteen other key stakeholders involved in election reporting, including editors, spin-doctors and politicians. Overall we interviewed the heads of television news or senior editors from the BBC, ITV, Sky, Channel 4 and Channel 5: Paul Royall (editor of BBC News at Six and Ten), Katy Searle (the BBC's Westminster editor), Sue Inglish (then head of BBC political programming), Geoff Hill (editor of ITV News at Ten), Michael Jermey (head of ITV news), Ben De Pear (head of Channel 4 News), Esme Wren (then head of politics at Sky News) and Cristina Squires (then head of Channel 5 News). We also interviewed four key spin-doctors – Chris Luffingham (Greens), Kevin Pringle (SNP), Alex Phillips (UKIP) and James Holt (Liberal Democrats) – and two MPs – Lucy Powell (a Labour shadow cabinet minister and vice-chair of the party's campaign strategy) and Craig Williams (who won a key marginal seat in Cardiff North for the Conservatives). Of course, this is not a representative sample of party political spin-doctors or senior campaign managers, but it provides a useful range of perspectives about how the impartiality of broadcast news should be interpreted and applied.

Our content analysis measured the impartiality of television news in three ways: first, stopwatch balance, which quantified the inclusion – and exclusion – of parties over the election campaign; second, issue balance, which explored which topics were addressed to assess whether a particular issue favoured one party over another; and, third, how far reporters rather than politicians appeared in coverage. While more airtime for reporters does not relate to an imbalance of party political perspectives, it does raise questions as to the impartiality of broadcast news, because coverage relies to a greater extent on journalistic judgements about campaign events and issues. We examined the most watched flagship evening newscasts over the six-week campaign, including BBC News at Ten, ITV News at Ten, Channel 4 News at 7 pm, Channel 5 at 5 pm and Sky News at Ten. Overall, 843 items were examined.

All interviewees agreed that impartiality should be maintained and not relaxed, despite the growing influence of online and social media platforms, which operate largely in an unregulated environment. As we explore further below, the impartiality of UK broadcasting was viewed as being particularly significant by some interviewees because much of the national press was so explicitly partisan. We then began to ask questions related to the findings of our television study of election coverage. As tables 4.6 and 4.7 reveal, coverage was relatively well balanced between the two main parties, Labour and the Conservatives, with both receiving the most airtime. But, on closer inspection, it was the SNP – designated by Ofcom a minor party in Great Britain – that received more visibility and attention in several newscasts than two of the major parties, UKIP and the Liberal Democrats.

Most of the party political interviewees did not take issue with the imbalance of SNP coverage or that it necessarily breached Ofcom's guidelines. However, Labour's Lucy Powell suggested that it had an important impact on the election outcome. She argued it promoted the possibility that Labour might enter into a coalition with the SNP, which the Conservative Party wanted to encourage. In her words:

it definitely altered the outcome of the election, it definitely had an impact . . . I don't think that Ofcom can justify . . . saying that [exercising news judgement] because it wasn't about the SNP talking about themselves . . . that had a news value. It was about another party [the Conservatives] trying to make the SNP the big story in the election, and that was permitted, basically, on quite a large scale.

Table 4.6 The proportion of airtime for political parties in television news coverage of the 2015 general election (percentages; seconds in parentheses)

	BBC	ITV	Ch. 4	Ch. 5	Sky	Total
Conservatives	28.3	28.3	26.4	32.9	25.6	27.8 (7,939)
Labour	27.5	24.7	28.3	24.2	24.2	26.4 (7,554)
Lib Dems	14.8	15.4	18.0	23.2	14.3	17.3 (4,936)
Greens	2.4	4.5	3.3	0.9	3.5	3.0 (862)
UKIP	6.4	10.2	14.7	8.8	10.9	11.3 (3,224)
SNP	15.3	13.8	5.2	7.6	18.3	10.4 (2,987)
Plaid Cymru	2.5	2.6	2.1	0.9	3.1	2.2 (638)
Others	3.0	0.5	1.9	1.5	—	1.6 (444)
Total	100.0	100.0	100.0	100.0	100.0	100.0
	(4,688)	(3,939)	(11,321)	(4,078)	(4,558)	(28,584)

Source: Adapted from Cushion and Thomas 2017.

Table 4.7 The proportion of news dominated by one political party in television news coverage of the 2015 UK general election (percentages; N in parentheses)

	BBC	ITV	Ch. 4	Ch. 5	Sky	Total
Conservatives	21.2	26.9	25.8	33.0	32.7	27.8 (147)
Labour	29.5	25.0	24.7	20.8	29.0	25.9 (137)
Lib Dems	13.1	13.5	13.5	16.0	8.4	12.8 (68)
Greens	2.5	1.9	2.2	1.9	1.9	2.1 (11)
UKIP	11.5	11.5	11.2	13.2	13.1	12.1 (64)
SNP	15.6	18.3	11.2	11.3	14.0	14.2 (75)
Plaid Cymru	1.6	2.9	3.4	1.9	0.9	2.1 (11)
Others	4.9	—	7.9	1.9	—	2.8 (15)
Total	100.0	100.0	100.0	100.0	100.0	100.0 (528)
	(122)	(104)	(89)	(106)	(107)	

Note: We have excluded instances when no party was dominant within a news item.
Source: Adapted from Cushion and Thomas 2017.

Again, none of the news editors considered that the SNP's prominence undermined broadcasters' impartiality. Apart from Channel 4's head of news, they all indicated that party balance was internally monitored without giving precise details about how. Most editors viewed the regulations as a guide that should broadly be followed, but not as a replacement for news values, which shaped editorial judgements about news selection:

> I don't think we, in a very formulaic way, follow major/minor parties, but it is a part of what informs us. But, actually, OFCOM's designation in recent elections has pretty well conformed with where the news story and where a sense of fairness would be, even without regulation. (Michael Jermey, ITV)

> We went into this election with . . . an approach that, if editorially we decide something needs to be done or reported, we will do it . . . I think that's obviously critical and really important. (Paul Royall, BBC)

This flexible approach to impartiality was acknowledged in our interviews with Ofcom and the BBC. Both perspectives explained how impartiality should be viewed more as a qualitative editorial judgement than as a quantitative exercise involving a stopwatch:

> So what is 'due' in an election is to be conscious of the fact . . . that your judgements about impartiality . . .[are] a reflection of different parties and different parts of the story . . . within a confined period – it's a very short period. So it's not just news values, as in there was an election going on, it's news values taking into account the particular circumstances that impartiality demands during an election. (Ric Bailey, BBC)

> Due impartiality does not mean equal division, and I suppose, carrying on with that, having major party status does not mean you give all major parties equal time. Gone are the days when you had people in studios with stopwatches . . . the major party framework, although you could say isn't it just a binary – you're either a major party or you're not . . . It doesn't mean equality of treatment. (Adam Baxter, Ofcom)

How both regulators interpret impartiality appear to be at odds with many scholarly accounts of policing political balance in UK broadcast news.

Our analysis then moved to issue balance, asking whether editors and regulators considered whether reporting particular topics might favour one party over another. Our study found, for example, that policy areas favoured by the Conservatives – the economy and business – were dominant across all broadcasters, making up almost half of all issue-based coverage (see table 4.8). Housing or the NHS – more Labour-'owned' issues – received far less coverage.

Our interviews explored how far issue balance influenced editorial decisions about impartiality. We asked whether broadcasters felt they could spend less time covering party political events and issues and instead pursue a more independently orientated agenda. All editors believed they had the freedom to decide their own agenda, although the BBC's Paul Royall did point out that 'it would be quite a big thing for BBC News to say we're not going to cover your [party] events and your speeches and everything else.' Meanwhile, Ofcom's Adam Baxter stated that agenda balance was not a regulatory concern, indicating that it was

Table 4.8 The proportion of policy-related news in television news coverage of the 2015 UK general election (percentages; N in parentheses)

	BBC	ITV	Ch. 4	Ch. 5	Sky	Total
Economy/business	45.5	41.9	38.3	53.6	40.5	44.2
Immigration	6.1	9.7	20.0	5.4	9.5	9.7
Housing	6.1	9.7	15.0	5.4	16.7	9.7
NHS	10.1	9.7	3.3	10.7	9.5	8.8
Unemployment/jobs/low pay	7.1	8.1	8.3	7.1	9.5	7.8
Europe	7.1	3.2	5.0	3.6	2.4	4.7
Welfare/benefits	5.1	8.1	—	7.1	2.4	4.7
Conflict/terror/defence/ foreign affairs	6.1	3.2	5.0	3.6	4.8	4.7
Other	7.1	6.5	5.0	3.6	4.8	5.6
Total	100.0	100.0	100.0	100.0	100.0	100.0
	(99)	(62)	(60)	(56)	(42)	(319)

Source: Adapted from Cushion and Thomas 2017.

very much dependent on the relationship between the broadcaster and the parties and how that relationship sorts itself out, and, of course, we shouldn't have any role in that relationship . . . It's a freedom of expression issue really [what the channels cover]. I think it would have to be . . . [although] we would be concerned clearly if a political editor or commentator was so partial.

Our study examined Baxter's final point about the role of political editors and the potential for commentary to be partial. As table 4.9 shows, we found that live two-ways made up nearly a quarter of television news coverage, with, typically, political editors interpreting the day's campaign events. Our analysis also explored which political party was dominant within these live two items (see table 4.10) and found that, once again, the SNP received more attention than either the Liberal Democrats or UKIP (two designated major parties within Great Britain or England and Wales).

Most of our interviewees did not consider that the enhanced role of political editors in live two-ways undermined the impartiality of broadcast news. Instead, they viewed it as an important shift in journalism, as reporters decoded the spin of politicians. However, the Green and Labour interviewees did raise concerns about the agenda-setting power of correspondents. As Powell revealed:

You've got to have more checks and balances in there, and I don't believe that happens. For example, the Norman Smith two-ways,

Table 4.9 The proportion of conventions used to report television news coverage of the 2015 UK general election (percentages; N in parentheses)

	BBC	ITV	Ch. 4	Ch. 5	Sky	Total
Anchor	16.2	15.6	10.3	30.1	22.3	18.4
Reporter package	65.2	53.9	49.4	43.1	49.6	53.1
Studio discussion	1.0	—	12.6	3.3	5.8	4.4
Live two-way	17.6	30.5	27.6	23.5	22.3	24.1
Total	100.0	100.0	100.0	100.0	100.0	100.0
	(210)	(167)	(174)	(153)	(139)	(843)

Source: Adapted from Cushion and Thomas 2017.

Table 4.10 The proportion of items dominated by one political party by conventions in television news coverage of the 2015 UK general election (percentages; N in parentheses)

	Anchor	Reporter package	Studio discussion	Live two-way	Total
Conservatives	15.6	31.9	31.6	31.3	27.8 (147)
Labour	16.4	29.1	15.8	31.3	25.9 (137)
Lib Dems	21.1	11.6	15.8	5.2	12.8 (68)
Greens	5.5	1.1	15.8	—	2.1 (11)
UKIP	21.9	9.1	5.3	7.3	12.1 (64)
SNP	7.8	14.3	15.8	21.9	14.2 (75)
Plaid Cymru	3.1	1.8	—	2.1	2.1 (11)
Others	8.6	1.1	—	1.0	2.8 (15)
Total	100.0 (128)	100.0 (285)	100.0 (19)	100.0 (96)	100.0 (528)

Source: Adapted from Cushion and Thomas 2017.

which is always on the *Today* programme [a leading radio programme] at 6.30 every morning, we'd all listen to that in the office before we had our first morning call, and that would often set the mood of the day. I don't know. Does anyone in the BBC systematically listen to all those things every day and say 'have we got that right?', have we got that balance right overall from our coverage?' I doubt very much if they do.

Nevertheless, BBC and Ofcom advisors viewed live two-ways as an issue of editorial freedom that would not undermine a broadcaster's impartiality unless there was clear evidence of bias. Ofcom's Adam Baxter reiterated the importance of broadcasters being allowed to follow news values rather than any formulaic rules about balancing party political perspectives: 'Once again, both regulators interpreted impartiality not as representing all sides of a political debate or giving equal time to different perspectives, but for journalists to exercise editorial judgements about what they consider to be the most significant and newsworthy.' Overall, it would appear that, rather than applying impartiality in a quantitatively precise way, the regulatory guidance encouraged broadcasters to exercise editorial judgements about what should – and should not – be included in coverage. We consider the wider implications of a more news-value approach in campaign coverage at the end of the chapter.

But, now, we continue this line of inquiry by asking whether the impartiality of UK broadcasters was compromised by the news values of the UK national press during the 2015 UK general election. Or, put another way, we consider how far the intermedia agenda-setting power of national newspapers influenced the editorial selection of campaign coverage.

Intermedia agenda-setting: the (continued) power of the UK national press

Agenda-setting *between* media (Rogers et al. 1993) forms a relatively new phase of agenda-setting research (McCombs 2004), with few empirical studies using this framework to examine the impact the media has on itself (Vliegenthart and Walgrave 2008). Since the media environment has expanded with new online and social media platforms, there has been a greater focus on exploring how far 'old' media are influenced by platforms such as Twitter or political blogs (Vonbun et al. 2015). As we explore further in chapter 5, studies have shown that intermedia effects have been multidirectional, with new and old media influencing each other to different degrees (Conway et al. 2015; Heim 2013; Sweetser et al. 2008). However, many studies have acknowledged that their largely quantitative approach to intermedia agenda-setting limits how far they can explain the editorial influences between media.

Our study developed both a quantitative and a qualitative approach to intermedia agenda-setting during the 2015 UK general election campaign. Above all, the aim was to explore the editorial influence of UK national newspapers on television newscasts (Cushion et al. 2016a). We drew on content analysis of evening newscasts – outlined earlier in the chapter – and interviews with the heads and/or senior editors of news or politics from each broadcaster to consider the editorial judgements about press power and how stories emanating from newspapers were framed by broadcasters. We cannot always clearly establish whether television newscasts *followed* particular newspaper headlines, but we can empirically determine how *similar* their agendas were and then question senior editors about their decision-making.

Although most recent intermedia agenda studies focus on the influence of online and social media platforms (Benkler et al. 2017), we examine newspapers because, in the UK, it is often claimed that the national press sets the political agenda in broadcast media (Toynbee 2016). The power of newspapers also extends into the online world, since most have websites that are both the most visited sources of news and those shared most widely on social media platforms (Newman et al. 2015). But, beyond speculation about newspaper influence, few studies have systematically traced how far they shape broadcasters' news agendas.

Since television newscasts have to remain impartial, following newspaper coverage – or being regularly informed by it – raises serious questions about agenda-setting power. After all, much of the UK national press is driven by right-wing editorial perspectives, with most not only supporting the Conservative Party but also vociferously attacking Labour. This was revealed by a study of the 2015 UK general election, which examined the tone of 1,050 leader columns in the national press. It found that '40 per cent of these expressed a view about the Conservatives (424 articles) and another 40 per cent a view about Labour. Yet, while more than half the leader columns that expressed a view about the Conservatives were positive (51 per cent), only 21 per cent of articles about Labour were positive' (Moore and Ramsay 2015: 44). Given this level of partisanship and political imbalance in the UK national newspaper market, relying on the press as a source of news could potentially compromise broadcasters' impartiality.

To examine the intermedia agenda-setting effect of newspapers during the 2015 general election, our content analysis compared which stories were reported the day after by evening newscasts. We limited this to *policy stories* because it was difficult to trace the editorial influence of process stories – such as a campaign event – between media. Many process stories tend to be about what happened *that day*, meaning that newspapers would not have reported it *the day before*. Overall, we examined over 800 election items on television news over the campaign and used relevant search terms in Nexis – a press archive – to ascertain if any policy stories had been reported the day before by UK national newspapers. We identified 140 different policy stories and 321 news items across five broadcasters.

In total, 44 of the 140 policy stories – 31.4 per cent – featured in newspapers the day before they made it to the evening newscasts. This represented 61.1 per cent of airtime when policy news was reported during the campaign. When we broke down which press stories appeared on television news during the campaign, we found that 62.4 per cent were from right-wing newspapers, notably *The Telegraph*, *The Times* and their Sunday versions (table 4.11). Given there are more right-wing than left-wing newspapers, it was not surprising that newscasts broadly shared their agenda. Yet it did empirically establish that the UK's evening newscasts during the campaign were more similar to the agenda of right- than of left-leaning newspapers. Sky News's agenda was most similar to that of national newspapers, with almost two-thirds of its policy news previously reported by the press (see table 4.12). Even though

Table 4.11 Percentage of television election-related policy stories reported by newspapers before being broadcast in UK national news

Newspaper	Percentage* of times broadcast story covered
Telegraph/Sunday Telegraph (Conservative supporting)	20.2
Times/Sunday Times (Conservative supporting)	16.3
Independent/Independent on Sunday (supported Conservative/Liberal Democrat coalition)	15.4
Mail/Mail on Sunday (Conservative supporting)	12.5
Guardian (Labour supporting)	12.5
Mirror (Labour supporting)	9.6
Express (Conservative supporting)	6.7
Sun/Sunday Sun (Conservative supporting)	6.7
Total*	100.0 (N = 104)

Note: *Percentages have been rounded up; total N represents policy stories covered by different newspapers and at least one television news bulletin (e.g., not all 140 policy stories on TV were reported by the press).
Source: Adapted from Cushion et al. 2016a.

Table 4.12 Percentage of election policy items in UK national television newscasts previously published in newspapers

Channel	Percentage* of TV news policy items that had been published in a newspaper article before being aired
BBC	51.6
ITV	60.9
Channel 4	51.6
Channel 5	56.6
Sky News	63.3
Total*	N = 321

Note: *Percentages have been rounded up; N represents the proportion of policy items reported by each broadcaster in stories covered by at least one newspaper.
Source: Adapted from Cushion et al. 2016a.

the BBC was had the most policy-driven news agenda of all the newscasts during the campaign, it was the broadcaster that *least* resembled the policy agenda of UK national newspapers.

Despite the symmetry between the agendas of newspapers and television newscasts, most interviewees challenged the notion that the press influenced their editorial agendas. However, the BBC's Westminster editor, Katy Searle, did reveal that newspapers were considered a legitimate source of information if they had a story with sufficient news value. In her words:

> Do I accept that we follow a newspaper agenda? Sometimes. I think it's as true today as it would have been during the campaign. There is, as you'll know, the 'feeding off each other' kind of mentality a little bit because, if someone's going to get a story, if it stands up, you're going to look at it. But I hope that that is the same as the other way round . . . my job is to make sure that we lead the news as much as possible but, of course, do we pick up stories from the papers? Of course we do. But did we slavishly follow their agenda? No, absolutely not.

Similarly, Sky's Esme Wren said that, if stories were

> out in the public domain, which they are if they've been printed in a newspaper, and they're significant enough and we think that they're

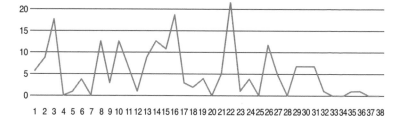

Figure 4.0 The number of policy stories during the election campaign covered by UK national television newscasts that were previously published in newspapers (30 March–6 May 2015)

capturing an audience or the public, of course we feel that we would want to report on that. But then, obviously, adding our own journalism to it, to say *The Telegraph* or *The Sun* have got this, here's our correspondent who's been speaking to sources or put it to the prime minister, and they've come back with this response, because we can't ignore a story if it's in the public domain.

Both perspectives indicated that the partisan agenda of most newspapers was overlooked if a published story was viewed as 'newsworthy'.

Our analysis also looked at how regularly newspaper stories about the election were reported by broadcasters during the campaign. As figure 4.0 shows, while the press's agenda was regularly in sync with the evening newscasts, there were striking moments – highlighted in the peaks of the graph – when 'big' stories were widely reported by newspapers and television newscasts.

Moore and Ramsay's (2015) study suggested that the Conservative Party colluded with some newspapers in the making of campaign announcements, such as the 'right to buy' policy and in letters of support from leading UK businesses. Our analysis showed that two stories, in particular, from Tory-supporting newspapers were reported prominently by television newscasts. The first included a front-page letter from *The Telegraph*, sent by over 100 business leaders supporting the Conservative Party. On closer inspection, none of the evening newscasts framed their coverage in a highly partisan way. Indeed, the ITV News at Ten expressly noted the party political tactics behind it at the end of one item:

> When David Cameron and George Osborne then turned up at Marsden's brewery in Wolverhampton, whose chief executive had put his name to the letter, the extent of the coordination become clear: there was nothing spontaneous about this. It was a carefully planned piece of electioneering to ensure their central economic message was hammered home . . . From the Conservatives' point of view, it means another day fighting on their chosen battleground: the economy. (31 March 2015)

Nonetheless, the business leaders' endorsement remained the main thrust of coverage on ITV and other television newscasts that night. Moreover, according to senior editors, it was perceived as a fair and impartial story to report, despite its being promoted by a right-wing newspaper. The BBC's Sue Inglish, for instance, said that 'it was a perfectly legitimate story to follow, and I think we reported it perfectly fairly. We were also very clear about where it came from, and we were completely clear about the fact that there'd been Conservative Party involvement in it.'

Likewise, Channel 5's Cristina Squires justified the story because, in her words, 'business leaders were writing letters . . . that is part of what's going on, that's part of the campaign, and therefore I feel no worry about reporting that at all.' When, later on in the campaign, *The Telegraph* published another front-page letter from 5,000 small businesses supporting the Conservative Party, the evening newscasts did not give it the same prominence. But, because of the news value of the letter, the BBC's Paul Royall still considered it a legitimate story for the News at Ten:

> The business letter, I know there was a bit of argument because it was driven from Conservative central office, but then, if 5,000 small and medium-sized business leaders still signed it, as long as you're clear about that, as long as you say the origin of this thing, it's still got 5,000

or however many it was to sign this thing. So I think there was a version of the story where it may have appeared that they all spontaneously got this thing together . . . they still managed to get these people.

Again, where the story originated – a right-wing Conservative-supporting newspaper, the *Daily Telegraph* – appeared to matter little if it was viewed as 'newsworthy'.

A second prominently reported television news story published by *The Times* involved a controversial interview with the Conservative defence secretary, Michael Fallon, who attacked the Labour leader personally, saying that: 'Miliband stabbed his own brother in the back to become Labour leader. Now he is willing to stab the United Kingdom in the back to become prime minister.' According to some reports, this was a classic 'dead cat' strategy orchestrated by the Conservative campaign manager, Lynton Crosby, with the aim of distracting the media from Labour's policy agenda (the logic being that the media – and thus voters – would be preoccupied by the dead cat and overlook other issues). It clearly worked, but, again, editors defended their coverage. According to ITV's Geoff Hill, the story was considered newsworthy because of *the conflict between political elites*. He said: 'it's difficult to ignore that kind of story when you've got a really high-profile member of party A making a really scathing personal attack about the leader of the opposition party.' While some broadcasters reframed coverage – rather than just focusing on the personal attack – the broader theme may well have reinforced the wider perception that the Labour leader was weak and flawed.

News values, above all, appeared to be the driving force behind the editorial selection of stories emanating from the right-wing press. On the face of it, professional judgements may seem a legitimate way of making decisions about news selection. But since right-wing newspapers outnumber left-wing titles and clearly favour one party over others, relying on them as a regular source of election news, in our view, undermines the impartiality of news judgements. Following the news values of newspapers, after all, means broadcasters' editorial decisions may be influenced by the perverseness of prominent right- (over left-)wing issues reported by much of the press. We now consider why following news values more generally can undermine the impartiality of broadcasters during election campaigns.

Why news values undermine impartial decision-making

In evaluating the fairness and balance of election reporting, our review of studies examining the most explicit forms of bias broadly found little evidence – apart from in the US – of any sustained favouritism towards one party over another. Our review, of course, was limited to just a handful of countries, and we focused on overt signs of bias rather than on the more subtle ways in which fair and balanced election news can be undermined. An obvious but important distinction between the US and other countries is that the former has no formal regulatory rules about policing balance or remaining impartial. However, a professional ethos of balancing the two main parties clearly informed US network campaign coverage. This was also the case in several other studies in the UK and across Europe, revealing a broadly shared political logic among broadcasters that the main parties should receive roughly equal time and treatment. Several studies showed that, across different types of election, minor parties tended to receive limited airtime during a campaign to advance their policy agendas. In that sense, the one clear bias across many advanced Western democracies is that the most established mainstream parties dominate the airwaves. Put another way, because of most countries' regulatory rules and professional sense of constructing balance, the ideological status quo of political parties is not radically challenged during an election campaign.

Needless to say, this paints only a broad-brush picture of how most political candidates and parties are reported during a campaign. Because of country-specific regulation rules, it is necessary to look more closely at election coverage and how balance is applied *within a national context*. As chapter 5 explores, for example, coverage of the primary election campaigns in the US was particularly imbalanced, with Donald Trump receiving significantly more airtime on network television than his Republican opponents. But even in the UK, where there are formal rules about balance and impartiality, this chapter showed that the guidelines were not strictly adhered to: there is evidence of minor parties receiving more coverage than major ones in television news coverage and an issue agenda that favoured one party over another. While our interviews with politicians and spin-doctors revealed some anxieties about how impartiality was interpreted by broadcasters, we also found that regulators adopted a relatively 'light touch' approach to regulation during the election campaign. This contradicted many scholarly accounts – including internationally comparative studies – that have suggested the UK's impartiality rules are regulated with a degree of quantitative precision. We would argue today's impartiality rules are highly flexible, allowing editors to make qualitative judgements based on news values.

This more relaxed interpretation of the rules represents a shift over recent decades in how impartiality has been regulated during election campaigns and, as a consequence, raises important issues about how impartiality is policed. Relying on news values, for example, may encourage broadcasters to focus on conflict between candidates or encourage parties to campaign in ways that appeal to a media logic rather than to develop an issue-based agenda. Our study showed that the focus on the SNP – a minor party – led to much speculation about a possible coalition deal with Labour (see also chapter 3). In doing so, it served the Conservatives' campaign logic, but it undermined the opportunity for other parties to advance their policy agendas. The Conservative Party's sophisticated campaign tactics clearly encouraged broadcasters to focus on a Labour–SNP coalition. Yet succumbing to a party's publicity machine or following the news values of particular types of stories and issues is unlikely to lead to maintaining a fair, balanced and impartial media agenda over the course of an election campaign. Caught up in the breathless speed of an election news cycle, it would be hard for most journalists to see the wood for the trees.

News values, of course, are not politically neutral, and following them rather than a more objective measure of balance has important implications for remaining impartial during an election campaign. Our study of the agenda-setting power of newspapers on television news, for example, raised concerns about the role news values have in undermining the impartial judgements of news selection. Over the course of the 2015 election campaign, we found television news had a broadly similar agenda to the UK's national press. But there were particular days when broadcasters ran prominent stories originating from right-wing newspapers. This was not interpreted as editors passively following the editorial line of openly partisan newspapers, as stories were often reframed on television and more objectively reported there than in the press. However, the underlying issue reported – such as big businesses endorsing the Conservative Party – still retained its prominence as *the election story* of the day. When we questioned editors about following this and other newspaper stories in the campaign and beyond, they appeared comfortable with reporting issues that had sufficient news value. Since, in the UK, right-wing newspapers outnumber left-wing ones – thus making news values far from an objective information source – we argued that broadcasters' impartiality would be compromised if they regularly relied on the press's news values to inform their agendas. Viewed in this context, the intermedia agenda-setting effect is to push broadcasters to the right of the political spectrum in campaign coverage and beyond.

Of course, the UK's news environment – particularly its tabloid press – is not representative of many other national media systems and journalism cultures. But similar intermedia agenda-setting influences are evident elsewhere, such as in the US's highly partisan cable news channels, in polemical blogs or in fake news online outlets (Benkler et al. 2017). As these and other news sources are increasingly shared online in largely unregulated markets, considerable pressure is placed on impartial broadcasters to resist the news values of competitors. Indeed, after the 2017 UK general election, it was the alt-left-wing news sites, such as *The Canary* and *Evolve Politics*, that were considered to be powerful agenda-setters for Labour voters (Jackson 2017). Post-election, this led to the editor of *The Canary* appearing on *Question Time* – the BBC political programme where audiences quiz politicians, journalists and celebrities. Since many broadcast journalists and politicians continue to rely on newspapers as a source of news, in our view the right-wing press continues to play a powerful agenda-setting role. But there are clearly new partisan sources of influence that may influence editorial judgements in future election campaigns.

A combination of our interviews with senior editors after the 2015 election campaign and a systematic content analysis was able to question the decisions behind the selection of news with a more objective review of coverage. Similarly, our content analysis findings were put to politicians, spin-doctors and regulators and uncovered a chasm between how scholars and practitioners interpreted 'due impartiality' in UK broadcasting. In our view, more election campaign research is needed to help explain the production and regulation of news rather than just describing it based on large content-analysis studies. This can not only help untangle the influence of agenda-setting power, it can also trace which logic shaped election news coverage.

The next chapter focuses on interpreting the logic shaping campaign coverage of the 2016 presidential election. As we reveal, Trump's campaigning was highly effective largely because of the US's highly commercialised and lightly regulated media system.

5

The Trumpification of Election News

[handwritten: heavy ill... to newspaper us]

The rise of partisan media, post–truth politics and the commercialisation of news values

Since US journalism is often viewed as a barometer for how media systems will evolve in the future (Hallin and Mancini 2004), this chapter focuses on how the 2016 presidential election campaign was reported and assesses the media logic of campaign coverage. The campaign was, of course, dominated by Republican candidate Donald Trump, a billionaire businessman and reality TV star of *The Apprentice*. Contrary to nationally representative opinion polls, many state surveys and most media commentators, Trump won the college vote by 304 to 227, although Hillary Clinton – his Democrat opponent – won the popular vote by almost 3 million votes (or a 2 per cent greater share). So what role did the news media play in reporting the campaign? This chapter explores the limited (at the time of writing) range of studies that have systematically explored the nature of campaign coverage during both the primary races and the election itself. We examine the characteristics of coverage – what we label a Trumpification of election reporting – against the rise of partisan media, post-truth politics and the increasing commercialisation of news values.

We begin by explaining how the US media system is, in many ways, exceptional when compared with those of most other Western nations. Whereas most advanced democracies have at least some rules about remaining balanced, impartial or objective during election campaigns (see chapter 4), US network and cable television channels are primarily market-driven and, over recent decades, have had their regulatory obligations lightened. Most significantly, from the mid-1980s, broadcasters no longer had to remain balanced, an intervention – we argue – that helped pave the way for more partisan news channels to emerge, such as Fox News and MSNBC. Since then, studies have shown that audiences have become less trusting of news and more ideologically selective in their viewing by tuning into programming that reflects their political beliefs (Stroud 2011). The consequences are potentially wide-ranging, with audiences growing increasingly intolerant of oppositional viewpoints, particularly when broadcast on partisan news channels. We explore how Trump further delegitimised the mainstream media during the campaign and examine the role played by fake news in shaping the outcome of the 2016 presidential election.

We then focus more specifically on Trump's campaign tactics, including his use of social media and his appearances on television news. We draw on studies that reveal the full extent of his media dominance during the primary race. Not only did Trump receive far more airtime, at times he was able to set the rules of engagement with broadcasters. This, we suggest, reflects the Trumpification of campaign coverage, with US broadcasters prioritising commercial news values above journalistic standards of balance and holding power to account. With news about policy making up only a fraction of the election agenda, the differences between Clinton and Trump during the general election were primarily about conflicts, controversies and their respective characters.

The chapter then turns to debates about post-truth politics and false balance, which resurfaced most prominently during the general election. Compared with past and present presidential candidates, Trump stands out as the politician most likely to make false statements, to disregard facts and to appeal to people's emotions. As we show, this represented a significant challenge to how journalists reported Trump's campaign. Despite independent fact-checking organisations pointing out that Trump was by far the most dishonest candidate, critics suggested that much of the mainstream media resorted to a 'he said, she said' model of reporting (Rosen 2016a) without always verifying competing claims. While journalists may argue that their aim was to grant both candidates an equal platform to air their views, this helped to normalise Trump – a candidate with a proven record of making false or misleading statements – and legitimised his credibility as a potential president. We then briefly explore coverage of the 2016 EU referendum in the UK, which also led to widespread discussion about false balance between claims made by the Leave and Remain campaign teams. Drawing on a systematic study of the ten-week campaign, we suggest impartiality was interpreted in a limited way, with many dubious claims often allowed to go unchallenged (Cushion and Lewis 2017).

Finally, we consider whether the Trumpification of election reporting is likely to spread around the world. Our primary focus, throughout the chapter, is on campaign coverage rather than wider (but important) issues that may have influenced the outcome of the 2016 presidential election. These questions concern the changing identity of American voters and the role played by political parties and their members, campaign teams, digital media advisors, corporate lobbyists, activists and non-partisan organisations, along with other key stakeholders that helped to select (and elect) Donald Trump. All of these factors (and many more) would have had an impact on both the election outcome and the campaign coverage. The Democrat Party's decision to nominate Hillary Clinton, for example, was also pivotal, since – rightly or wrongly – she was widely mistrusted by voters after being in the media spotlight for many decades. After all, one of the biggest stories of the 2016 election vote – but overlooked as the media narrative focused on Trump's underdog victory – was the dramatic fall in the number of Democrats who voted for Clinton compared with those who voted for Obama in 2012 (she received nearly 5 million *fewer* votes overall). This was strikingly the case in several key swing states that opted for Trump by a small but significant margin.

Nevertheless, while our analysis of election reporting alone cannot explain Trump's electoral success, the evidence suggests that the US's media environment and the nature of campaign coverage clearly benefited Trump more than Clinton. The Trumpification of election news, in this respect, should be considered a significant factor in the creation and election of Trump both as the Republican presidential candidate and as the forty-fifth president of the US.

US exceptionalism: the commercialisation of American media and the polarisation of news audiences

In order to understand the 2016 American presidential election and whether other countries would adopt a similar logic towards campaign coverage, it is necessary to understand how the US news environment has evolved over recent decades. As previous chapters have evidenced, the American media system is exceptional compared with those in many other Western countries (Curran 2011). Above all, most people rely on news from market-driven outlets which have no public service obligations or requirements to be impartial in their coverage of politics (Cushion 2012a). Public service broadcasting does exist in the form of organisations such as NPR and PBS, but, between them, they make up a fraction of the audience share of radio and television news programming. In short, most people in the US are not exposed to the kind of public service broadcasting that, as studies have repeatedly shown, enhances greater knowledge and understanding of politics and public affairs than does commercial media (Curran et al. 2009; Cushion 2012a; Strömbäck 2016).

The market-driven nature of US broadcasting was not a natural or inevitable development. As media historians have long argued, since radio began life in the 1920s, corporate interests have been at the heart of broadcasting policy, limiting how far programming should be required to serve the public good (Douglas 1987; McChesney 1993). Listeners were viewed largely as consumers rather than citizens, with sponsorship and advertising driving editorial decisions about news and public affairs programming. By contrast, when the Sykes Broadcasting Committee considered how to develop the UK's broadcasting system in the 1920s, they attached, in their words, 'great importance to the maintenance of a high standard of broadcast programmes . . . we think that advertisements would lower the standard . . . This would be too high a privilege to give to a few big advertisers at the risk of lowering the standard of broadcasting' (Sykes 1923, para. 41). This led to the UK's long-standing commitment towards public service broadcasting, which then and over time has influenced how other Western countries have developed their media systems (Cushion 2012b).

However, it is important not to overlook some of the regulatory obligations in news programming that did shape US broadcasting throughout the twentieth century. So, for example, the 1927 Radio Act ensured licences were issued on the basis of delivering public interest by including an equal-time rule that, in theory, required broadcasters to offer the same amount of free airtime to all political candidates. In practice, this was difficult to achieve and, over the years, was subject to repeated legal challenges. A legal battle at the end of the 1950s led to certain types of television news programming – newscasts most notably – being excused from the equal-time rule. Against the backdrop of Nazi propaganda, Pickard (2014) has suggested that, in the post-Second World War period, there was a public appetite for tighter regulation to ensure partisanship did not inform US broadcasting. In 1949 the Federal Communications Commission (FCC) had also put in place another regulatory attempt to balance political coverage with the Fairness Doctrine, which was a more robust attempt (in the era of television) than the equal-time rule to regulate a balance of opinions in political and public affairs programming. But, once again, the FCC's regulation was subject to a number of legal challenges, most famously in 1969, when the Supreme Court ruled against its being unconstitutional. In 1987 – when Ronald Regan was president – the FCC revoked the law, as critics claimed it undermined free speech in the US, and in 2011 the FCC finally repealed the Fairness Doctrine from its rulebook.

It is, of course, difficult to measure precisely the impact of the equal-time rule not being applied to particular news programmes since the 1960s or the abolition of the Fairness Doctrine in the 1980s. As the previous chapter explored, studies have shown that American network news does not exhibit *any clear or sustained signs of bias during recent election campaigns towards one party.* However, in 2016, US cable news channels, including Fox News and MSNBC, did stand out, with political partisanship brazenly on display. It was no coincidence, in this sense, that both channels were launched less than a decade *after* the Fairness Doctrine was rescinded. Unquestionably, the deregulation of rules about balance laid the groundwork for cable channels to adopt a more partisan approach to journalism. At the same time, however, talk radio stations were gaining popularity throughout the 1980s, with notably strong conservative perspectives. It is in this context that cable news channels were born and developed a new brand of opinion-based journalism that did not comply with age-old traditions, such as equal time for candidates or allowing for opposing perspectives (Cushion 2012b). After 9/11 and the wars in Afghanistan and Iraq, cable news also became more patriotic in its coverage, with Fox News in particular abandoning any attempt to report military and diplomatic affairs objectively. MSNBC, meanwhile, began its life with a less slanted approach when it launched in 1996, but by the mid-2000s it recognised the market logic of adopting a more liberal position. Viewing for cable news channels spiked at various points in the 2000s, with events such as election campaigns further increasing people's exposure to them.

But more significant than the audience size for cable news channels was the polarising effect they had on people's news consumption habits. As Stroud (2011) has convincingly documented, as partisan channels on different platforms have grown in reach and stature, a phenomenon known as partisan selective exposure has become more evident. Broadly put, this relates to individuals seeking out news in line with their own ideological understanding of the world and avoiding information that may challenge or undermine their pre-existing beliefs. While this kind of media effect may have some benefits in engaging viewers not necessarily interested in politics, it can have significant consequences for citizens at election time. They could, after all, be starved of the issues that may be in their interest or be fed false information about opposition parties that might appeal to them. As Stroud (2011: 10) has pointed out, 'it may lead people to question the political legitimacy of public affairs not sharing their political perspective.' Indeed, exploiting conservative attacks on the so-called liberal bias of mainstream US media, it is in this context that Fox News entered the market and has long claimed to be 'fair and balanced'. As mentioned in chapter 4, trust in the credibility of media has fallen sharply in the life-span of a post-Fairness Doctrine and cable news environment. For instance, a Gallup (2016a) poll found that, between 1993 and 2016, the proportion of people trusting television news a great deal or quite a lot fell from 46 to 21 per cent (in 2014 it fell as far as 18 per cent).

Of course, Fox News cannot be singled out as the cause of declining levels of trust in television news *generally*. There has been a downturn in network news viewing (Mitchell and Holcomb 2016) and, by and large, Americans have become more suspicious of institutions such as the media (Riffkin 2015). But while attacks against the mainstream media and a perceived liberal bias have been cultivated over many decades by conservative and Republican critics, they were perhaps on display most vociferously in the run-up to the 2016 presidential election. Trump repeatedly and aggressively attacked the mainstream media for their perceived bias on social media platforms and in interviews and rallies, and he even attacked journalists and banned news organisations from attending his campaign events. Thus, when his often dubious claims and campaign plans were criticised by the mainstream media, he was able to deflect negative coverage by portraying it as evidence of liberal media bias. As a billionaire businessman with no political baggage, Trump more cynically exploited this climate of mistrust towards the mainstream media than previous Republican presidential candidates. This was even acknowledged by a former conservative radio talk show host, Charles Sykes, not long after Trump became president. His testimony chillingly reveals the long-term effects of the partisan media environment in the US, where 'facts' could be so brazenly dismissed and propaganda could so easily be pedalled:

> I played a role in that conditioning by hammering the mainstream media for its bias and double standards. But the price turned out to be far higher than I imagined. The cumulative effect of the attacks was to delegitimize those outlets and essentially destroy much of the right's immunity to false information. We thought we were creating a savvier, more skeptical audience. Instead, we opened the door for President Trump, who found an audience that could be easily misled. (Sykes 2017)

Later sections in this chapter consider how Trump was reported during the campaign and, for much of the contest, was able to evade questioning and scrutiny about specific claims. But it is first necessary to put into context the polarisation of election news audiences during the presidential race, because it shows how people's media ecosystems varied according to whether they voted for Trump or Clinton. As table 5.0 indicates, a poll that asked people to *name* their main source of news found that 18 and 9 per cent of Clinton supporters' namechecked CNN and MNSBC, respectively, while 40 per cent of Trump supporters singled out Fox News.

Fox News's brand recognition perhaps helps explain why so many respondents named it. But this also reflects how Fox, in comparison with other cable news stations, was most stridently in favour of a candidate once the primaries were over and the general election had begun. In other words, Fox News's conservative brand of politics stands out as the dominant source for Republicans and right-of-centre voters, whereas MSNBC – a liberal and more sympathetic Democrat-supporting channel – does not register the same recognition among more left-leaning voters. Indeed, studies of previous presidential election campaigns have found evidence of a relationship between viewing Fox News and the likelihood

Table 5.0 Percentage of principal named source of election news during the 2016 presidential campaign

	All voters	*Trump voters*	*Clinton voters*
Fox	19	40	3
CNN	13	8	18
Facebook	8	7	8
Local TV	7	5	8
NBC	5	6	4
MSNBC	5	—	9
ABC	5	3	6
NPR	4	—	7
CBS	4	3	5
New York Times	3	—	5
Local newspapers	3	—	4
Local radio	—	3	—

Source: Adapted from Gottfried et al. 2017.

of voting Republican (DellaVigna and Kaplan 2007; Hopkins and Ladd 2014).

But we should not inflate the influence of Fox News on people's understanding of (or voting preferences during) the 2016 presidential election campaign or politics more generally. As the introduction to the book explained, there has long been an echo chamber of more conservative media outlets – from radio programmes such as the *Rush Limbaugh Show* to newspapers such as the *Wall Street Journal* – that have favoured Republicans, opposed liberals and undermined the credibility of mainstream media (Jamieson and Cappella 2008). But in 2016 the issue of fake news raised further debate about the distortion of information, with a high proportion of pro-Trump and anti-Clinton stories appearing across many online and social media platforms, and Facebook in particular. While 'real' and 'fake' news are not always easy to distinguish, the latter is viewed as the deliberate publication of false information with the aim of attracting online traffic and spreading lies. In the weeks after the US presidential election, *Buzzfeed* reported more people were engaging with the most popular fake news stories – by commenting or sharing them – than with more established news organisations such as the *Washington Post* and *New*

York Times. Although the methodology of the research reported – notably the media sample – has rightly been questioned, the study led to claims and considerable media commentary that fake news sites played a major role in the outcome of the election. At the time of writing, there was limited evidence to support this proposition. Indeed, Allcott and Gentzkow's survey of people's engagement with news during the election punctured much of the hyperbole about the decisive nature of fake news during the campaign. In their words:

> Our data suggest that social media were not the most important source of election news, and even the most widely circulated fake news stories were seen by only a small fraction of Americans. For fake news to have changed the outcome of the election, a single fake news story would need to have convinced about 0.7 percent of Clinton voters and non-voters who saw it to shift their votes to Trump, a persuasion rate equivalent to seeing 36 television campaign ads. (Allcott and Gentzkow 2017: 22)

Nevertheless, the rise of fake news remains an important issue to consider in future elections, as are partisan online news sites that may not be explicitly 'fake' but which spread (mis)information without context for political purposes. If the filter bubble of most Americans continues to be divided according to ideological and partisan loyalties, and people shift away from legacy mainstream media, then fake news could become an even bigger issue in future election campaigns.

For all the hype and hyperbole surrounding the role played by online and social media platforms during the campaign, studies before and after it actually found that television news was by far the *main* source of information about the 2016 US presidential election, particularly for older people – the most likely age group to vote (Allcott and Gentzkow 2017; Gottfried et al. 2016). Since television news remains so central to the public's understanding of the election campaign, the next section focuses on how the primaries and presidential race were reported, exploring how the TV news agenda was influenced by Trump over the course of the campaign.

'It may not be good for America, but it's damn good for CBS': the Trumpification of news values

At the Morgan Stanley Technology, Media & Telecom Conference in San Francisco in February 2016, the CBS Chief Executive, Leslie Moonves, declared that 'It may not be good for America, but it's damn good for CBS' (cited in Weprin 2016). He was referring to Donald Trump's ascendancy in the race to be the presidential candidate and the advertising revenue generated from the Republican primaries. Moonves went on to argue that, despite the campaign being a 'circus', it was going to be 'a very good year for us [CBS]. Sorry. It's a terrible thing to say. But, bring it on, Donald. Keep going' (ibid.). As the previous section established, given the market-driven nature of US television, on one level it is not surprising that broadcast executives were celebrating the commercial success of Trump's role in the election campaign. But, on another level, the logic of putting profit above everything else is brazenly at odds with many long-held values and standards in professional journalism. It reveals how the editorial selection of news items pertaining to the election was motivated, above all, by the desire to maximise commercial revenue from a controversial candidate rather than the challenge of how to report the politics of Trump's campaign.

Studies exploring network television news coverage of the primary races have indicated that it was not just CBS which was putting Trump front and centre of the campaign (see table 5.1). For example, *Tyndall Report* research shows that, from 2015 to 26 February 2016, while Trump attracted over 400 minutes of airtime on CBS, ABC and NBS, his main competitors – Ted Cruz and Marco Rubio – received around more than eight times less. Meanwhile, Clinton occupied less than half the amount of airtime that Trump did in this period, with Bernie Sanders – her main Democrat competitor – also receiving over eight times less coverage than Trump.* Broadcasters may argue, of course, that it was

---

* This is our analysis from Andrew Tyndall's raw data.

not just ratings that elevated Trump's position within the news agenda. Since he was the clear front-runner in the Republican race – favoured by 41 per cent according to a CNN poll in late January 2016 – broadcasters were reflecting voters' preferences. But, in allowing one candidate so much airtime, it arguably perpetuated Trump's ability to set the agenda and maintain his lead in the polls. This is borne out by his lower poll ranking as of June 2015 – not long after he declared he would run as a Republican candidate – which put him in second place behind Jeb Bush, at just 11 per cent. And yet, according to Tyndall's (2016a) analysis of network news coverage between January and the end of November 2015, Trump was 'by far the most newsworthy storyline of Campaign 2016, alone accounting for more than a quarter of all coverage (234 mins or 27%), more than the entire Democratic contest combined. The other GOP candidates, in order of prominence, were Jeb Bush (56 mins), Ben Carson (54), Marco Rubio (22).' In other words, it would be difficult not to conclude that network news helped *construct* Trump's public support during the primary race rather than simply *reflecting* it.

As Patterson (2016a) has pointed out, the media attention and prominence shown towards Trump should not necessarily be viewed as new or surprising. Even if it is challenged by critics, as a candidate Trump represented a new brand of anti-establishment politics, a departure from the rhetoric of candidates long tied to a political party. Accordingly, Patterson's (2016c) analysis of pre-

Table 5.1 Network television airtime allotted to the main 2016 primary candidates[1]

2015 to 26 February 2016, by network (minutes)	ABC	CBS	NBC	Total
Democrats				
Hillary Clinton	57	41	79	177
Bernie Sanders	14	27	17	58
Republicans				
Donald Trump	159	102	163	424
Ted Cruz	18	17	18	53
Marco Rubio	12	11	14	37

[1] This is our analysis from Andrew Tyndall's raw data.

primary coverage of the 2016 campaign led to him to conclude that:

> Reporters are attracted to the new, the unusual, the sensational, the outrageous – the type of story material that can catch and hold an audience's attention. Trump fit that interest as has no other candidate in recent memory. Trump is arguably the first bona fide media-created presidential nominee. Although he subsequently tapped a political nerve, journalists fueled his launch.
>
> Journalists seemed unmindful that they and not the electorate were Trump's first audience. Trump exploited their lust for riveting stories . . . The politics of outrage was his edge, and the press became his dependable if unwitting ally.

true

In other words, campaign coverage was guided predominantly by commercial news values that superseded journalistic standards about fair and balanced reporting of the primary candidates before each party's presidential nominations.

Of course, Trump's campaign style and tactics played an instrumental role in generating attention and appealing to the news values of market-driven media. As many commentators and scholars have already pointed out, Trump effectively used digital media to deliver key campaign messages by regularly communicating to voters via an array of social media platforms – Twitter, Instagram and Facebook – to help set the agenda (Chadwick and Stromer-Galley 2016; Ott 2016; Wells et al. 2016). This does not mean, as Trump admitted post-election, that broadcast media did not provide an important platform for his messaging. When asked if he would continue tweeting as the president, Trump not only revealed in a January 2017 interview that he would, but that it also served an important intermedia agenda-setting function:

> I've got 46 million people right now including Facebook, Twitter and ya know, Instagram, so I'd rather just let that build up and just keep it @realDonaldTrump, it's working – and the tweeting, I thought I'd do less of it, but I'm covered so dishonestly by the press – so dishonestly – that I can put out Twitter – and it's not 140, it's now 280 – I can go

bing bing bing . . . and they put it on and as soon as I tweet it out –
this morning on television, Fox – 'Donald Trump, we have breaking
news'. (Cited in Griffin 2017)

Indeed, the time series analysis by Wells et al. (2016: 672) of
Trump's use of Twitter during the primaries showed that, when
the Republican candidate was not generating news stories, he
'unleashes "tweetstorms" when his coverage is low'.

Trump's ability to court media attention was evident beyond
social media platforms. Many of his campaign speeches and rallies
were highly provocative, with negative soundbites that attacked
opponents – Republican and Democrat alike – and included controversial policies such as the proposals to ban all Muslims from
entering the US and to build a wall on the border with Mexico
(which Mexico would pay for). Trump also eschewed many of the
traditional ways candidates communicated in mainstream media,
notably allowing journalists to pose questions in regular press conferences (which Hillary Clinton, incidentally, also did), and would
phone in rather than appearing live on television network and cable
talk shows. So, for example, table 5.2 shows how Trump not only
featured in more Sunday morning interviews during the primaries
than all his Republican and Democrat competitors, but that he alone
was granted the opportunity to phone in. In March 2016, Chuck
Todd (from NBC's *Meet the Press*) refused to agree to any more pre-
scheduled telephone interviews with Trump. According to the *New
York Times* columnist Jim Rutenberg, not appearing live in the studio
to face robust journalistic questioning has important implications:

For decades they have served as proving grounds where candidates
must show up on camera, ideally in person, to handle questions without
aides slipping them notes, their facial reactions and body language on
full display. It's why the programs were named 'Face the Nation' and
'Meet the Press' – not 'Call the Nation' or 'Phone the Press.'

And yet, as the campaign began in earnest, all of the shows went
along with Mr. Trump's insistence that he 'appear' by phone – all
except one, 'Fox News Sunday with Chris Wallace'. (Rutenberg
2016)

Table 5.2 Interviews with presidential candidates on the five Sunday shows (1 January 2015 to 27 March 2016)

	On-camera interviews	Phone interviews	Total
Donald Trump	35	30	65
Bernie Sanders	58		58
John Kasich	43	—	43
Ted Cruz	26	—	26
Hillary Clinton	17	—	17

Source: Adapted from Savillo 2016.

Table 5.3 Type of interviews with Donald Trump on the five Sunday shows

	On-camera interviews	Phone interviews	Total
ABC This Week	4	11	15
CBS Face the Nation	9	7	16
NBC Meet the Press	8	6	14
FOX News Sunday	6	—	6
CNN State of the Union	8	6	14

Source: Adapted from Savillo 2016.

Indeed, as table 5.3 confirms, with the exception of Fox News, different cable and network outlets allowed Trump, to varying degrees, to phone in rather than appear live. It is yet another indication of how *broadcasters allowed Trump to depart from the conventional rules of engagement with the press and let him set the news agenda.*

According to Patterson's analysis, journalists explained their focus on Trump over Clinton because of the former's willingness to appear in election coverage. But, as he pointed out, 'availability has never been the standard of candidate coverage. If that were so, third–party candidates and also-rans would dominate coverage' (Patterson 2016a). As chapter 2 confirmed, the Green or Libertarian candidates received a fraction of the airtime afforded to Trump. Instead, Patterson (2016b) argued that 'Trump's dominant presence in the news stemmed from the fact that his words and actions were ideally suited to journalists' story needs ... Both nominees tweeted heavily during the campaign but journalists monitored his tweets more closely. Both nominees delivered speech after speech on the campaign trail but journalists followed his speeches more intently.' As table 5.4 shows, over the course of 2016, Donald Trump's campaign was by far the top story on US network coverage, generating more than twice as much airtime as Hillary Clinton. Further still, Trump received more specific candidate focus than Clinton and comfortably received more network airtime than any other presidential hopeful since 1988 (see table 5.5). But, beyond the dominance of Trump's appearances in broadcast media, how was he portrayed in coverage and what evidence is there that he set the campaign news agenda?

Patterson (2016b) examined coverage of the 2016 presidential campaign between mid-August and the day before polling day

Table 5.4 Top twenty stories of 2016 on US network news (minutes of coverage)

	ABC	CBS	NBC	Total
2016 Donald Trump campaign	434	317	393	1,144
2016 Hillary Clinton campaign	199	149	159	506
Mosquitoes spread zika virus	57	124	75	255
Syria civil war: siege of Aleppo	26	139	74	238
Rio de Janeiro Olympic Games	62	40	128	230
Trump administration transition	79	76	70	225
Winter weather	91	53	68	212
Gay club massacre in Orlando	50	66	47	163
Hurricane Matthew	55	46	56	158
2016 Republican convention	38	50	48	137
Brussels terrorist bomb attacks	46	43	43	132
Hillary Clinton emails	39	50	41	130
Russian cyber-espionage, hacking	30	45	55	129
2016 general election	43	43	41	127
2016 Bernie Sanders campaign	26	52	37	115
Iraqi civil war: battle for Mosul	18	66	31	115
2016 presidential debates	39	32	40	111
2016 Iowa caucuses	38	29	39	106
2016 Democratic convention	39	29	35	103
Tornado season	49	27	26	101
Total top 20 stories	1,458	1,476	1,506	4,437
Total 2016 campaign stories	1,151	1,042	1,112	3,304

Source: Adapted from Tyndall 2016a.

Table 5.5 The focus on presidential candidates between 1998 and 2016 (minutes across three networks)

Year	Total minutes	Democrat candidate	Mins	Republican candidate	Mins
2016	3,304	Hillary Clinton	506	Donald Trump	1,144
2012	2,016	Barack Obama	157	Mitt Romney	479
2008	3,677	Barack Obama	745	John McCain	531
2004	2,433	John Kerry	445	George W. Bush	352
2000	3,102	Al Gore	297	George W. Bush	339
1996	1,883	Bill Clinton	174	Bob Dole	337
1992	3,040	Bill Clinton	448	George H. W. Bush	461
1988	3,117	Michael Dukakis	421	George H. W. Bush	388

Source: Adapted from Tyndall 2016a.

2016 on CBS, NBC and Fox, as well as in the *Los Angeles Times*, the *New York Times*, *USA Today*, the *Wall Street Journal* and the *Washington Post*. He found, contrary to allegations of a liberal bias in the press, that over the full campaign period (1 January 2015 to 7 November 2016) Clinton was more negatively reported than Trump – 62 compared to 56 per cent, respectively. Since much negative coverage – particularly from journalists – was anti-establishment, vilifying Washington politics and attacking previous governments, much of it reinforced Trump's campaign messages. So, for example, Trump's mantra of 'Draining the Swamp' – to rid Washington of establishment figures – for example, reinforced an anti-government message (even though his appointed cabinet was far from a group out of 'outsiders'), while his 'Make America Great Again' slogan romanticised a mythical past when government *was* effective. Since so much negativity shaped election coverage, it promoted a message more likely to resonate with Trump and Republican voters that political institutions were failing.

A lack of coverage about issues and policy solutions and a focus on horserace-driven campaign news should also be seen not as neutral and partisan free but as ideologically consequential in itself. As chapter 2 confirmed, coverage of policy issues – from healthcare to foreign policy – barely featured during the 2016 presidential campaign, meaning voters were not regularly exposed (beyond the personalities of candidates) to how each contender

Table 5.6 Coverage of policy issues vs. Hillary Clinton's emails on broadcast evening news, 1 January–21 October 2016 (percentages)

	World News Tonight	NBC Nightly News	CBS Evening News	Total
Policy coverage	8	8	16	32
Email coverage	29	31	40	100

Source: Adapted from Boehlert 2016.

would practically run the government if elected. This lack of policy debate was perhaps most noticeable and, arguably, most consequential in the final weeks of the campaign, when the FBI reopened an investigation into Hillary Clinton's misuse of emails when she was secretary of state. It was subsequently dropped just days before the election, but, as table 5.6 shows, the investigation generated far more media attention in the closing stages of the campaign than the policy differences between competing candidates.

Needless to say, it is beyond the scope of this chapter to consider how far coverage of the FBI investigation impacted on the election outcome, but the evidence suggests a late swing towards Trump in the key battleground states that Clinton lost. According to Nate Silver – a pollster who accurately predicted previous election results – 'Comey [the director of the FBI] had a large, measurable impact on the race . . . Clinton would almost certainly be President-elect if the election had been held on Oct. 27 (day before Comey letter)' (cited in Savransky 2016). Indeed, of all the controversies throughout the election – the misogynistic comments by Trump or his failure to release his tax returns – it was Clinton's investigation by the FBI that most people could remember. In fact, 79 per cent of registered voters – according to one poll – had 'heard a lot about' the FBI just before election day, more than for any other candidate-specific issue (McElwee et al. 2017).

Of the two candidates, it was Trump who supplied the fewest policy proposals during the campaign. Associated Press, for example, reported that 'Trump's campaign has posted just seven policy proposals on his website, totalling just over 9,000 words', whereas there were '38 on Clinton's "issues" page, ranging from efforts to cure Alzheimer's disease to Wall Street and criminal justice reform, and her campaign boasts that it has now released 65 policy fact sheets, totalling 112,735 words' (Colvin 2016). This meant that a negative, process-driven news agenda served Trump's campaign ideologically more effectively than Clinton's. But it raises questions – which the next section now explores – as to why journalists did not more regularly challenge Trump over his many controversial and dubious claims during the campaign. We develop this discussion in the context of debates about post-truth politics and false balance and move beyond the US elections to consider campaign coverage of the 2016 EU referendum in the UK.

Trump, Brexit and 'alternative facts': reporting in a post-truth media environment

In 2016, Oxford Dictionaries declared that 'post-truth' – an adjective defined as 'relating to or denoting circumstances in which objective facts are less influential in shaping public opinion than appeals to emotion and personal belief' – was their word of the year. While they conceded the concept had been used over the previous decade, there had, in their words, been a spike 'in frequency this year in the context of the EU referendum in the United Kingdom and the presidential election in the United States' (Oxford Dictionaries 2016). Since presenting 'facts' is central to reporting candidate positions during an election, the enhanced prominence of post-truth politics (often used interchangeably with 'post-factual') in 2016 suggests that both campaigns were particularly challenging for journalists. Of course, politicians have also always stretched the 'truth' when campaigning in elections, but the decision to make 'post-truth' the word of the year suggests the current generation have even more disregard for facts. As a consequence, concepts such as objectivity, impartiality and balance – as explored in chapter 4 – have regained critical attention, prompting debates about how news media should hold politicians to account.

Donald Trump made many false statements during the presidential campaign, such as denying the existence of climate change,

Table 5.7 The veracity of public statements by the main Democrat and Republican primary candidates between 1 January 2015 and 30 January 2016

	True	Mostly true	Half true	Mostly false	False	Pants on fire
Hillary Clinton	12	45	16	12	14	—
Bernie Sanders	11	42	18	21	8	—
Jeb Bush	16	25	27	24	5	2
Marco Rubio	8	23	23	25	17	4
Ted Cruz	7	20	5	34	24	5
Donald Trump	1	4	16	19	41	18

Source: Adapted from PolitiFact 2016.*

stating that Muslims celebrated in New York after 9/11, claiming he opposed the war in Iraq (when footage clearly reveals that he supported it), suggesting that President Obama was not a US citizen, and maintaining that Obama and Hillary Clinton created ISIS. As table 5.7 indicates, PolitiFact found that, while all of the major candidates during the primaries (from 1 January 2015 to 30 January 2016) told 'half-truths, mostly false, false or pants on fire' statements, Trump made the most false statements. Despite (or perhaps because of) Trump's persistent false or misleading statements during the campaign, he received far more airtime than other candidates.

At the time of writing, no research has systematically tracked how far reporters countered Trump's false statements in media coverage of the election. We know, however, that fact-checking organisations, such as Factcheck.org, PolitiFact and the *Washington Post*'s Fact Checker, studiously verified candidates' statements throughout the campaign and were made use of by many media organisations – notably during the three TV debates. Nevertheless, as a fact checker at Poynter pointed out at the beginning of the campaign, 'Cable news polluted the airwaves with uncritical and senseless Trump coverage. Pundits didn't bother to dig beyond the smart take on their Twitter feed' (Mantzarlis 2016). It was only *after* the general election had begun – once Trump and Clinton

---

* This table was constructed from data collected on the PolitiFact website.

had been formally nominated as presidential candidates – that there appeared to be greater pressure on journalists to 'call out' Trump's dubious claims.

This was demonstrated in September 2016, when false balance became a debating point in media coverage. It was suggested that the news media were sticking to their long-standing convention of 'he said, she said' reporting that (falsely) balanced Clinton's controversies – such as the FBI investigation – with Trump's more egregious behaviour and deceitful claims. Critics argued that this helped normalise Trump and legitimise him as a credible presidential candidate, while overlooking his erratic behaviour, his many misdemeanours and his serial disregard for telling the truth. This is also despite many senior Republicans – such as Paul Ryan, the speaker of the House of Representatives – beginning to cast doubt on Trump's integrity ahead of election day. Nevertheless, media critics pointed out that much of the news media – with the exception of partisan outlets – continued to be even-handed in their treatment of Trump and Clinton. According to Jay Rosen (2016b), departing from long-standing norms of objectivity during election campaigns represents a radical departure for most journalists. In the US's two-party political system, he suggested, most reporters stick rigidly to a long-held symmetry where both perspectives are represented: 'Asymmetry between the major parties fries the circuits of the mainstream press.' Further, referring to Trump, he argued:

> A political style that mocks the idea of a common world of facts – and gets traction with that view – is an attack on the very possibility of honest journalism. Campaign journalists have to find a way to oppose this style without becoming election-season opponents of Trump himself, which is not, I think, their proper role. Nothing in their training or tradition would have prepared them for this moment.

The Trumpification of election news, viewed in this light, reflects an attack on the conventional rules of journalism, since it requires reporters to make judgements about the veracity of claims and counter-claims that may single out a candidate. As the *New York Times* public editor pointed out, the danger of correcting a perceived false balance is that liberal opinions or even partisanship could supersede more objective ways of reporting one candidate differently from another (Spayd 2016). But, from the limited evidence available, far from a liberal bias shaping election reporting, the weight of coverage of each candidate's controversies was stacked against Clinton rather than Trump. As Patterson's (2016b) study concluded:

> Clinton's controversies got more attention than Trump's (19 percent versus 15 percent) and were more focused. Trump wallowed in a cascade of separate controversies. Clinton's badgering had a laser-like focus. She was alleged to be scandal-prone. Clinton's alleged scandals accounted for 16 percent of her coverage – four times the amount of press attention paid to Trump's treatment of women and sixteen times the amount of news coverage given to Clinton's most heavily covered policy position.

Since both presidential candidates appeared to be marred by scandals, Patterson suggested that the news media interpreted them as equally newsworthy. In his view more objective treatment of case-by-case scandals was needed, because 'When journalists can't, or won't, distinguish between allegations directed at the Trump Foundation and those directed at the Clinton Foundation, there's something seriously amiss.'

Of course, since many Republican and pro-Trump supporters have become increasingly suspicious of the mainstream media over recent years, it remains debatable whether fact-checking Trump more aggressively would have had any material effect on voters' attitudes. In other words, a more radical asymmetrical approach of the kind Rosen (2016b) advocated may not be the magic bullet likely to restore people's immediate trust in US news media. There are clearly deep ideological and party-political divisions in the US, and, over many decades, the news media environment has become part of (rather than independent from) this partisanship. In the next chapter, we consider how the logics behind election reporting can be rethought to restore public trust, engagement and knowledge in politics. However, in the hostile media and political environment of the US, the challenge is perhaps greater than in most other Western democracies.

In the president elect's first press conference in January 2017, for example, he labelled CNN a 'fake news' outlet and refused to answer a question from its senior White House correspondent, Jim Acosta. Meanwhile, in his first press briefing, the White House press secretary, Sean Spicer, made false claims (clearly contradicted by images) about the size of the crowd at Trump's presidential inauguration. Days later, he defended this claim to journalists by saying that 'Sometimes we can disagree with facts' (cited in Foran 2017). This echoed comments by presidential aide Kellyanne Conway the day before, when she suggested that Spicer was using 'alternative facts' to explain the difference in crowd sizes (cited in Revesz 2017). Conway gained particular infamy in the early weeks of the Trump administration after she claimed (although subsequently clarified) that a terrorist attack had taken place in 'Bowling Green', when no such attack had ever occurred (cited in Smith 2017). In other words, Trump's communication team continued to challenge the premise of objective truth just as he himself had done throughout the campaign, undermining the credibility of mainstream news media and delegitimising their democratic role. In the era of Trump's administration, it would appear that post-truth politics is more likely to increase than diminish. Future election campaigns may become even more contentious as the battle for (and interpretation of) the 'truth' becomes ever murkier among rival parties, partisan media outlets and voters.

Many of the debates about post-truth or false balance reporting during the US presidential election were foreshadowed by events in the UK less than five months earlier, during the campaign ahead of the June 2016 referendum about remaining in or leaving the EU. This involved many dubious and exaggerated claims and counter-claims made by rival campaign groups. Independent bodies, such as the Parliamentary Treasury Committee and the UK Statistics Authority, drew particular attention to the Leave campaign's (mis)use of statistics (BBC 2016). Perhaps most controversial was the claim that the UK government sends £350m to the EU every week. As independent observers such as fact-checking organisations repeatedly pointed out, this figure did not include the UK's rebate, as well as various EU grants and subsidies the UK received. Nevertheless, the claim featured prominently in the campaign – emblazoned on the side of the Leave's battle bus – along with the idea of spending the £350m saving on the National Health Service.

A systematic study of the major UK evening newscasts over the ten-week campaign found that, for the most part, broadcasters remained balanced in reporting the Leave and Remain campaigns (Cushion and Lewis 2017). However, both campaign groups – though notably the Leave camp – often made misleading statistical claims that went unchallenged by journalists. So, for example, just over one in five statistical claims were challenged by a journalist or a political or independent source – though many of the challenges were from rival campaigns. This meant that coverage often featured a statistical tit-for-tat exchange between rival politicians, with limited journalistic scrutiny of either side's claims.

Under pressure from both campaign groups and a hostile commercial sector – particularly from powerful pro-Brexit newspapers (Deacon et al. 2016) – broadcasters appeared to interpret impartiality as simply balancing competing perspectives. But, in doing so, they did not always verify competing source claims, despite independent bodies challenging some of their messaging, in particular from the Leave campaign. This appeared to serve the latter's aim, which was to discredit the views of experts about EU membership. As Michael Gove, a leading Leave campaigner, acknowledged in a television interview: 'people in this country have had enough of experts' (cited in Deacon 2016).

Of course, not all issues could be clearly fact-checked, since many debates about EU membership were contentious. However, on some issues there was a weight of expert opinion that could have been used to inform debates or to challenge claims more robustly. Indeed, we should not overlook the effects that such claims can have on the outcome of elections. As Dominic Cummings (2017), director of the Vote Leave campaign, revealed in a blog posting about the Brexit victory: 'Would we have won without £350m/NHS? All our research and the close result strongly suggests No.'

Given that an Ipsos MORI survey (2016) discovered that close to half of people before the referendum believed that £350 million was sent to Brussels every week, challenging this campaign claim more regularly may have better informed the public. Although UK broadcasters had to remain impartial during the referendum, this misconception suggests they could have more effectively communicated news and more robustly held campaigners to account.

The effect of an even more blatant political deception was witnessed in the aftermath of Trump's 2017 temporary ban on people entering the US from seven Muslim majority countries. Defending the policy, Trump aide Kellyanne Conway claimed it was needed to prevent events such as the 'Bowling Green terrorist attack'. But, as established earlier in the chapter, this massacre never actually took place. Yet, days later in February 2017, when a representative poll asked: 'Do you agree or disagree with the following statement – "the Bowling Green massacre shows why we need Donald Trump's executive order on immigration?"' – 51 per cent of Trump supporters agreed it was needed (Public Policy Polling 2017). Conway's fake terrorist attack was immediately countered by news organisations (prompting an immediate correction by Conway on Twitter). But the example illustrates how many people in the US follow their *ideological convictions* when making sense of politics, even when independent evidence contradicts their own perceptions (Flynn et al. 2017).

Towards a Trump logic in election reporting? News values, regulation and professional journalism

Since cross-national comparative studies have suggested that the US acts as a barometer for future developments in media and political systems (Hallin and Mancini 2004), the chapter began by asking whether other advanced Western democracies would follow the logic of US campaign coverage. As shown, Trump's victory and campaign strategy were far from 'normal'. But, given the rise of populist political communication over recent years (Aalberg et al. 2017), there are clearly lessons to be learnt about the media logic of reporting a candidate such as Trump.

On the face of it, Trump's logic may appear to be relatively new. But it does not fit neatly into conventional theory about media logic (Strömbäck and Esser 2014). A businessman and former reality TV star turned anti-establishment politician, Trump mastered the art of what Esser (2013) calls 'self-mediatisation': the ability to set the media agenda by appealing to the news values of mainstream journalists. As this chapter showed, from provocative speeches to negative soundbites, Trump dominated the airwaves, particularly during the primaries, when many candidates competed for the Republican nomination. This, we argued, represented a Trumpification of election reporting because networks appeared happy to grant Trump far more airtime then rival candidates in order to attract viewers and generate advertising revenue. News values, in other words, outweighed the journalistic need to balance the views of competing candidates or to counter dubious claims with facts.

Indeed, despite independent fact-checkers establishing that Trump shamelessly made false statements throughout the campaign and was by far the least honest candidate of all the primary contenders – regularly making (up) claims without supporting evidence – critics suggested that campaign coverage often created a false balance between Clinton and Trump perspectives (Rosen 2016a). Since news about policy made up a tiny fraction of the news agenda during the campaign (Tyndall 2016b), much of the coverage was about the horserace or controversies about each candidate (Patterson 2016a). Even though Trump was involved in several different controversies, both his and Clinton's misdemeanours were treated even-handedly, with the FBI's investigation into the Democrat candidate generating most media attention (ibid.). Whereas balance was not policed in coverage of candidates during the primary campaigns, during the general election – when the opposing candidates from the main two parties were battling it out – journalists appeared to take impartiality more seriously and adopted a 'he said, she said' approach to political reporting.

Of course, past presidential candidates have all sought to court media attention and, to a greater or lesser extent, evade complex policy issues, attack opponents, and deny or defend involvement in controversies. But, while debates about the mediatisation of politics largely assume candidates want to discuss policy debates, Trump's logic was to skate over issues and focus on the process of politics ('to Make America Great Again' or 'Drain the Swamp'). That so much coverage focused on these processes and on the horserace between candidates is consistent with well-established trends of media and political logic in election reporting identified in previous chapters. Where the 2016 election – and the Trumpification of reporting – appears to have departed from old norms is in the emergence of a more tangible political logic in post-truth or post-factual campaigning. While the 2012 US election may have also been characterised as a post-truth campaign, Trump's more blatant disregard for facts represents an even more serious challenge for American journalists. Trump's logic, in short, rewrote the rules of election campaigning not only by exploiting the US's dominant media logic but also in appealing to the increasingly partisan logic of news audiences and voters' political identities.

But is a Trumpification of election reporting likely to spread *US style* to other Western countries? As previous chapters have explored, *might* most broadcasters in different countries have formal rules policing election reporting. While this does not necessarily mean that each mainstream party receives equal time during a campaign, it does mitigate against the possibility of one candidate overwhelmingly dominating the airwaves. After all, US election reporting was driven by commercial news values during the primaries, elevating Trump above all other candidates and, for much of the time, legitimating his presidential credentials without always probing and challenging his policy positions. As previous chapters have concluded, while relying on news values might appear a reasonable professional strategy for selecting stories in a competitive industry, it is far from politically neutral. It limits the range of candidates and issues being debated and rewards populist politicians for their campaigning style and performance. In other words, compared to countries with a stronger tradition of public service media and greater regulatory oversight, the US's commercialised system helped create the conditions for a Trumpification of election news to flourish.

Since the US has an *exceptionally* light regulatory system that is driven by commercial aims, it would appear less likely that, in most other Western countries, one candidate could receive so much more airtime than their rivals. Of course, populist parties and candidates have attracted attention in many countries, such as UKIP in the UK, the Front National in France, and Lijst Pim Fortuyn in the Netherlands (Aalberg et al. 2017). But because of the public service broadcasting ecology of many Western nations – notably in Europe – and their more independent and impartial approach to election reporting, it could be argued that journalists would have dealt more effectively with Trump's brand of post-truth campaigning. That said, the final part of this chapter explored coverage of the UK's 2016 EU referendum and found that many of the dubious claims made by campaigners were not always challenged, and that rival politicians were often left to argue between themselves. Impartiality, in this context, was interpreted largely as balancing the perspectives of Leave and Remain campaigners. But since UK broadcasters operate under 'due impartiality' guidelines, greater editorial discretion could have been applied in order to report the referendum campaign more accurately and objectively (Cushion and Lewis 2017). Faced with a blizzard of statistics about the benefits or pitfalls of EU membership, viewers may have been better served by television newscasts fact-checking the claims and counter-claims of the campaigners (Cushion et al. 2016c). Polls showed both confusion about the issues and that many people felt they were not adequately informed ahead of the vote. Fact-checking politicians, in this respect, might seem the obvious solution to raising people's knowledge of issues, particularly in the UK, where approximately three-quarters of people say they trust television newscasts (Williams 2016). As the next chapter explores, fact-checking offers one way of putting the 'truth' back into post-factual politics.

However, in the more partisan news environment of the US, where trust is increasingly shaped by the ideological beliefs of audiences, how far the public would be receptive to believing fact-checkers remains debatable. While it is not easy to resolve the credibility of information sources in the US or elsewhere, the final chapter now turns to examine how campaigns *could* be reported to enhance voters' engagement with and understanding of election coverage. Drawing on evidence throughout the book, we suggest a public logic should play a greater role in election reporting, where the agenda of voters takes centre stage in the campaign and the policies of respective political parties receive more airtime and independent scrutiny.

Conclusion:
Rethinking Election Reporting

Understanding the logic of campaign coverage and the democratic needs of citizens

The aim of this book was to understand the logic of campaign coverage and consider the value of election reporting. Informed by more than a hundred studies drawn on throughout the book, this chapter now reflects on these findings and considers how well the news media enhance people's engagement with and understanding of politics ahead of different elections. In doing so, we consider how the logic of campaign coverage can be rethought in ways that better serve the democratic needs of citizens. The news media, after all, have a fundamental role to play in democratic systems. For most people they are the primary source of election information during a campaign.

Many book-length studies about election reporting have been nationally oriented and dealt with first-order elections, such as presidential or general elections (Strömbäck and Kaid 2008). Our scope was more internationally comparative and included second-order elections, such as EU and local elections. While we examined campaign coverage in a range of Western democracies, as well as different media and political systems, the main focus was *disputed?* on election reporting in the UK and the US. In order to explore coverage in comparative detail, we primarily analysed campaign reporting on television news. While online and social media platforms play an increasingly important part of people's information diet, *television continues to be one of the most popular sources of news* *that informs most people about election campaigns* (Bold 2015; Even 2015; Gottfried et al. 2016). We also drew on our research about the reporting of elections over the past decade (Cushion 2017a, 2017b, 2017c, 2017d; Cushion and Thomas 2016; Cushion et al. 2006, 2009, 2015a, 2015b, 2016a, 2016b). This was supported by interviews we conducted in 2015 and 2016 with the heads and/ *not* *well* *used* or senior editors at the BBC, ITV, Sky News, Channel 4 and Channel 5, and with media regulators and senior party officials, including spin-doctors (Cushion et al. 2016a, 2016b; Cushion and Thomas 2017). This allowed us to consider the editorial decisions behind the selection of election news and interpret the campaign logic behind them. Overall, the book asked:

How are different types of electoral contests reported? What is the main logic shaping news agendas during election campaigns?

How well do the media serve citizens during an election campaign? How can the logic of campaign coverage be rethought to better inform and engage voters?

Different chapters entered into interrelated debates about media systems and information environments, media ownership and regulation, political news and horserace journalism, objectivity and impartiality, agenda-setting and intermedia agenda-setting, and the relationship between media and democracy more generally. But the overarching focus of this book was about *understanding the media logic of campaign coverage* and interpreting the degree of mediatisation in election news (Strömbäck 2008; Strömbäck and Esser 2014).

By 'media logic', we mean the organising principles behind the editorial selection and communication of election campaign coverage. In debates about the mediatisation of politics, there are competing logics that shape political coverage (Strömbäck and Esser 2014), but (as argued in chapter 1) election reporting tends to revolve around three central actors – political parties, news media and the public. In exploring each of these logics, we considered how campaign coverage would be analysed in subsequent chapters. In light of debates about the mediatisation of politics, this final chapter examines the evidence concerning which logic prevails at election time and considers more broadly how campaign coverage can be rethought in ways that better reflect the democratic needs of citizens.

From process to policy coverage: towards more independent and informative election campaign news values

Contrary to the prevailing wisdom of many mediatisation scholars, Brants and van Praag (2015: 405) have asked whether, 'instead of a media logic – in which media dominate politics – we are witnessing a logic of or driven by the public, or that the latter are too fragmented and too contradictory to speak of a logic.' They suggested that theorising any type of logic – public, media or political – is ultimately fruitless because there is no 'one single dominating logic, but an often unpredictable interaction between public, media and politics, with mutual influence and changing positions of power' (ibid.). While it is hard empirically to disentangle agenda-setting power between media, politics and the public, of the hundred+ news studies examined throughout this book, we found little evidence of any clear or sustained public logic influencing campaign coverage. Election reporting, in this sense, was not 'unpredictable' (ibid.) but fairly uniform across different types of electoral contests in many Western democracies, with coverage increasingly about the processes of the campaign rather than policies of competing parties. When policy debates were addressed, they tended to be within the narrow ideological confines of the mainstream parties, with limited airtime being given to alternative political views or for experts to interpret coverage. Far from the public exerting 'mutual influence' on the election news agenda, as Brants and van Praag argued, overall the weight of evidence in each chapter pointed towards a media and political logic dominating campaign coverage.

Above all, the news media have long been criticised in the run-up to an election for their preoccupation with reporting campaign process rather than covering more substantive policy issues (Katz 1971; Patterson 1993). While there is evidence that process-type election news, such as horserace reporting, may engage audiences (Iyengar et al. 2004), it also limits the opportunities for citizens *regularly to learn* about competing party positions ahead of election day. It is a familiar critique most often associated with American election journalism (Patterson 1993). But the evidence amassed in this book shows that, nearly two decades into the twenty-first century, *process-driven news remains the overriding logic of campaign coverage in most Western democracies.* As chapter 2 demonstrated, many countries have a relatively high degree of process-orientated coverage during election campaigns (above 40 per cent share of the news agenda), and longitudinal studies have revealed a steady (if not necessarily uniform) reduction in policy-related reporting over time. This was evident not just in the razzmatazz of presidential or general election campaigns but also in relatively low-profile second-order elections. Our comparative analysis of EU and local election news in the UK, for example, established that campaign coverage then was more process driven than during the general election (Cushion and Thomas 2016).

But while the rise of process news was not limited to US elections, American campaign coverage stood out internationally as being the least policy driven. This was most striking in the coverage of the 2016 campaign, where, according to several studies, there was an almost complete absence of policy debates (Patterson 2016a; Tyndall 2016b). As discussed in chapter 5, given the hyper-commercialised media system in the US, this may not appear all that surprising, since the news agenda is geared primarily towards audience ratings rather than raising people's understanding of policy issues. Several studies showed that, during election campaigns, public service broadcasters tended to report a higher degree of policy-orientated news than their commercial counterparts (Strömbäck and van Aelst, 2010; Strömbäck and Dimitrova 2011; Cushion 2012a; Rafter et al. 2014; Cushion and Thomas 2016; Cushion et al. 2016b; Strömbäck 2016). At the same time, we drew on evidence that revealed public service broadcasters have also reduced their policy agenda in recent election campaigns (Cushion et al. 2016b; Cushion and Thomas 2017). In other words, while the degree of process-driven coverage may be different between media systems and electoral contests, the prevailing logic of campaign coverage is to report less policy news in the run-up to an election day.

[handwritten margin note: let's hope they are not favouring a unit model]

Since the news media play a crucial role in reporting election campaigns and (at least in first-order contests) report them extensively, it does not necessarily follow that they would deliberately starve citizens of vital information. According to the mediatisation of politics framework (Strömbäck and Esser 2014), prioritising process above policy news reflects a media superseding a political logic in campaign coverage. On the basis of twenty-two chapters exploring how different countries' campaigns were reported, Strömbäck and Kaid's edited volume, *The Handbook of Election News Coverage around the World*, concluded that a media logic was a prominent and, indeed, 'dominant' characteristic of election coverage, with horserace news, campaign events or party political strategy increasingly part of news agendas (2008: 425). In national studies, too, media logic has been widely used to explain why journalists relegate policy for news about the process of election campaigns. Brants and van Praag's assessment of elections in the Netherlands over several decades, for example, argued that 'the 2003 campaign showed clear signs of media logic: performance driven campaign communication, media orientation on the public, on the whole less substantive and more horserace and poll driven reporting, journalistic dominance' (2006: 38).

The media logic of prioritising process above policy coverage, according to conventional mediatisation of politics theory, is driven by market incentives and more commercial editorial decision-making (Strömbäck 2008). As Moog and Sluyter-Beltrao (2001: 34) put it well over a decade ago, 'as political actors are becoming more and more dependent on television as a means of communication, national broadcasting systems are being transformed by the expansion of commercial television. As a result, political coverage increasingly is coming to be dominated by what we will call "commercial media logic".' Similarly, Kriesi (2014: 366) has observed that 'journalists' practices in a professionalised and commercialised media system . . . mainly tend to focus on the political contest at the detriment of the policies' substantive content.' Plasser (2005), meanwhile, viewed 'progressive commercialism' as encouraging an 'increasing focus upon horse race journalism'. In short, horserace reporting is fuelled, above all, by a market-driven media logic.

However, as suggested in several chapters, and supported by our interviews with UK news editors, *media logic alone cannot account for the rise in campaign-process coverage.* In recent UK and US elections, candidates and political parties no longer held regular press conferences, thus limiting the opportunities for journalists to scrutinise parties' policies (Cushion et al. 2016b). Despite its being customary after being elected, Donald Trump refused to hold a press conference for many weeks after election day. He instead relied heavily on communicating via his own social media platforms and granted one-on-one interviews only with selected broadcasters. We also suggested that *horserace reporting was not entirely a media-driven logic.* While the polls (incorrectly) informed journalists during the 2015 UK general election campaign that the race between the two main parties was close, there was also a clear political logic promoting this narrative because it favoured the Conservatives' campaign strategy. In doing so, it influenced the election news agenda, promoting stories about coalition deals and marginalising policy debates.

From a different perspective, horserace news also played a role in how the 2016 US presidential election campaign was reported, with most polls predicting that Hillary Clinton would beat Donald Trump. While they were broadly accurate in the popular vote, the polls in several swing states were not. As with the 2015 UK general election, this will have informed campaign coverage. Since turnout among likely Democrat voters was far lower than expected in many states, the 'Clinton-ahead narrative' may have demotivated people from turning out. Horserace coverage, in other words, is not ideologically inconsequential, since it could have affected people's engagement with the 2016 US presidential election. Indeed, far from process news being a neutral campaign story, free from any political bias – as editors may claim – it fosters an information environment largely devoid of policy issues and is centred primarily on the main political parties. As a consequence, this type of election coverage does little to enhance people's understanding of policy issues and maintains the ideological status quo, with the horserace narrative largely focused on the party or candidate 'ahead' in the polls. So, for example, during the 2016 presidential election campaign – but evident in past contests also – a tiny fraction of airtime was granted to the Libertarian or Green Party candidates. Likewise, during the 2017 UK general election campaign, broadcast coverage was given largely to the Conservatives and Labour, leaving little space for parties such as the Greens, UKIP, the SNP and Plaid Cymru (Cushion 2017a). Of course, broadcasters (and regulators) may argue that their job is to reflect the democratic will of the people and not to construct it. The news media, in this sense, have a difficult balancing act in reflecting the views of the main political parties while not drowning out alternative voices and policy perspectives. However, the weight of evidence amassed throughout this book suggests they do well on the former but less so on the latter.

So, for example, our analysis of the 2015 UK general election revealed that broadcasters and regulators had, over recent campaigns, moved from quantitatively balancing coverage of the main parties to making more qualitative judgements about news selection (Cushion and Thomas 2017). The editors we interviewed indicated they relied primarily on news values to make judgements about the election agenda. On the face of it, news values may appear a reasonable way of selecting stories, since they imply editors rely on an objective set of criteria free from partisan influence. But, as argued throughout the book, news values are not ideologically innocent and can have a major bearing on the election agenda. For instance, the decision by US networks to grant Trump far greater coverage than his Republican and Democrat opponents – even when he was repeatedly making false claims – helped him set the agenda throughout both the primaries and the general election. The overwhelmingly negative tone of campaign coverage also favoured Trump. As Patterson (2016a) argued, Trump's anti-establishment message chimed with many Republican voters because they tend to be more mistrusting of government than Democrats. But we also identified more subtle influences which went beyond commercial news values. During the 2015 UK general election campaign, for example, broadcasters at times shared the news values of national newspapers, which overwhelmingly supported the Conservative Party and favoured reporting right-wing issues. In doing so, newspapers played an intermedia agenda-setting role, which – we argued – undermined the impartiality of television news during the election campaign.

Overall, our analysis suggests that the reliance on news values promoted either a media or a political logic, or both. A public logic was difficult to trace because election coverage was largely devoid of policy or reflective of the voters' issue preferences. But how can a public logic more effectively shape election campaign coverage?

Resetting the election agenda: questioning the parties' campaigns and pursuing a public logic

Research has long revealed the close ties between the agendas of political parties and the media in election campaign coverage (Brookes et al. 2004; Strömbäck and Kaid 2008). In order for an agenda that is more bottom-up than top-down to emerge, in our view broadcasters need to free themselves from the *campaign logic* of the main political parties and pursue a more independently informed *public agenda.* This would represent a radical but important departure from the logic that has typically underpinned campaign coverage. Dutifully following the campaign logic of political parties was well illustrated in an interview with the journalist Sarah Sands, now editor of BBC Radio 4's *Today* programme, when she defended her coverage of the London mayoral campaign during her time as editor of the London *Evening Standard*. Her exchange with the interviewer on Radio 4's *Media Show* on 1 February 2017 went as follows:

> *Interviewer:* Let's look a little bit at the qualities of the *Evening Standard*, where you've just come from as editor. There was criticism over the way that you treated Sadiq Khan in the run-up to the mayoral elections . . . there was talk about links to extremists and there was a feeling that you weren't being fair to a Muslim candidate. What would you say to that?

> *Sarah Sands:* We report the news, and so the accusations that were made . . . were made by the Tory Party . . . those were news stories, so if Cameron stands up and says something then it's clearly a story. In the election campaign it became an issue because the Tory Party chose to make it an issue, and therefore we reflected that.

In other words, the logic of campaign coverage was intimately tied to the agenda of one of the main political parties. Systematic research has shown that, in following the Conservative Party's agenda, the *Evening Standard*'s coverage of the 2016 London mayoral campaign was often unfair, misleading or factually questionable (Media Reform Coalition 2016).

Since political parties and candidates have become increasingly sophisticated in handling the media and managing campaign events, from limiting questions from (or even banning) journalists to evading questions about their policy proposals, we would argue that the news media should not be so complicit in their logic. After all, if the news media seek to better inform people about the respective policies of competing parties, what democratic value does it serve to report election news devoid of issues or that is misleading? After the 2015 UK general election, the head of BBC News, James Harding, conceded that the parties held significant sway in shaping campaign coverage: 'we have to ask ourselves whether we did enough to hold in check the political machines of each party. With each election, the political operations of all parties become more controlled, [and] there is ever greater effort put into news management.' 'Sometimes', he added, 'the result wasn't news, but messaging' (BBC 2015). Our interviews with UK editors revealed how frustrated many were with the parties' over-controlling spin tactics and limited access to journalists, with some indicating they would reconsider campaign reporting in future contests (Cushion et al. 2016b). At the same time, there was a reluctance to limit the airtime granted to political parties during the campaign. Since representative democracies rely on political parties representing the public, we would agree that they should remain the lead protagonists in campaign coverage. But, instead of accepting the logic of political parties, the media could, where necessary, expose the spin behind their campaigning and lead with an issue-based agenda that includes the perspectives of parties but is independent from their control. Whether it be healthcare or education, the economy or crime, *issues* could become the central logic of coverage that parties *responded to* rather than defined on their terms.

Pursuing this logic, of course, may appear to run counter to campaign coverage being entertaining as well as informative, turning viewers off. But sacrificing process for policy news does not have to translate into dull but worthy election reporting that lacks drama or human interest. As even the oft-cited study by Iyengar et al. (2004: 174) about the consumer demand for horse-race news concluded: 'our results suggest that an "all issues" news outlet is unlikely to survive past the first issue', but that 'One approach might be to piggyback information about issue positions onto stories dealing with the personal side of the candidates. Alternatively, polling on the issues allows reporters to file policy-oriented horserace stories.' In other words, campaign coverage needs to find ways to *connect to voters' democratic interests* without abandoning their democratic needs.

So, for example, ahead of the 2015 general election, a *Guardian/ ICM* poll found that, while more than two-thirds of the electorate rated the NHS as the single most important issue, it made up a tiny fraction of television news coverage (Cushion and Sambrook

2015a). Other issues of concern – education, the environment, pensions and transport – were pushed to the very margins of coverage. While polls go up and down and media coverage can play a role in constructing rather than reflecting public opinion (Lewis 2001), in our view journalists could follow people's issue preferences more closely ahead of election day. Indeed, as table 6.0 shows, a representative study found a majority of Americans thought there was too little coverage of the candidates' stance on various issues and too much about their comments, personal lives and who was 'winning' the race. Of course, just because people claim to want more issue-based news, it does not follow they will watch it (after all, online metrics can now track people's preferences for chickbait celebrity news ahead of more serious news coverage).

In an increasingly soft news environment, the challenge for journalists is to find ways of being engaging *and* informative by arousing people's interest in *as well as* raising their understanding of politics. Not only do many prominent national journalists often underestimate an audience's knowledge about politics and public affairs (Philo and Berry 2004), their concerns and anxieties can appear distant from those of the wider public. Indeed, BBC audience research in the UK has shown that, the further away audiences live from London, the more likely they are to believe news is not relevant to them (King 2008). Being 'inside the Washington beltway' or in the 'Westminster bubble' are phrases that have long been used to reflect how the political and/or media agenda are out of sync with 'ordinary folk'. But in our view reporters could find more effective ways of closing the gap between voters' concerns and the news agenda during election campaigns.

The disconnect between election journalism and voters was dramatically revealed after the UK voted to leave the EU in June 2016 and, just a few months later, when Trump was elected US president. A year later, another political earthquake was felt when, contrary to many opinion polls, Labour won a much greater share of votes than expected in the 2017 UK general election. Each one of these appeared to represent a shock to many commentators and reporters, despite opinion polls showing that the eventual out-

Table 6.0 Percentage of people who say there is too much, too little or about the right amount of coverage about aspects of the 2016 US presidential campaign

	Too much	Too little	About the right amount
Candidates' comments	44	15	39
Candidates' personal lives	43	19	35
Which candidate is leading	37	13	46
Candidates' moral characters	30	34	33
Candidates' experience	15	45	37
Candidates' issue stances	3	55	30

Source: Adapted from Gottfried 2016.

comes were distinctly possible, even that of the 2017 UK election, had pollsters included the likelihood of young people voting. As far as the EU referendum and the 2016 US election were concerned, this was perhaps because many who voted Leave or who backed Trump were outside the major cities – in northern towns, say, or beltway states that were rarely if ever frequented by mainstream journalists or connected to their filter bubbles. This was revealed in a 2016 Showtime TV documentary, *The Circus*, which filmed three journalists covering the presidential campaign over many months. Baffled about Trump's shock victory, as the results came in one journalist exclaimed: 'I'm gonna go on TV tomorrow and have to say, hey man, I was wrong. I gotta figure out why I was wrong – we've all gotta figure it out.' It was a moment that visibly exposed the disconnect between the media commentariat and many millions of American voters.

There was less soul-searching from journalists after Labour won a greater share of votes than anticipated in the 2017 UK general election. There appeared to be a conventional wisdom among many journalists that the leader of the Labour Party, Jeremy Corbyn, was not widely liked by the public, despite champion-ing many popular policies. Live two-ways with correspondents, for example, often appeared to cast doubt on Corbyn's electa-bility (Cushion 2017a). This was also apparent in the editorial construction of vox pops during the campaign. Despite Labour and its leader gradually improving in the polls over the campaign, vox pops often focused on Corbyn's character rather than on the policies he was advocating (Cushion 2017b).

After both the UK and the US elections there were calls for a more blue-collar approach to journalism (Nieman Lab Staff 2017), a shift away from a metropolitan agenda of issues to better reflect the democratic needs of 'ordinary' people from different regions and communities. As *The Guardian*'s US features editor acknowledged in a job advertisement in March 2017, 'This [US] election has highlighted why covering communities from the inside out, instead of from the outside in, matters. This year, I am keen to work with journalists who want to report on their own communities – places and people they already know well' (Reed 2017). The aim, according to the headline of the advert, was to go 'beyond the bubble' and 'write for Guardian US about the places that others ignore'. In principle, it would be difficult to argue against journalists' *understanding the electorate* better (rather than forecasting how they will vote or employing commentators to debate how they think). But this means going beyond 'parachute' journalism – flying in journalists to swing states or marginal constituencies at election time – and employing reporters in communities throughout the US for sustained periods of time (as *The* Guardian advert advocated). This could help diversify the elction agenda, putting people's issues at the centre of the campaign and asking political elites to respond to them. It may also go some way, as the next section now explores, towards rebuilding the credibility of news media, which – in the US most strikingly – have become an increasingly mistrusted source of information.

Policing the boundaries of election coverage: reinterpreting impartiality in the age of post-truth politics

On the face of it, we found little explicit or sustained evidence beyond the US cable news channels of broadcasters being biased

<u>towards or against one party</u>. Broadly speaking, most remained balanced or impartial, with different national regulatory rules (with the exception of the US) policing the boundaries of how the mainstream parties were reported during the election campaign. Thus we argued that the ideological status quo of the main political parties was not radically challenged during an election campaign, with smaller parties, such as Green candidates, having been granted limited airtime.

However, we also acknowledged that this broad-brush approach to examining bias failed to expose more subtle influences shaping campaign coverage. While there are similarities between many country's regulatory guidelines about political balance in news programming (Strömbäck and Kaid 2008), there are nationally specific factors that help explain imbalances in how political parties are reported. As our UK case study explored, rather than following regulatory guidelines about ensuring due prominence to major and minor parties or whether certain issues favour one party over another, broadcasters relied on news values when selecting campaign stories (Cushion and Thomas 2017). This more flexible approach to interpreting impartiality – endorsed by the regulator – places greater discretion on journalists when judging balance. Indeed, the decision in March 2017 by Ofcom – the UK's media regulator – to cease issuing major and minor party status before election campaigns granted broadcasters even more freedom to select stories according to news values (Ofcom 2017). However, as we argued in chapter 4, in the breathless speed of an election news cycle, relying on news values alone can lead to an agenda of campaign-process news that is conflict driven or personality based. Moreover, it encourages parties to campaign in ways that appeal to a media logic rather than promoting policy perspectives that merit debate. In this way, coverage of party political perspectives could become imbalanced over a campaign, with newsworthy stories undermining the impartiality of news agendas. As already discussed, <u>news values are not politically neutral and can influence election coverage in ways that favour candidates or political parties,</u> such as granting Trump a bigger platform to launch his presidential bid or allowing right-wing newspapers to set the campaign agenda.

At the same time, sticking rigidly to a crude impartiality framework can undermine the balance of campaign coverage and limit how far journalists hold political parties and candidates to account. So, for example, during the 2016 EU referendum campaign, while broadcasters gave equal time to Leave and Remain perspectives, nearly eight out of ten political sources were from the Conservative Party and UKIP (a centre-right and right-wing party, respectively) (Cushion and Lewis 2017). Labour, the SNP, the Liberal Democrats and the Greens were notably granted little airtime to put forward their more centre-left-wing views on the merits of remaining in or leaving the EU. The BBC issued impartiality guidelines reminding journalists that 'referendums are seldom fought purely on the basis of just two opposing standpoints – on each side, where there is a range of views or perspectives, that should be reflected appropriately during the campaign.' But perhaps because of the pace of the news cycle, while broadcasters maintained an equal balance between Leave and Remain campaigners, they overlooked the broader range of views that could have informed debates about EU membership. Moreover, as chapter 5 explored, both sides of the debate made dubious claims during the campaign that were often left unchallenged by journalists. This resulted in many stories featuring a statistical tit-for-tat between rival politicians, with knowledge-based sources such as academics, economists, think tanks, business representatives and trade unionists being granted limited opportunities to inform relevant debates or verify competing claims. Many experts from these professions favoured remaining in the EU, but the weight of evidence they might have given about issues from the economy to immigration were left to campaigners to argue about. Independent evidence, in other words, was sidelined, and a greater focus was placed on the claims and counter-claims of each campaign.

This kind of 'he said, she said' approach to election reporting was evident during the 2016 US presidential election, with each candidate's claims often being accepted rather than challenged. Despite, as chapter 5 showed, independent analysts revealing how pervasively Trump – compared to other candidates – made false or misleading statements, throughout much of the campaign many of these went unopposed in media coverage. Once at the general election stage of the campaign, it was suggested that a 'false balance' was set up between the claims and counter-claims made by Trump and Clinton (Rosen 2016a). Indeed, although Trump was involved in many controversies during the campaign, these were often counterbalanced by less significant scandals involving Clinton (for example, the Trump Foundation vs. the Clinton Foundation – see Patterson 2016b). Put simply, journalists appeared reluctant to break free from the objectivity norm and interpret the weight of evidence about particular issues or events. To paraphrase Jay Rosen, to report opposing candidates asymmetrically fries the brains of most journalists (Rosen 2016b).

In an era of post-truth (or post-factual) politics, where emotions and opinions are increasingly replacing 'facts', clearly sticking to age-old conventions represents a challenge to how objectivity or impartiality has usually been interpreted. Compared to most (past and present) presidential candidates, Trump made many more false or misleading statements and limited the freedom of the press to scrutinise his behaviour or policy proposals during the campaign. Fact-checkers actually revealed that Trump made, on average, four false statements a day in his first 100 days in office. In speeches, remarks or statements, on Twitter or Facebook, in interviews and news conferences, the US president's claims have been regularly discredited. As many commentators have pointed out, Trump's behaviour is not 'normal' for a president (or even for a candidate), but, given his electoral success, it may become the blueprint for future campaigning (and governing).

As a consequence, it is important to understand Trump's campaign logic, since it challenges an underlying premise of how the mediatisation of political news is interpreted. After all, while a media logic represents a fascination with the processes of an election campaign, a political logic reflects the ability of candidates and parties to make *their issues* part of the news agenda. As Strömbäck and Dimitrova (2011: 36) theorised, 'If politicians were allowed to decide, they would mainly talk about and focus on the issues.' Of course, most politicians will, at some point, evade specific policy questions or overlook criticisms about their agenda, but

Trump's logic is to campaign with relatively superficial references to substantive issues. In attacking his opponents – both politicians and the media – engaging with horserace stories or talking in broad generalities ('to Make America Great Again'), Trump's soundbites appeal to the frenetic pace of US news values. His brand of campaigning, viewed in this light, represents the climax of the mediatisation of the political process. According to the four phases of mediatisation of politics, the final phase is reached 'when political or other social actors not only adapt to the media logic and the predominant news values, but also *internalize* these values and, more or less consciously, allow the media logic and the standards of newsworthiness to become a built-in part of the governing process' (Strömbäck and Kaid 2008: 4; original emphasis). As chapter 5 showed, Trump instantly transferred his style of campaigning to government, whether in speeches, in interviews, in his use of Twitter or in his more general behaviour to the press.

However, Trump's reasoning appears more pernicious than merely exploiting the logic of the media to gain campaign coverage and achieve electoral success. Undermining the credibility of the news media with repeated claims of fake news, both during the campaign and in his early days as president, Trump challenged the basic tenors of journalism to establish the 'facts' and seek out the 'truth'. Echoing Richard Nixon's comments in the 1960s, in one speech Trump called the media 'enemies of the people' (BBC 2017). This full-frontal attack on the media institutions that govern people's understanding of the world represents far more than a passive acceptance of news values for political gain.

Needless to say, the implications of Trump delegitimising journalism have far-reaching implications for the relationship between media and democracy in the US and beyond. One immediate effect was how the White House's press corps would operate in a more hostile environment. While threats to move the White House press room to another building were resisted by the Trump administration, the press secretary changed the rules of his briefings, with senior front-row reporters no longer having the privilege of asking the first questions. These are now often asked by sympathetic right-wing outlets, such as OANN, the *Daily Caller* or *Townhall*. On one occasion, some media organisations, including CNN, the *New York Times*, *Politico*, *Buzzfeed* and the BBC, were excluded from an informal private briefing known as a 'gaggle'. In the opening weeks of Trump's administration, the then press secretary, Sean Spicer, was increasingly using 'gaggles' to disseminate information and answer journalists' questions (Nussbaum and Gold 2017)

Not long into Trump's administration, then, the historically close relationship between the press and the president was being redefined. Even after the very first press briefing, a *Washington Post* media columnist argued that 'White House press briefings are "access journalism," in which official statements – achieved by closeness to the source – are taken at face value and breathlessly reported as news. And that is over. Dead' (Sullivan 2017). In other words, many journalists could no longer trust the president's office to tell the truth. Of course, the press's role as a conduit between the president and the people represents an important democratic function. But, in our view, loosening the ties between the press and administration, and casting greater doubt on government statements, represents a healthy development in holding power to account. Moreover, it reinforces our earlier argument that *campaign coverage needs to be rethought in ways that weaken the ability of political parties to set the election agenda.* As we now see, drawing on a greater range of knowledge-based sources could enhance the scrutiny of each party's policy proposals and widen the news agenda beyond the narrow range of issues that typically shape campaign coverage.

Expanding the voices of campaign coverage and standing up to power at election time

Studies have long shown that, in election reporting, the leaders and candidates of the *main* political parties dominate campaign coverage. During the 2017 UK general election, for example, political parties were the dominant source of television news, with few experts used to challenge their claims (Cushion 2017d). Of course, given the reach and power of broadcasters, it would be dangerous for representative democracy if political parties were marginalised from or placed at the periphery of campaign coverage. But the *overwhelming focus* of political elites in campaign coverage, in our view, limits both the range of issues addressed in election news agendas and how far journalists can scrutinise the relative merits of political parties' claims and counter-claims.

It is not just politicians that dominate the airwaves during election campaigns. Media pundits, typically political journalists, are regularly used to interpret campaign news and help set the parameters of discussion (Cushion and Sambrook 2015b). As Hopmann and Strömbäck's (2010: 956) analysis of Swedish election reporting between 1994 and 2007 discovered, there was a 'rise of the punditocracy', with politicians appearing less and journalists and media commentators featuring more. While journalists can play an important interpretive role in political coverage, their commentary tends to revolve around a narrow set of (party political) concerns rather than a broad range of policy issues (Cushion 2015). Moreover, reporters do not necessarily have the knowledge or expertise to pass judgement on complex policy debates. The degree to which journalists can interpret issues, particularly at election time, is also limited by rules about impartiality or a professional commitment towards objectivity.

In our view, however, a more evidenced-based approach to election reporting need not undermine impartial or objective journalism but could, rather, enhance it by more effectively holding power to account and improving the accuracy of campaign coverage. As we suggested in chapter 5, a weight of evidence approach to reporting would move beyond the 'he said, she said' paradigm of campaign coverage, encouraging journalists to draw on a wider range of expertise and expand the election agenda. Of course, interpreting the weight of evidence on particular issues is not always straightforward. In coverage of climate change, for instance, where there is a clear scientific consensus that human behaviour causes global warming, reporters can rely on experts *within* this consensus to inform coverage. But there is no clear consensus about how more bread-and-butter issues, such as dealing with social care, crime, education or the economy, should be resolved.

Nevertheless, journalists could draw more regularly on independent experts to fact-check the parties' proposals or to explore alternative ways of addressing policy issues. No source may be viewed as truly 'independent', but there remain many knowledge-rich experts, from think tanks, the academy, industry, science, medicine and other professions, that could be used to interpret evidence without being partisan. Moreover, journalists could spend time researching competing evidence between relevant experts (not political parties) and communicate the parameters of this debate in campaign coverage. From a viewer's perspective, listening to the leading experts about the relative merits of various political parties' policy positions or spending promises can only help them make a more informed decision at the ballot box.

Of course, this kind of fact-checking is not a particularly novel development in journalism. Many media organisations use fact-checkers in election campaign coverage. But often these are for special events – such as a TV leaders' debate or a set-piece campaign speech – rather than day-to-day reporting in newscasts. Moreover, fact-checkers often acknowledge that facts can be difficult to establish one way or another, so regularly relying on a wider pool of expert sources to interpret evidence or politicians' claims would also help keep power in check *throughout* the campaign. Broadcasters have clearly become more aware of reporting politics in a post-factual political environment. In a BBC Trust review of how statistics were reported, for example, the regulator recommended the corporation 'help audiences make sense of the statistical evidence in an impartial way. That involves being willing, more than at present, to weigh, interpret and explain the statistical evidence and, when appropriate, challenge and correct when it is misused.' The BBC, the report added, 'needs to get better and braver in interpreting and explaining rival statistics and guiding the audience' (BBC Trust 2016: 11).

In rethinking campaign coverage, it remains important to consider the wider context in which journalism operates. In the UK and many Western democracies, the broadcast media and most knowledge-based professions remain relatively well trusted by the public. During the EU referendum campaign, Leave voters' trust towards experts did fall, but this was arguably a consequence of long-standing scepticism towards the European Union fuelled by negative television and press coverage (Copeland and Copsey 2017; Wahl-Jorgensen et al. 2013). Generally speaking, academics, think tanks, scientists and other information-rich sources remain credible figures of authority in the UK. In the more partisan culture of US politics, however, experts are viewed more suspiciously. As Blank and Shaw's (2015) research established, many Americans, notably Republican voters, often reject scientific recommendations that are contrary to their own political views. Evidence or facts, in other words, are outweighed by deep-rooted ideological convictions. As a wide-ranging report into fact-checking pointed out, 'Rather than draining power from negative campaigning and partisan politics, fact checking can fuel it' (Stencel 2015). Indeed, Shin and Thorson's research into social media behaviour during the 2012 election campaign found a partisan (mostly Republican) hostility towards fact-checking organisations. The authors established that 'partisans selectively share fact checking messages that cheerlead their own candidate and denigrate the opposing party's candidate, resulting in an ideologically narrow flow of fact checks to their followers' (Shin and Thorson 2017: 1). In other words, in a culture where media and politics are shaped so heavily by people's ideological convictions, audiences appear reluctant to accept independent analysis if it contradicts their own perceptions (Blank and Shaw 2015). Nevertheless, there is some evidence that the rigorous fact-checking of politicians, as Nyhan and Reifler (2014) discovered, can lead to more honest campaigning. Regularly exposing people to accurate information can also – eventually – challenge their partisan preconceptions (Redlawsk et al. 2010), particularly if coverage does not repeat false accusations but affirms truthful statements (Nyhan and Reifler 2009).

Of course, the media alone cannot explain people's understanding and interpretation of politics. US society, including many of its institutions, has become increasingly politicised, and people's lifestyles and beliefs have polarised many communities (Bishop 2008). Voters' identities, in this sense, are shaped by wider cultural influences that make people more or less receptive to political information and election reporting (Flynn et al. 2017). Nevertheless, the US's increasingly partisan media system remains a significant source of influence during election cycles, with factional coverage fuelling misconceptions about political issues. Moreover, it appears to be enhancing a more conservative political information environment. Benkler et al.'s (2017) study of 1.25 million online stories on social media between 1 April 2015 and 8 November 2016 suggested that right-wing online news sites – in particular Breitbart – played a significant intermedia agenda-setting role during the US presidential election. They found 'Pro-Clinton audiences were highly attentive to traditional media outlets, which continued to be the most prominent outlets across the public sphere, alongside more left-oriented online sites. But pro-Trump audiences paid the majority of their attention to polarized outlets that have developed recently, many of them only since the 2008 election season.' Further still, their news analysis suggested that the 'right-wing media was . . . able to bring the focus on immigration, Clinton emails, and scandals more generally to the broader media environment. A sentence-level analysis of stories throughout the media environment suggests that Donald Trump's substantive agenda – heavily focused on immigration and direct attacks on Hillary Clinton – came to dominate public discussions.'

As explored in chapter 4, intermedia agenda-setting effects are subtle and indirect but become potent because of the *news values of mainstream media*. As Rosen (2017) has observed, accusations rather than facts often act as the news hook in political reporting. In doing so, they help legitimise the credibility of the story irrespective of any supporting evidence. So, for example, when Trump was under pressure about his campaign's relationship with Russian officials in March 2017, he tweeted the following: 'Terrible! Just found out that Obama had my "wires tapped" in Trump Tower just before the victory. Nothing found. This is McCarthyism!' Although he offered no evidence to support the claim, the accusation was nonetheless widely reported. Fox News, for example, had a banner 'WIRETAPPING FROM THE WH', reporting the story more as a fact than an unsubstantiated accusation. Other mainstream media organisations did lead with more subtle headlines (for example, the *New York Times* said, 'Trump, offering no evidence, says Obama tapped his phones'), but even a BBC breaking news tweet – 'President Trump urges Congress to examine whether Obama abused presidential powers as part of Russia probe' – helped legitimise the claim. Tracing the origins of the claim, Baker and Haberman (2017) established that the accusation began on a conservative talk show, was reported by Breitbart news, and then appeared in a Trump tweet. In other words, a baseless allegation had spread within a 48-hour news cycle not just on right-wing partisan news outlets but in the mainstream US media, as well as via the Twitter feed of an internationally impartial public service media outlet.

Viewed in this light, the emergence of a post-truth political environment has enhanced the power of political elites to set the agenda. As a consequence, the political logic underpinning the mediatisation of politics theory has been challenged (Strömbäck 2008). After all, some politicians may not want their policies pushed up the news agenda (Strömbäck and Dimitrova 2011) and would prefer instead to revel in the razzmatazz of campaign coverage. Media-savvy politicians have not only learnt the rules of gaining media attention, they have rewritten the rulebook to shape more effectively a political logic in campaign coverage. As a consequence, those in the journalism profession are now debating how to report post-truth politics against the backdrop of more partisan media, disinformation online and selective news exposure. This was acknowledged in an open letter from the White House press corps just days before Trump was inaugurated: 'You [Trump] have forced us to rethink the most fundamental questions about who we are and what we are here for' (cited in Pope 2017). While Trump's political logic represents a threat to the free press, his election victory has prompted critical and timely questions about how journalism can effectively hold power to account. It has even led to a surge in news ratings across a wide range of news media (Rajan 2017).

In rethinking the logic of political coverage, however, we would argue that it should be driven not just by the behaviour of populist politicians but by *the democratic needs of citizens*, particularly during election campaigns. Above all, citizens need reliable information about the policies of competing political parties before election day. They need journalists to establish the facts behind politicians' campaigns and to expose any falsehoods. A ruthless commitment to objectivity, in this sense, will eventually outweigh political deceit, with politicians paying the (electoral) price for not being honest about their actions or promises. In our view, for news media to enhance people's understanding and engagement with election campaigns, they could *rethink the emphasis placed on process-driven news and the attention paid to the parties' campaign agendas*. Following the horserace between parties – who's up or down in the polls – is often the focal point of campaign coverage. But, as recent electoral contests have revealed, relying so heavily on opinion polls about the campaign horserace can be more misleading than informative, pushing issues to the margins and glossing over voters' concerns. Instead, if journalists were more in tune with the public's mood and anxieties and drew on a wider range of actors to interrogate politicians' claims, a more independent news agenda might emerge. This will not be a quick-fix solution, but over time it may encourage a public logic in campaign coverage that better connects with people's democratic needs.

References

Aalberg, T., van Aelst, P., and Curran, J. (2010) Media systems and the political information environment: a cross-national comparison, *International Journal of Press/Politics* 15(3): 255–71.

Aalberg, T., Strömbäck, J., and de Vreese, C. H. (2012) The framing of politics as strategy and game: a review of concepts, operationalizations and key findings, *Journalism* 13(2): 162–78.

Aalberg, T., Esser, F., Reinemann, C., Strömbäck, J., and de Vreese, C. H. eds (2017) *Populist Political Communication in Europe*. Abingdon: Routledge.

Allcott, H., and Gentzkow, M. (2017) Social media and fake news in the 2016 election, *Journal of Economic Perspectives* 31(2): 211–36; https://web.stanford.edu/~gentzkow/research/fakenews.pdf.

Altheide, D. L. (2016) Media logic, *International Encyclopaedia of Political Communication*. Wiley online, pp.1–6.

Annenberg Public Policy Center (2016) America's knowledge of the branches of government is declining, www.annenbergpublicpolicy center.org/americans-knowledge-of-the-branches-of-government-is-declining/.

Baker, P., and Haberman, M. (2017) A conspiracy theory's journey from talk radio to Trump's Twitter, *New York Times*, 5 March, https://mobile.nytimes.com/2017/03/05/us/politics/trump-twitter-talk-radio-conspiracy-theory.html?smid=tw-share&_r=0&referer=https://t.co/IiXE5Lf20Y.

Banducci, S., and Hanretty, C. (2014) Comparative determinants of horse-race coverage, *European Political Science Review* 6(4): 621–40.

Banville, L. (2016) *Covering American Politics in the 21st Century: An Encyclopedia of News Media Titans, Trends, and Controversies*. Santa Barbara, CA: ABC-CLIO.

BBC (2014) *Draft Election Guidelines: Election Campaigns for the General Election across the UK Local Government in England*, http://downloads.bbc.co.uk/bbctrust/assets/files/pdf/our_work/election_guidelines/2014/draft_election_guidelines.pdf.

BBC (2015) James Harding Speech at VLV Conference 2 June 2015, www.bbc.co.uk/mediacentre/speeches/2015/james-harding-speech-vlv-2-june-2015.

BBC (2016) EU referendum campaigns 'misleading voters', 27 May, www.bbc.co.uk/news/uk-politics-eu-referendum-36397732.

BBC (2017) 'Enemies of the people': Trump remark echoes history's worst tyrants, 18 February, www.bbc.co.uk/news/world-us-canada-39015559.

BBC Trust (2016) *BBC Trust Impartiality Review: Making Sense of Statistics*. London: BBC Trust.

Benkler, Y., Faris, R., Roberts, H., and Zuckerman, E. (2017) Study: Breitbart-led right-wing media ecosystem altered broader media agenda, *Columbia Journalism Review*, 3 March, www.cjr.org/analysis/breitbart-media-trump-harvard-study.php.

Bennett, W. L. (1990) Toward a theory of press–state relations in the United States, *Journal of Communication* 40(2): 103–27.

Bishop, B. (2008) *The Big Sort: Why the Clustering of Like-Minded America is Tearing Us Apart*. Boston: Houghton Mifflin.

Blank, J. M., and Shaw, D. (2015) Does partisanship shape attitudes toward science and public policy? The case for ideology and religion, *Annals of the American Academy of Political and Social Science* 658(1): 18–35.

Blumler, J. G., and Coleman, S. (2010) Political communication in free-fall: the British case – and others? *International Journal of Press/Politics* 15(2): 139–54.

Blumler, J. G. and Cushion, S. (2014) Normative perspectives on journalism studies: stock-taking and future directions, *Journalism* 15(3): 259–72.

Blumler, J. G., and Gurevitch, M. (2001) 'Americanization' reconsidered: UK–US campaign communication comparisons across time, in W. L. Bennett and R. M. Entman, eds, *Mediated Politics*. Cambridge: Cambridge University Press, pp. 380–406.

Boehlert, E. (2016) The media isn't for Hillary Clinton: her emails have been covered more than all policy proposals, *Salon*, 3 November, www.salon.com/2016/11/03/the-media-isnt-for-hillary-clinton-her-emails-have-been-covered-more-than-all-policy-proposals/.

Bold, B. (2015) TV most influential media in general election, *Campaign*, 11 May, www.campaignlive.co.uk/article/tv-influential-media-general-Election/1346475.

Boyd, M., and Bahador, B. (2015) Media coverage of New Zealand's 2014 election campaign, *Political Science* 67(2): 143–60.

Brants, K., and van Praag, P. (2006) Signs of media logic: half a century of political communication in the Netherlands, *Javnost – The Public* 13(1): 25–40.

Brants, K., and van Praag, P. (2015) Beyond media logic, *Journalism Studies* 18(4): 395–408.

Broh, C. A. (1980) Horse-race journalism: reporting the polls in the 1976 presidential election, *Public Opinion Quarterly* 44(4): 514–29.

Brookes, R., Lewis, J., and Wahl-Jorgensen, K. (2004) The media representation of public opinion: British television news coverage of the 2001 general election, *Media, Culture & Society* 26(1): 63–80.

Cappella, J. N., and Jamieson, K. H. (1997) *Spiral of Cynicism: The Press and the Public Good*. Oxford: Oxford University Press.

Chadwick, A. (2013) *The Hybrid Media System: Politics and Power*. Oxford: Oxford University Press.

Chadwick, A., and Stromer-Galley, J. (2016) Digital media, power, and democracy in parties and election campaigns: party decline or party renewal? *International Journal of Press/Politics* 21(3): 283–93.

Christians, C. G., Glasser, T. L., McQuail, D., Nordenstreng, K., and White, R. A. (2009) *Normative Theories of the Media: Journalism in Democratic Societies*. Urbana: University of Illinois Press.

Clement, S. and Craighill, P. M. (2015) Gallup isn't doing any horserace polling in 2016: here's why, *Washington Post*, 7 October, www. washingtonpost.com/news/the-fix/wp/2015/10/07/gallup-isnt-do ing-any-horserace-polling-in-2016-heres-why/?utm_term=.fcbac65 9b941.

Colvin, J. (2016) Trump's deportation waffle highlights campaign weak- nesses, *US News*, 30 August, www.usnews.com/news/politics/articles /2016-08-30/trumps-deportation-waffle-highlights-campaign-weak nesses.

Conway, B. A., Kenski, K., and Wang, D. (2015) The rise of Twitter in the political campaign: searching for intermedia agenda-setting effects in the presidential primary, *Journal of Computer-Mediated Communication* 20(4): 363–80.

Copeland, P., and Copsey, N. (2017) Rethinking Britain and the European Union: politicians, the media and public opinion reconsidered, *Journal of Common Market Studies*, 55(4): 709–26, http://onlinelibrary.wiley. com/doi/10.1111/jcms.12527/pdf.

Cowley, P., and Kavanagh, D. (2016) *The British General Election of 2015.* Basingstoke: Palgrave Macmillan.

Cummings, D. (2017) How the Brexit referendum was won, *The Spectator*, 9 January, https://blogs.spectator.co.uk/2017/01/dominic- cummings-brexit-referendum-won/#.

Curran, J. (2011) *Media and Democracy.* Abingdon: Routledge.

Curran, J., Iyengar, S., Brink Lund, A., and Salovaara-Moring, I. (2009) Media system, public knowledge and democracy: a comparative study, *European Journal of Communication* 24(1): 5–26.

Curran, J., Coen, S., Soroka, S., Aalberg, T., Hayashi, K., Hichy, Z., Iyengar, S., Jones, P., Mazzoleni, G., Papathanassopoulos, S., Woong Rhee, J., Rojas, H., Rowe, D., and Tiffen, R. (2014) Reconsidering 'virtuous circle' and 'media malaise' theories of the media: an 11-nation study, *Journalism* 15(7): 815–33.

Cushion, S. (2012a) *The Democratic Value of News: Why Public Service Media Matter.* Basingstoke: Palgrave Macmillan.

Cushion, S. (2012b) *Television Journalism.* London: Sage.

Cushion, S. (2015) *News and Politics: The Rise of Live and Interpretive Journalism.* London: Routledge.

Cushion, S. (2017a) Were broadcasters biased against Jeremy Corbyn? It's the details that count, *New Statesman*, 21 June, www.newstatesman.

com/politics/june2017/2017/06/were-broadcasters-biased-against-jer
emy-corbyn-its-details-count.

Cushion, S. (2017b) TV news coverage of the 2017 election isn't
giving you the full picture – especially about Jeremy Corbyn, *The
Conversation*, 12 May, https://theconversation.com/tv-news-
coverage-of-the-2017-election-isnt-giving-you-the-full-pic
ture-especially-about-jeremy-corbyn-77632.

Cushion, S. (2017c) It's time journalists exposed the spin behind politicians' campaign rallies, *The Independent*, 8 May, www.independent.
co.uk/voices/media-election-politics-news-journalism-expose-the-
spin-a7718141.html.

Cushion, S. (2017d) TV election coverage needs more experts and less
squabbling, *Total Politics*, 19 May, www.totalpolitics.com/articles/
opinion/stephen-cushion-tv-election-coverage-needs-more-experts-
and-less-squabbling.

Cushion, S., and Lewis, J. (2017) Impartiality, statistical tit-for-tats and
the construction of balance: UK television news reporting of the 2016
EU referendum campaign, *European Journal of Communication* 32(3):
208–23.

Cushion, S., and Sambrook, R. (2015a) The 'horse-race' contest
dominated TV news election coverage, www.electionanalysis.uk/
uk-election-analysis-2015/section-1-media-reporting/the-horse-race-
contest-dominated-tv-news-election-coverage/.

Cushion, S., and Sambrook, R. (2015b) How the TV news let the Tories
fight the election on their own terms, *The Guardian*, 15 May, www.
theguardian.com/media/2015/may/15/tv-news-let-the-tories-fight-
the-election-coalition-economy-taxation.

Cushion, S., and Sambrook, R., eds (2016) *The Future of 24-Hour News:
New Directions, New Challenges*. Oxford: Peter Lang.

Cushion, S., and Thomas, R. (2016) Reporting different second order
elections: a comparative analysis of the 2009 and 2013 local and EU
elections on public and commercial UK television news bulletins,
British Politics 11(2): 164–83.

Cushion, S., and Thomas, R. (2017) From quantitative precision to
qualitative judgements: professional perspectives about the impartiality
of television news during the 2015 UK general election, *Journalism*,
http://journals.sagepub.com/doi/pdf/10.1177/1464884916685909.

Cushion, S., Franklin, R., and Court, G. (2006) Citizens, readers and local newspaper coverage of the UK 2005 general election, *Javnost – The Public* 13(1): 41–60.

Cushion, S., Lewis, J., and Groves, C. (2009) Prioritizing hand-shaking over policy-making: a study of how the 2007 devolved elections was [*sic*] reported on BBC UK network coverage, *Cyfrwng: Media Wales Journal* 6: 7–32.

Cushion, S., Thomas, R., and Ellis, O. (2015a) Interpreting UKIP's 'earthquake' in British politics: UK television news coverage of the 2009 and 2014 EU election campaigns, *Political Quarterly* 86(2): 314–22.

Cushion, S., Thomas, R., and Ellis, O. (2015b) The mediatization of second-order elections and party launches: UK television news reporting of the 2014 European Union campaign, *International Journal of Communication* 9: 1523–43.

Cushion, S., Thomas, R., Kilby, A., Morani, M., and Sambrook, R. (2016a) Newspapers, impartiality and television news: interpreting intermedia agenda-setting during the 2015 UK general election, *Journalism Studies*, www.tandfonline.com/doi/pdf/10.1080/1461670X.2016.1171163?needAccess=true.

Cushion, S., Thomas, R., Kilby, A., Morani, M., and Sambrook, R. (2016b) Interpreting the media logic behind editorial decisions: television news coverage of the 2015 UK general election campaign, *International Journal of Press/Politics* 21(4): 472–89.

Cushion, S., Lewis, J., and Callaghan, R. (2016c) Data journalism, impartiality and statistical claims, *Journalism Practice*, www.tandfonline.com/doi/full/10.1080/17512786.2016.1256789.

D'Alessio, D. (2012) *Media Bias in Presidential Election Coverage, 1948–2008: Evaluation via Formal Measurement*. Lanham, MD: Lexington Books.

D'Alessio, D., and Allen, M. (2000) Media bias in presidential elections: a meta-analysis, *Journal of Communication* 50(4): 133–56.

Deacon, M. (2016) Michael Gove's guide to Britain's greatest enemy . . . the experts, *The Telegraph*, 10 June, www.telegraph.co.uk/news/2016/06/10/michael-goves-guide-to-britains-greatest-enemy-the-experts/.

Deacon, D., and Stanyer, J. (2014) Mediatization: key concept or conceptual bandwagon? *Media, Culture & Society* 36(7): 1031–44.

Deacon, D., and Wring, D. (2005) Election unspun? The mediation of the campaign, in A. Geddes and J. Tonge, eds, *Britain Decides: The UK General Election 2005*. Basingstoke: Palgrave Macmillan, pp. 208–33.

Deacon D., and Wring, D. (2011) Reporting the 2010 general election: old media, new media – old politics, new politics, in D. Wring, R. Mortimore and S. Atkinson, eds, *Political Communication in Britain: The Leader's Debates, the Campaign and the Media in the 2010 General Election*. Basingstoke: Palgrave Macmillan, pp. 281–303.

Deacon, D., Golding, P., and Billig, M. (2001) Press and broadcasting: 'real issues' and real coverage, *Parliamentary Affairs* 54(4): 666–78.

Deacon, D., Wring, D., Billig, M., Downey, J., Golding, P., and Davidson, S. (2005) *Reporting the 2005 UK General Election*, Loughborough University, https://dspace.lboro.ac.uk/dspace-jspui/bitstream/2134/3171/1/D.pdf.

Deacon, D., Wring, D., Harmer, E., Stanyer, J., and Downey, J. (2016) Hard evidence: analysis shows extent of press bias towards Brexit, *The Conversation*, 16 June, http://theconversation.com/hard-evidence-analysis-shows-extent-of-press-bias-towards-brexit-61106.

DellaVigna, S., and Kaplan, E. (2007) The Fox News effect: media bias and voting, *Quarterly Journal of Economics* 122(3): 1187–234.

de Vreese, C. H. (2003) Television reporting of second-order elections, *Journalism Studies* 4(2): 183–98.

de Vreese, C. H. (2005) The spiral of cynicism reconsidered, *European Journal of Communication* 20(3): 283–301.

de Vreese, C. H. (2009) Second-rate election campaigning? An analysis of campaign styles in European parliamentary elections, *Journal of Political Marketing* 8(1): 7–19.

de Vreese, C. H., and Boomgaarden, H. (2006) News, political knowledge and participation: the differential effects of news media exposure on political knowledge and participation, *Acta Politica* 41(4): 317–41.

de Vreese, C. H., and Elenbaas, M. (2008) Media in the game of politics: effects of strategic metacoverage on political cynicism, *International Journal of Press/Politics* 13(3): 285–309.

de Vreese, C. H., Banducci, S. A., Semetko, H. A., and Boomgaarden, H. G. (2006) The news coverage of the 2004 European parliamentary election campaign in 25 countries, *European Union Politics* 7(4): 477–504.

de Vreese, C. H., Esser, F., and Hopmann, D. N. (2017) *Comparing Political Journalism*. London: Routledge.

Diddi, A., Fico, F., and Zeldes, G. A. (2014) Partisan balance and bias in TV network coverage of the 2000, 2004, and 2008 presidential elections, *Journal of Broadcasting and Electronic Media* 58(2): 161–78.

Dimitrova, D. V., and Kostadinova, P. (2013) Identifying antecedents of the strategic game frame: a longitudinal analysis, *Journalism and Mass Communication Quarterly* 90(1): 75–88.

Douglas, S. (1987) *Inventing American Broadcasting, 1899–1922*. Baltimore: Johns Hopkins University Press.

Downey, J., and Neyazi, T. A. (2014) Complementary and competitive logics of mediatization: political, commercial, and professional logics in Indian media, *International Journal of Press/Politics* 19(4): 476–95.

Dunaway, J. (2011) Poll-centered news coverage: causes and consequences, in K. Goidel, ed., *Political Polling in the Digital Age: The Challenge of Measuring and Understanding Public Opinion*. Baton Rouge: Louisiana State University Press, pp. 71–84.

Ekström, M., and Patrona, M., eds (2011) *Talking Politics in Broadcast Media*. Amsterdam: John Benjamins.

Electoral Commission (2004) *Public Opinion and the 2004 Elections: A Study of Attitudes towards Elections for the European Parliament and London's Mayor and Assembly*, www.electoralcommission.org. uk/_data/assets/electoral_commission_pdf_file/0009/16110/ FinalVote2004Reportupdated2_18922-8545__E__N__S__W__.pdf.

Electoral Commission (2009) *European and Local Elections 2009: Summary Report*, www.electoralcommission.org.uk/__data/assets/pdf_file/000 9/81828/Post-election-survey-European-and-local-elections-2009-ICM-summary-report.pdf.

Enli, G. (2017) Twitter as arena for the authentic outsider: exploring the social media campaigns of Trump and Clinton in the 2016 US presidential election, *European Journal of Communication* 32(1): 50–61.

Entman, R. (1993) Framing: toward clarification of a fractured paradigm, *Journal of Communication* 43(4): 51–8.

Esser, F. (2008) Dimensions of political news cultures: sound bite and image bite news in France, Germany, Great Britain, and the United States, *International Journal of Press/Politics* 13(4): 401–28.

Esser, F. (2013) Mediatization as a challenge: media logic versus political logic, in H. Kriesi, S. Lavenex, F. Esser, J. Matthes, M. Bühlmann and D. Bochsler, eds, *Democracy in the Age of Globalization and Mediatization*. Basingstoke: Palgrave Macmillan, pp. 155–76.

Esser, F., and D'Angelo, P. (2003) Framing the press and the publicity process: a content analysis of meta-coverage in campaign 2000 network news, *American Behavioral Scientist* 46(5): 617–41.

Esser, F., and Hanitzsch, T. (2012) *Handbook of Comparative Communication Research*. London: Routledge.

Esser, F., and Strömbäck, J., eds (2014) *Mediatization of Politics: Understanding the Transformation of Western Democracies*. Basingstoke: Palgrave Macmillan.

Esser, F., de Vreese, C. H., Strömbäck, J., van Aelst, P., Aalberg, T., Stanyer, J., Lengauer, G., Berganza, R., Legnante, G., Papathanassopoulos, S., Salgado, S., Sheafer, T., and Reinemann, C. (2012a) Political information opportunities in Europe: a longitudinal and comparative study of thirteen television systems, *International Journal of Press/Politics* 17(3): 247–74.

Esser, F., Strömbäck, J., and de Vreese, C. H. (2012b) Reviewing key concepts in research on political news journalism: conceptualizations, operationalizations, and propositions for future research, *Journalism* 13(2): 139–43.

Even, M. (2015) *Reflections on campaign TV coverage of UK elections 2015*, Reuters Institute for the Study of Journalism, 26 May, http://reu tersinstitute.politics.ox.ac.uk/news/reflections-campaign-tv-cove rage-uk-Elections-2015.

Farnsworth, S. J., and Lichter, S. R. (2011a) *The Nightly News Nightmare: Media Coverage of U.S. Presidential Elections, 1988–2008*. Lanham, MD: Rowman & Littlefield.

Farnsworth, S. J., and Lichter, S. R. (2011b) Network television's coverage of the 2008 presidential election, *American Behavioral Scientist* 55(4): 354–70.

Farnsworth, S. J., and Lichter, S. R. (2014) News coverage of US presidential campaigns: reporting on primaries and general elections, 1988–2012, *APSA 2014 Annual Meeting Paper*, https://papers.ssrn. com/sol3/papers2.cfm?abstract_id=2454423.

Figenschou, T. U., and Thorbjørnsrud, K. (2015) Backstage media–

government negotiations: the failures and success of a government pitch, *International Journal of Communication* 9: 1947–1965.

FiveThirtyEight (2016) *National Polls*, 16 November, https://projects.fivethirtyeight.com/2016-election-forecast/national-polls/.

Flynn, D., Nyhan, B., and Reifler, J. (2017) The nature and origins of misperceptions: understanding false and unsupported beliefs about politics, *Political Psychology* 38(s1): 127–50.

Foran, C. (2017) Kellyanne Conway and the Bowling Green massacre that wasn't, *The Atlantic*, 3 February, www.theatlantic.com/politics/archive/2017/02/kellyanne-conway-bowling-green-massacre-alternative-facts/515619/.

Franklin, M. (2004) *Voter Turnout and the Dynamics of Electoral Competition in Established Democracies since 1945*. Cambridge: Cambridge University Press.

Friedman, U. (2016) American elections: how long is too long?, *The Atlantic*, 5 October, www.theatlantic.com/international/archive/2016/10/us-Election-longest-world/501680/.

Gaber, I. (2011) The transformation of campaign reporting: the 2010 UK general election, revolution or evolution?, in D. Wring, R. Mortimore, and S. Atkinson, eds, *Political Communication in Britain: The Leader's Debates, the Campaign and the Media in the 2010 General Election*. Basingstoke: Palgrave Macmillan, pp. 261–80.

Gallup (2016a) Media use and evaluation, www.gallup.com/poll/1663/media-use-evaluation.aspx.

Gallup (2016b) Americans' trust in mass media sinks to new low, 14 September, www.gallup.com/poll/195542/americans-trust-mass-media-sinks-new-low.aspx.

Gamson, W. (2001) Promoting political engagement, in W. L. Bennett and R. M. Entman, eds, *Mediated Politics*. Cambridge: Cambridge University Press, pp. 56–74.

Gibson, R. K., and Römmele, A. (2009) Measuring the professionalization of political campaigning, *Party Politics* 15(3): 321–39.

Gottfried, J. (2016) Most Americans already feel election coverage fatigue, *Pew Research Center*, 14 July, www.pewresearch.org/fact-tank/2016/07/14/most-americans-already-feel-election-coverage-fatigue/.

Gottfried, J., Barthel, M., Shearer, E., and Mitchell, A. (2016) The 2016 presidential campaign – a news event that's hard to miss, *Pew Research*

Center, 4 February, www.journalism.org/2016/02/04/the-2016-pres
idential-campaign-a-news-event-thats-hard-to-miss/.

Gottfried, J., Barthel, M., and Mitchell, A. (2017) Trump, Clinton voters
divided in their main source for election news, *Pew Research Center*,
18 January, www.journalism.org/2017/01/18/trump-clinton-voters-
divided-in-their-main-source-for-election-news/.

Grabe, M. E., and Bucy, E. P. (2009) *Image Bite Politics: News and the
Visual Framing of Elections*. Oxford: Oxford University Press.

Griffin, A. (2017) Donald Trump will keep using his own Twitter as
US president because he can 'go bing bing bing', *The Independent*, 16
January, www.independent.co.uk/life-style/gadgets-and-tech/news/
donald-trump-keep-using-own-twitter-tweets-us-president-inaugura
tion-us-president-go-bing-white-a7529281.html.

Hallin, D. C. (1992) Sound bite news: television coverage of elections,
1968–1988, *Journal of Communication* 42(2): 5–24.

Hallin, D. C., and Mancini, P. (2004) *Comparing Media Systems: Three
Models of Media and Politics*. Cambridge: Cambridge University
Press.

Hanretty, C., and Banducci, S. (2016) Party competition and news cov-
erage of European Parliament elections, in W. van der Brug and
C. H. de Vreese, eds, *(Un)intended Consequences of European Parliamentary
Elections*. Oxford: Oxford University Press, pp. 36–51.

Hansen, K. M., and Pederson, R. T. (2014) Campaigns matter: how
voters become knowledgeable and efficacious during election campaigns, *Political Communication* 31(2): 303–24.

Harcup, T., and O'Neill, D. (2001) What is news? Galtung and Ruge
revisited, *Journalism Studies* 2(2): 261–80.

Harcup, T., and O'Neill, D. (2016) What is news? News values revisited
(again), *Journalism Studies*, www.tandfonline.com/doi/pdf/10.1080/
1461670X.2016.1150193?needAccess=true.

Harding, T. (2001) TV stations put away stopwatches, *The Telegraph*,
18 May, www.telegraph.co.uk/news/uknews/1330735/TV-stations-
put-away-stopwatches.html.

Heim, K. (2013) Framing the 2008 Iowa Democratic caucuses: political
blogs and second-level intermedia agenda setting, *Journalism & Mass
Communication Quarterly* 90(3): 500–19.

Hencke, D. (2006) Ministers say 24/7 news demands 3,200 press officers,

The Guardian, 31 August, www.theguardian.com/politics/2006/aug/31/uk.media.

Herman, E. S., and Chomsky, N. (1988) *Manufacturing Consent: The Political Economy of the Mass Media*. New York: Pantheon Books.

Holt, K., Shehata, A., Strömbäck, J., and Ljungberg, E. (2013) Age and the effects of news media attention and social media use on political interest and participation: do social media function as leveller?, *European Journal of Communication* 28(1): 19–34.

Hopkins, D. J., and Ladd, J. M. (2014) The consequences of broader media choice: evidence from the expansion of Fox News, *Quarterly Journal of Political Science* 9(1): 115–35.

Hopmann, D. N., and Strömbäck, J. (2010) The rise of the media punditocracy? Journalists and media pundits in Danish election news 1994-2007, *Media, Culture & Society* 32(6): 943–60.

Hopmann, D. N., de Vreese, C. H., and Albæk, E. (2011) Incumbency bonus in election news coverage explained, *Journal of Communication* 61(2): 264–82.

Hopmann, D. N., van Aelst, P., and Legnante, G. (2012) Political balance in the news: a review of concepts, operationalizations and key findings, *Journalism* 13(2): 240–57.

Hopmann, D. N., Shehata, A., and Strömbäck, J. (2015) Contagious media effects: how media use and exposure to game-framed news influence media trust, *Mass Communication and Society* 18(6): 776–98.

Ipsos MORI (2016) Immigration is now the top issue for voters in the EU referendum, 16 June, www.ipsos.com/ipsos-mori/en-uk/immigration-now-top-issue-voters-eu-referendum?language_content_entity=en-uk.

Iyengar, S., and Hahn, K. S. (2009) Red media, blue media: evidence of ideological selectivity in media use, *Journal of Communication* 59(1): 19–39.

Iyengar, S., Norpoth, H., and Hahn, K. S. (2004) Consumer demand for election news: the horserace sells, *Journal of Politics* 66(1): 157–75.

Jackson, D. (2014) Time to get serious? Process news and British politics, in M. J. Broersma and C. Peters, eds, *Retelling Journalism: Conveying Stories in a Digital Age*. Leuven: Peeters; http://eprints.bournemouth.ac.uk/22555/1/Jackson%20Time%20to%20get%20serious%20.pdf.

Jackson, J. (2017) Hyper-partisan Corbynite websites show how the left can beat the tabloids online, *New Statesman*, 24 June, www. newstatesman.com/politics/media/2017/06/hyper-partisan-corbyni te-websites-show-how-left-can-beat-tabloids-online.

Jamieson, K. H., and Cappella, J. N. (2008) *Echo Chamber: Rush Limbaugh and the Conservative Media Establishment*. Oxford: Oxford University Press.

Johnson, T. (2014) *Agenda Setting in a 2.0 World: New Agendas in Communication*. Abingdon: Routledge.

Joslyn, R. (1984) *Mass Media and Elections*. New York: Random House.

Kanter, J. (2017) TV news broadcasters have ditched general election polls as a 'total waste of time', *Business Insider UK*, 2 June, http:// uk.businessinsider.com/bbc-itv-channel-4-channel-5-and-sky-news-shun-election-polls-2017-6.

Katz, E. (1971) Platforms & windows: broadcasting's role in election campaigns, *Journalism Quarterly* 48(2): 304–14.

Kevill, S. (2002) *'Beyond the Soundbite': BBC Research into Public Disillusion with Politics*. London: BBC.

King, A. (2008) *The BBC Trust Impartiality Report: BBC Network News and Current Affairs Coverage of the Four UK Nations*, http://downloads. bbc.co.uk/bbctrust/assets/files/pdf/review_report_research/impartia lity/uk_nations_impartiality.pdf.

Kohut, A. (2009) But what do the polls show?, *Pew Research Center*, 14 October, www.pewresearch.org/2009/10/14/but-what-do-the-polls-show/.

Kolbeins, G. H. (2016) Public opinion polls and experts in election news, *Icelandic Review of Politics and Administration* 12(1): 127–50.

Kreiss, D. (2012) *Taking our Country Back: The Crafting of Networked Politics from Howard Dean to Barack Obama*. Oxford: Oxford University Press.

Kreiss, D. (2014) Seizing the moment: the presidential campaigns' use of Twitter during the 2012 electoral cycle, *New Media & Society* 18(8): 1473–90; https://danielkreiss.files.wordpress.com/2010/05/kreiss_sei zingthemoment.pdf.

Kreiss, D. (2016) *Prototype Politics: Technology-Intensive Campaigning and the Data of Democracy*. Oxford: Oxford University Press.

Kriesi, H. (2014) The populist challenge, *West European Politics* 37(2) 361–78.

Landerer, N. (2013) Rethinking the logics: a conceptual framework for the mediatization of politics, *Communication Theory* 23(3): 239–58.

Lawrence, R. G. (2000) Game-framing the issues: tracking the strategy frame in public policy news, *Political Communication* 17(2): 93–114.

Lepore, J. (2015) Politics and the new machine: what the turn from polls to data science means for democracy, *New Yorker*, 16 November, www.newyorker.com/magazine/2015/11/16/politics-and-the-new-machine.

Lewis, J. (2001) *Constructing Public Opinion: How Political Elites Do What They Like and Why We Seem to Go Along with It*. New York: Columbia University Press.

Lewis, J., and Morgan, M. (1992) Issues, images & impact: a FAIR survey of voters' knowledge, http://fair.org/extra/issues-images-amp-impact/.

Lewis, J., Inthorn, S., and Wahl-Jorgensen, K. (2005) *Citizens or Consumers? What the Media Tell Us about Political Participation*. Maidenhead: Open University Press.

Lichter, S. R., Rothman, S., and Lichter, L. S. (1986) *The Media Elite: America's New Powerbrokers*. Bethesda, MD: Adler & Adler.

Lilleker, D. G., and Negrine, R. (2002) Professionalization: of what? Since when? By whom?, *International Journal of Press/Politics* 7(4): 98–103.

Lloyd, J. (2004) *What the Media Do to our Politics*. London: Robinson.

Loughborough University (2015) Media coverage of the 2015 campaign (report 5), http://blog.lboro.ac.uk/crcc/general-Election/media-coverage-of-the-2015-campaign-report-5/.

Loughborough University (2017) Media coverage of the 2017 general election campaign (report 4), Centre for Research in Communication and Culture, http://blog.lboro.ac.uk/crcc/general-election/media-coverage-of-the-2017-general-election-campaign-report-4/.

McChesney, R. W. (1993) *Telecommunications, Mass Media, & Democracy: The Battle for the Control of US Broadcasting, 1928–1935*. Oxford: Oxford University Press.

McCombs, M. (1997) Building consensus: the news media's agenda-setting roles, *Political Communication* 14(4): 433–43.

McCombs, M. (2004) *Setting the Agenda: The Mass Media and Public Opinion*. Cambridge: Polity.

McCombs, M. (2014) *Setting the Agenda: Mass Media and Public Opinion.* 2nd edn, Cambridge: Polity.

McElwee, S., McDermott, M., and Jordan, W. (2017) 4 pieces of evidence showing FBI director James Comey cost Clinton the election, *Vox*, 11 January, www.vox.com/the-big-idea/2017/1/11/14215930/comey-email-election-clinton-campaign.

McLuhan, M. (1964) *Understanding Media: The Extensions of Man.* London: Routledge & Kegan Paul.

McNair, B. (2000) *Journalism and Democracy: An Evaluation of the Public Sphere.* London: Routledge.

Mantzarlis, A. (2016) Fast-checking under President Trump, 10 November, www.poynter.org/news/fast-checking-under-president-trump.

Media Focus (2016) *Media Masters – Isabel Oakeshott, Political Editor-at-Large, Daily Mail*, 14 April, www.mediafocus.org.uk/isabel-oakeshott.

Media Reform Coalition (2016) *The Bias of Objectivity: An Analysis of Coverage of the 2016 London Mayoral Race in the London Evening Standard*, www.mediareform.org.uk/wp-content/uploads/2016/04/The-Bias-of-Objectivity-final-final.pdf.

Mendes, E. (2013) In U.S., trust in media recovers slightly from all-time low, *Gallup*, 19 September, www.gallup.com/poll/164459/trust-media-recovers-slightly-time-low.aspx.

Mitchell, A., and Holcomb, J. (2016) *State of News Media 2016*, Pew Research Center, www.journalism.org/2016/06/15/state-of-the-news-media-2016/.

Moog, S., and Sluyter-Beltrao, J. (2001) The transformation of political communication?, in B. Axford and R.Huggins, eds, *New Media and Politics*. London: Sage, pp. 30–63.

Moore, M., and Ramsay, G. (2015) *UK Election 2015: Setting the Agenda*, King's College London, www.kcl.ac.uk/sspp/policy-institute/publications/MST-Election-2015-FINAL.pdf.

Negrine, R. (2008) *The Transformation of Political Communication.* Basingstoke: Palgrave Macmillan.

Newman, N., Levy, D. A. L., and Nielsen, R. K. (2015) *Reuters Institute Digital News Report 2015*, https://reutersinstitute.politics.ox.ac.uk/sites/default/files/Reuters%20Institute%20Digital%20News%20Report%202015_Full%20Report.pdf.

Newman, N., Fletcher, R., Levy, D. A. L., and Nielsen, R. K. (2016) *Reuters Institute Digital News Report 2016*, https://reutersinstitute.politics.ox.ac.uk/sites/default/files/Digital-News-Report-2016.pdf.

Newman, N., Fletcher, R., Kalogeropoulos, A., Levy, D. A. L., and Nielsen, R. K. (2017) *Reuters Institute Digital News Report 2017*, https://reutersinstitute.politics.ox.ac.uk/sites/default/files/Digital%20News%20Report%202017%20web_0.pdf.

Newton, K. (1999) Mass media effects: mobilization or media malaise?, *British Journal of Political Science* 29(4): 577–99.

Nichols, J., and McChesney, R. W. (2013) *Dollarocracy: How the Money and Media Election Complex is Destroying America*. New York: Nation Books.

Nielsen, R. K. (2012) *Ground Wars: Personalized Communication in Political Campaigns*. Princeton, NJ: Princeton University Press.

Nielsen, R. K., and Sambrook, R. (2016) *What is Happening to Television News? Digital News Project 2016*, Reuters Institute for the Study of Journalism, https://reutersinstitute.politics.ox.ac.uk/sites/default/files/What%20is%20Happening%20to%20Television%20News.pdf.

Nieman Lab Staff (2017) 'I think that journalism needs to rediscover its roots as a blue-collar profession', Nieman Foundation at Harvard, www.niemanlab.org/2017/02/i-think-that-journalism-needs-to-rediscover-its-roots-as-a-blue-collar-profession/.

Nord, L. W., and Strömbäck, J. (2014) It didn't happen here: commercialization and political news coverage in Swedish television 1998–2010, in M. J. Canel and K. Voltmer, eds, *Comparing Political Communication across Time and Space: New Studies in an Emerging Field*. Basingstoke: Palgrave Macmillan, pp. 214–33.

Norris, P. (2000) *A Virtuous Circle: Political Communications in Postindustrial Societies*. Cambridge: Cambridge University Press.

Norris, P. (2009) Comparative political communications: common frameworks or Babelian confusion?, *Government and Opposition: An International Journal of Comparative Politics* 44(3): 321–40.

Norris, P. (2014) *Why Electoral Integrity Matters*. Cambridge: Cambridge University Press.

Norris, P., Curtice, J., Sanders, D., Scammell, M., and Semetko, H. A. (1999) *On Message: Communicating the Campaign*. London: Sage.

Nussbaum, M., and Gold, H. (2017) The disappearing Sean Spicer,

Politico, 6 March, www.politico.com/story/2017/03/sean-spicer-trump-white-house-235737.

Nyhan, B., and Reifler, J. (2009) *The Effects of Semantics and Social Desirability in Correcting the Obama Muslim Myth*. Working paper, Dartmouth University.

Nyhan, B., and Reifler, J. (2014) The effect of fact-checking on elites: a field experiment on U.S. state legislators, *American Journal of Political Science* 59(3): 628–40.

Oates, S. (2008) *Television, Democracy and Elections in Russia*. London: Routledge.

Ofcom (2017) *Ofcom's Rules on Due Impartiality, Due Accuracy, Elections and Referendums*, www.ofcom.org.uk/__data/assets/pdf_file/0030/98148/Due-impartiality-and-elections-statement.pdf.

Ott, B. (2016) The age of Twitter: Donald J. Trump and the politics of debasement, *Critical Studies in Media Communication* 34(1): 59–68.

Oxford Dictionaries (2016) Word of the year: post-truth, https://en.oxforddictionaries.com/word-of-the-year/word-of-the-year-2016.

Patterson, T. E. (1993) *Out of Order*. New York: Vintage Books.

Patterson, T. E. (2016a) News coverage of the 2016 presidential primaries: horse race reporting has consequences, Shorenstein Center on Media, Politics and Public Policy, 11 July, http://shorensteincenter.org/news-coverage-2016-presidential-primaries/.

Patterson, T. E. (2016b) News coverage of the 2016 general election: how the press failed the voters, Shorenstein Center on Media, Politics and Public Policy, 7 December, https://shorensteincenter.org/news-coverage-2016-general-election/.

Patterson, T. E. (2016c) Pre-primary news coverage of the 2016 presidential race: Trump's rise, Sanders' emergence, Clinton's struggle, Shorenstein Center on Media, Politics and Public Policy, 13 June, https://shorensteincenter.org/pre-primary-news-coverage-2016-trump-clinton-sanders/.

Pew Research Center (2012) Frame: which aspects of the race got attention, and which ones didn't?, 1 November, www.journalism.org/2012/11/01/frame-which-aspects-race-got-attention-and-which-ones-didnt/.

Philo, G. (1990) *Seeing and Believing: The Influence of Television*. London: Routledge.

Philo, G., and Berry, M. (2004) *Bad News from Israel*. London: Pluto Press.

Pickard, V. W. (2014) *America's Battle for Media Democracy: The Triumph of Corporate Libertarianism and the Future of Media Reform*. Cambridge: Cambridge University Press.

Plasser, F. (2005) From hard to soft news standards? How political journalists in different media systems evaluate the shifting quality of news, *International Journal of Press/Politics* 10(2): 47–68.

PolitiFact (2016) Statements we say are pants on fire!, www.politifact. com/truth-o-meter/rulings/pants-fire/.

Poniewozik, J. (2016) Was that a debate? Or were the candidates just trying to go viral? *New York Times*, 10 October, www.nytimes.com/ 2016/10/11/arts/television/donald-trump-hillary-clinton-second-debate.html?_r=0.

Pope, K. (2017) An open letter to Trump from the US press corps, *Columbia Journalism Review*, 17 January, www.cjr.org/covering_trump/ trump_white_house_press_corps.php.

Public Policy Polling (2017) Americans now evenly divided on impeaching Trump, 10 February, www.publicpolicypolling.com/pdf/2017/ PPP_Release_National_21017.pdf.

Rafter, K. (2015) Regulating the airwaves: how political balance is achieved in practice in election news coverage, *Irish Political Studies* 30(4): 575–94.

Rafter, K., Flynn, R., McMenamin, I., and O'Malley, E. (2014) Does commercial orientation matter for policy-game framing? A content analysis of television and radio news programmes on public and private stations, *European Journal of Communication* 29(4): 433–48.

Rajan, D. (2017) Donald Trump, media saviour, 7 February, www.bbc. co.uk/news/entertainment-arts-38854711.

Redlawsk, D. P., Civettini, A. J., and Emmerson, K. M. (2010) The affective tipping point: do motivated reasoners ever 'get it'?, *Political Psychology* 31(4): 563–93.

Reed, J. (2017) Beyond the bubble: write for Guardian US about the places that others ignore, *The Guardian*, 17 March, www.theguardian.com/ media/2017/mar/17/how-to-write-for-guardian-us-pitch-guide.

Reif, K., and Schmitt, H. (1980) Nine second-order national elections – a conceptual framework for the analysis of European election results, *European Journal of Political Research* 8(1): 3–44.

Revesz, R. (2017) Donald Trump's presidential counsellor Kellyanne Conway says Sean Spicer gave 'alternative facts' at first press briefing, *The Independent*, 22 January, www.independent.co.uk/news/world/americas/kellyanne-conway-sean-spicer-alternative-facts-lies-press-briefing-donald-trump-administration-a7540441.html.

Riffkin, R. (2015) Americans' trust in media remains at historical low, *Gallup*, 28 September, www.gallup.com/poll/185927/americans-trust-media-remains-historical-low.aspx.

Rogers, E., Dearing, J., and Bregman, D. (1993) The anatomy of agenda-setting research, *Journal of Communication* 43(2): 68–84.

Rosen, J. (2010) Seven questions for Jay Rosen, *The Economist*, 28 August, www.economist.com/blogs/democracyinamerica/2010/08/jay_rosen_media.

Rosen, J. (2016a) He said, she said journalism: lame formula in the land of the active user. *PressThink*, 12 April, http://archive.pressthink.org/2009/04/12/hesaid_shesaid.html.

Rosen, J. (2016b) Asymmetry between the major parties fries the circuits of the mainstream press, *PressThink*, 25 September, http://pressthink.org/2016/09/asymmetry-between-the-major-parties-fries-the-circuits-of-the-mainstream-press/.

Rosen, J. (2017) Evidence-based vs. accusation-driven reporting, *Storify*, https://storify.com/jayrosen_nyu/evidence-based-vs-accusation-driven-reporting.

Rosenstiel, T., Mitchell, A., and Jurkowitz, M. (2012) Winning the media campaign 2012, 2 November, *Pew Research Center*, www.journalism.org/files/legacy/Winningthemediacampaign2012.pdf.

Ross, H. (2004) *Media and Elections: An Elections Reporting Handbook*. IMPACS – Institute for Media, Policy and Civil Society, www.unesco.org/fileadmin/MULTIMEDIA/HQ/CI/CI/pdf/media_+_elections_an_elections_reporting_handbook_en.pdf.

Rutenberg, J. (2016) The mutual dependence of Donald Trump and the news media, *New York Times*, 20 March, www.nytimes.com/2016/03/21/business/media/the-mutual-dependence-of-trump-and-the-news-media.html.

Sambrook, R. (2012) *Delivering Trust: Impartiality and Objectivity in the Digital Age*. Oxford: Reuters Institute for the Study of Journalism.

Savillo, R. (2016) Study: Trump the only candidate to swamp the Sunday

shows with phone interviews, *Media Matters*, 18 March, https://medi
amatters.org/blog/2016/03/18/study-trump-the-only-candidate-to
-swamp-the-sun/209363.

Savransky, R. (2016) Nate Silver: Clinton 'almost certainly' would've
won before FBI letter, *The Hill*, 11 December, http://thehill.com/
homenews/campaign/309871-nate-silver-clinton-almost-certainly-
wouldve-won-if-election-were-before.

Schuck, A. R. T., Xezonakis, G., Elenbaas, M., Banducci, S. A., de
Vreese, C. H. (2011) Party contestation and Europe on the news agenda:
the 2009 European parliamentary elections, *Electoral Studies* 30(1):
41–52.

Schuck, A. R. T., Vliegenthart, R., Boomgaarden, H. G., Elenbaas, M.,
Azrout, R., van Spanje, J., and de Vreese, C. H. (2013) Explaining
campaign news coverage: how medium, time, and context explain
variation in the media framing of the 2009 European parliamentary
elections, *Journal of Political Marketing* 12(1): 8–28.

Schuck, A. R. T., Vliegenthart, R., and de Vreese, C. H. (2016) Who's
afraid of conflict? The mobilizing effect of conflict framing in campaign news, *British Journal of Political Science* 46(1): 177–94.

Schudson, M. (2001) The objectivity norm in American journalism,
Journalism 2(2): 149–70.

Searles, K., Ginn, M. H., and Nickens, J. (2016) For whom the poll
airs: comparing poll results to television poll coverage, *Public Opinion
Quarterly* 80(4): 943–63.

Semetko, H. A. (2000) Great Britain: the end of News at Ten and
the changing news environment, in R. Gunther and A. Mughan,
eds, *Democracy and the Media: A Comparative Perspective*. Cambridge:
Cambridge University Press, pp. 343–74.

Semetko, H. A., Blumler, J. G., Gurevitch, M., and Weaver, D. H.
(1991) *The Formation of Campaign Agendas: A Comparative Analysis of
Party and Media Roles in Recent American and British Elections*. Hillsdale,
NJ: Erlbaum.

Shehata, A. (2014) Game frames, issue frames, and mobilization: disen-
tangling the effects of frame exposure and motivated news attention on
political cynicism and engagement, *International Journal of Public Opinion
Research* 26(2): 157–77.

Shin, J., and Thorson, K. (2017) Partisan selective sharing: the biased diffusion of fact checking messages on social media, *Journal of Communication* 67(2): 233–55.

Sigelman, L., and Bullock, D. (1991) Candidates, issues, horse races, and hoopla: presidential campaign coverage, 1888–1988, *American Politics Research* 19(1): 5–32.

Smith, D. (2017) Kellyanne Conway's fictitious 'Bowling Green massacre' not a one-time slip of the tongue, *The Guardian*, 6 February, www.theguardian.com/us-news/2017/feb/06/kellyanne-conway-fake-bowling-green-massacre-three-times.

Spayd, L. (2016) The truth about 'false balance', *New York Times*, 10 September, www.nytimes.com/2016/09/11/public-editor/the-truth-about-false-balance.html?_r=1.

Stencel, M. (2015) How fact-checking journalism is changing politics, *American Press Institute*, 13 May, www.americanpressinstitute. org/publications/reports/survey-research/fact-checking-journalism-changing-politics/.

Strömbäck, J. (2008) Four phases of mediatization: an analysis of the mediatization of politics, *International Journal of Press/Politics* 13(3): 228–46.

Strömbäck, J. (2009a) Selective professionalisation of political campaigning: a test of the party-centred theory of professionalised campaigning in the context of the 2006 Swedish election, *Political Studies* 57(1): 95–116.

Strömbäck, J. (2009b) Vox populi or vox media? Opinion polls and the Swedish media, 1998–2006, *Javnost – The Public* 16(3): 55–70.

Strömbäck, J. (2011) Mediatization of politics: toward a conceptual framework for comparative research, in E. P. Bucy and R. L. Holberg, eds, *Sourcebook for Political Communication Research: Methods, Measures, and Analytical Techniques*. London: Routledge, pp. 367–82.

Strömbäck, J. (2016) Does public service TV and the intensity of the political information environment matter?, *Journalism Studies*, www. tandfonline.com/doi/pdf/10.1080/1461670X.2015.1133253?need Access=true.

Strömbäck, J., and Dimitrova, D. (2011) Mediatization and media interventionism: a comparative analysis of Sweden and the United States, *International Journal of Press/Politics* 16(1): 30–49.

Strömbäck, J., and Esser, F. (2014) Mediatization of politics: towards a theoretical framework, in F. Esser and J. Strömbäck, eds, *Mediatization of Politics: Understanding the Transformation of Western Democracies*. Basingstoke: Palgrave Macmillan, pp. 3–28.

Strömbäck, J., and Kaid, L., eds (2008) *The Handbook of Election News Coverage around the World*. London: Routledge.

Strömbäck, J., and van Aelst, P. (2010) Exploring some antecedents of the media's framing of election news: a comparison of Swedish and Belgian election news, *International Journal of Press/Politics* 15(1): 41–59.

Strömbäck, J., and van Aelst, P. (2013) Why political parties adapt to the media: exploring the fourth dimension of mediatization, *International Communication Gazette* 75(4): 341–58.

Strömbäck, J., Negrine, R., Hopmann, D. N., Jalali, C., Berganza, R., Seeber, G. U. H., Seceleanu, A., Volek, J., Dobek-Ostrowska, B., Mykkänen, J., Belluati, M., and Maier, M. (2013) Sourcing the news: comparing source use and media framing of the 2009 European parliamentary elections, *Journal of Political Marketing* 12(1): 29–52.

Stroud, N. (2011) *Niche News: The Politics of News Choice*. Oxford: Oxford University Press.

Sullivan, M. (2017) The traditional way of reporting on a president is dead, and Trump's press secretary killed it, *Washington Post*, 22 January, www. washingtonpost.com/lifestyle/style/the-traditional-way-of-reporting-on-a-president-is-dead-and-trumps-press-secretary-killed-it/2017/01/22/75403a00-e0bf-11e6-a453-19ec4b3d09ba_story.html?utm_term=.5d22820906cd.

Sweetser, K. D., Golan, G. J., and Wanta, W. (2008) Intermedia agenda setting in television, advertising, and blogs during the 2004 election, *Mass Communication and Society* 11(2): 197–216.

Sweney, M. (2011) Ed Miliband TV interviewer reveals shame over 'absurd' soundbites, *The Guardian*, 1 July, www.theguardian.com/politics/2011/jul/01/ed-miliband-interviewer-shame-strike-soundbites.

Sykes, C. J. (2017) Why nobody cares the president is lying, *New York Times*, 4 February, www.nytimes.com/2017/02/04/opinion/sunday/why-nobody-cares-the-president-is-lying.html.

Sykes, F. (1923) *The Broadcasting Committee: Report*. London: HMSO.

Takens, J., van Atteveldt, W., van Hoof, A., and Kleinnijenhuis, J. (2013) Media logic in election campaign coverage, *European Journal of Communication* 28(3): 277–93.

Tankard, J. W. (2001) The empirical approach to the study of media framing, in S. D. Reese, O. H. Gandy and A. E. Grant, eds, *Framing Public Life: Perspectives on Media and our Understanding of the Social World*. Mahwah, NJ: Lawrence Erlbaum Associates, pp. 95–106.

Tenscher, J., Mykkänen, J., and Moring, T. (2012) Modes of professional campaigning: a four-country comparison in the European parliamentary elections, 2009, *International Journal of Press/Politics* 17(2): 145–68.

Toff, B. (2015) How poll-driven is contemporary news about American politics? Results from two content analyses, Paper presented at the annual meeting of the International Communication Association, San Juan, Puerto Rico, May.

Toynbee, P. (2016) The rightwing press can't be allowed to bully us out of the EU, *The Guardian*, 4 February, www.theguardian.com/commentisfree/2016/feb/04/eu-referendum-rightwing-newspapers-cameron-fate.

Traugott, M. (2005) The accuracy of the national pre-election polls in the 2004 presidential election, *Political Opinion Quarterly* 69(5): 642–54.

Tyndall, A. (2016a) Year in review, *Tyndall Report*, http://tyndallreport.com/.

Tyndall, A. (2016b) Issues? What issues?, *Tyndall Report*, http://tyndallreport.com/comment/20/5778/.

Vaccari, C. (2008) From the air to the ground: the internet in the 2004 US presidential campaign, *New Media & Society* 10(4): 647–65.

Valentino, N. A., Beckmann, M. N., and Buhr, T. A. (2001) A spiral of cynicism for some: the contingent effects of campaign news frames on participation and confidence in government, *Political Communication* 18(4): 347–67.

van Aelst, P., Maddens, B., Noppe, J., and Fiers, S. (2008) Politicians in the news: media or party logic? Media attention and electoral success in the Belgian election campaign of 2003, *European Journal of Communication* 23(2): 193–210.

van Aelst, P., Strömbäck, J., Aalberg, T., Esser, F., de Vreese, C. H., Matthes, J., Hopmann, D., Salgado, S., Hubé, N., Stępińska, A., Papathanassopoulos, S., Berganza, R., Legnante, G., Reinemann, C., Sheafer, T. and Stanyer, J. (2017) Political communication in a high-choice media environment: a challenge for democracy?, *Annals of the International Communication Association* 41(1): 3–27.

Vliegenthart, R., and Walgrave, J. (2008) The contingency of intermedia agenda setting: a longitudinal study in Belgium, *Journalism and Mass Communication Quarterly* 85(4): 860–77.

Vonbun, R., Kleinen-von Königslöw, K., and Schoenbach, K. (2015) Intermedia agenda-setting in a multimedia news environment, *Journalism* 17(8): 1054–73.

Wahl-Jorgensen, K., Sambrook, R., Berry, M., Moore, K., Bennett, L., Cable, J., Garcia-Blanco, I., Kidd, J., Dencik, L., and Hintz, A. (2013) *BBC Breadth of Opinion Review: Content Analysis*, http://downloads.bbc.co.uk/bbctrust/assets/files/pdf/our_work/breadth_opinion/content_analysis.pdf.

Waterson, J., and Phillips, T. (2017) People on Facebook only want to share pro-Corbyn, anti-Tory news stories, *Buzzfeed*, 7 May, www.buzzfeed.com/jimwaterson/people-on-facebook-only-want-to-share-pro-corbyn-news?utm_term=.iqrN44xyw#.ksk0MM1ED.

Weber Shandwick (2017) New poll unpacks social media and GE2017, 31 May, http://webershandwick.co.uk/social-media-ge2017/.

Wells, C., Shah, D. V., Pevehouse, J. C., Yang, J., Pelled, A., Boehm, F., Lukito, J., Ghosh, S., and Schmidt, J. L. (2016) How Trump drove coverage to the nomination: hybrid media campaigning, *Political Communication* 33(4): 669–76.

Weprin, A. (2016) CBS CEO Les Moonves clarifies Donald Trump 'good for CBS' comment, *Politico*, 19 October, www.politico.com/blogs/on-media/2016/10/cbs-ceo-les-moonves-clarifies-donald-trump-good-for-cbs-comment-229996.

West, D. M. (2014) *Air Wars: Television Advertising and Social Media in Election Campaigns, 1952–2012*. 6th edn, Washington, DC: CQ Press.

Williams, E. (2016) Why trust matters, Reuters Institute for the Study of Journalism, www.digitalnewsreport.org/essays/2016/why-trust-matters/.

Witschge, T. (2014) Passive accomplice or active disruptor, *Journalism Practice* 8(3): 342–56.

Young, S. (2011) *How Australia Decides: Election Reporting and the Media.* Cambridge: Cambridge University Press.

Zeh, R., and Hopmann, D. N. (2013) Indicating mediatization? Two decades of election campaign television coverage, *European Journal of Communication* 28(3): 225–40.

Zelizer, B. (1993) Journalists as interpretive communities, *Critical Studies in Mass Communication* 10(3): 219–37.

Zelizer, B., and Allan, S. (2010) *Keywords in News and Journalism Studies*. Maidenhead: Open University Press.

Index